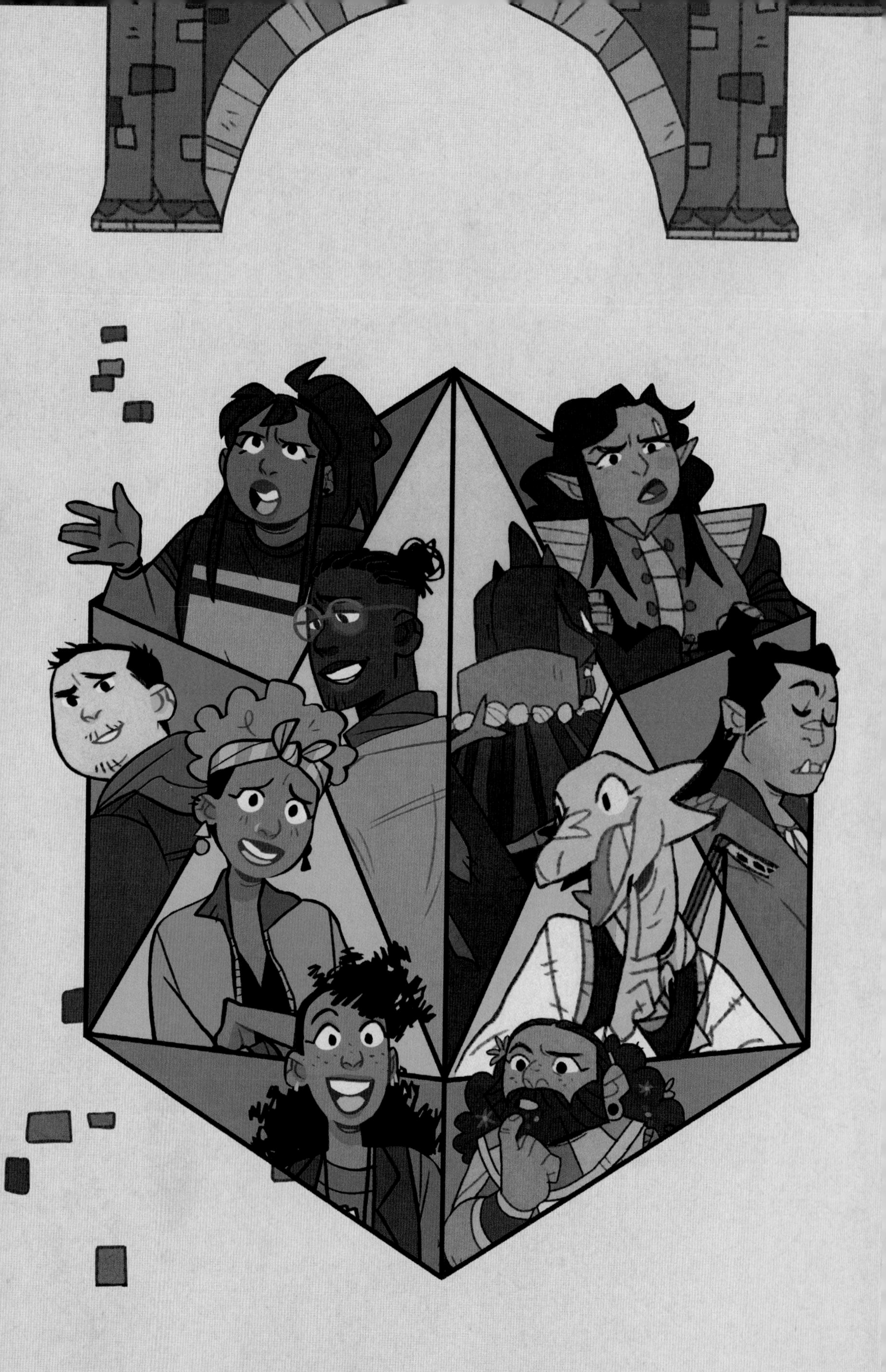

THE LAST SESSION

JASMINE WALLS
WRITER

DOZERDRAWS
ARTIST

MICAH MYERS
LETTERER

MICHAEL MOCCIO
EDITOR

DAVID REYES
BOOK & LOGO DESIGNER

Laura Chacón
Founder

Mark London
CEO and Chief Creative Officer

Mark Irwin
VP of Business Development

Chris Fernandez
Publisher

Cecilia Medina
Chief Financial Officer

Allison Pond
Marketing Director

Giovanna T. Orozco
Production Manager

Miguel Angel Zapata
Design Director

Chas! Pangburn
Senior Editor

Maya Lopez
Marketing Manager

Brian Hawkins
Editor

Diana Bermúdez
Graphic Designer

David Reyes
Graphic Designer

Adriana T. Orozco
Interactive Media Designer

Nicolás Zea Arias
Audiovisual Production

Frank Silva
Executive Assistant

Pedro Herrera
Retail Associate

Stephanie Hidalgo
Office Manager

FOR MAD CAVE COMICS, INC.

The Last Session™ published by Mad Cave Studios, Inc. 8838 SW 129th St. Miami, FL 33176. © 2023 Mad Cave Studios, Inc. All rights reserved. Contains materials originally published in single magazine form as The Last Session™ (2021-2022) #1 - 5.

Second Printing. Printed in Canada.
ISBN: 978-1-952303-19-7

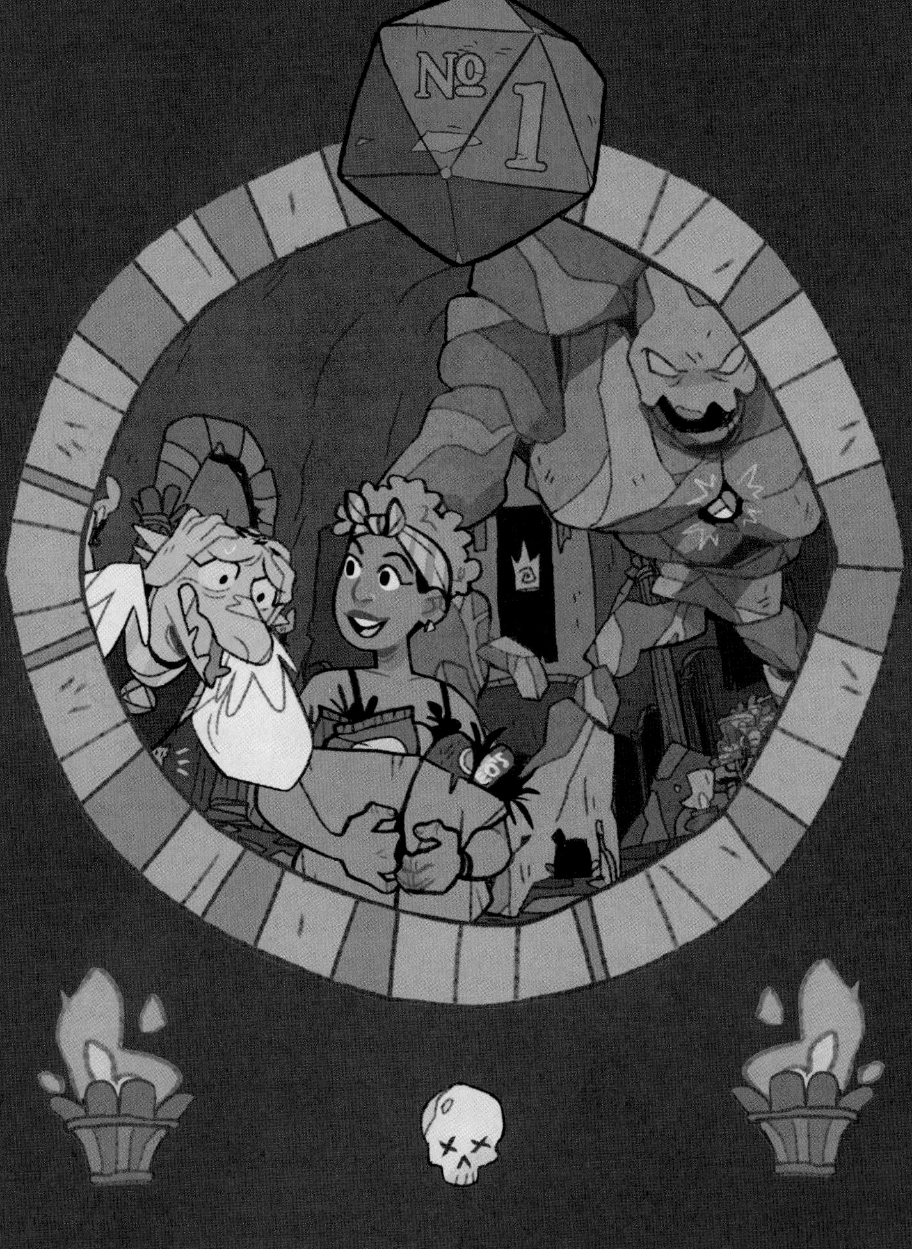
№ 1

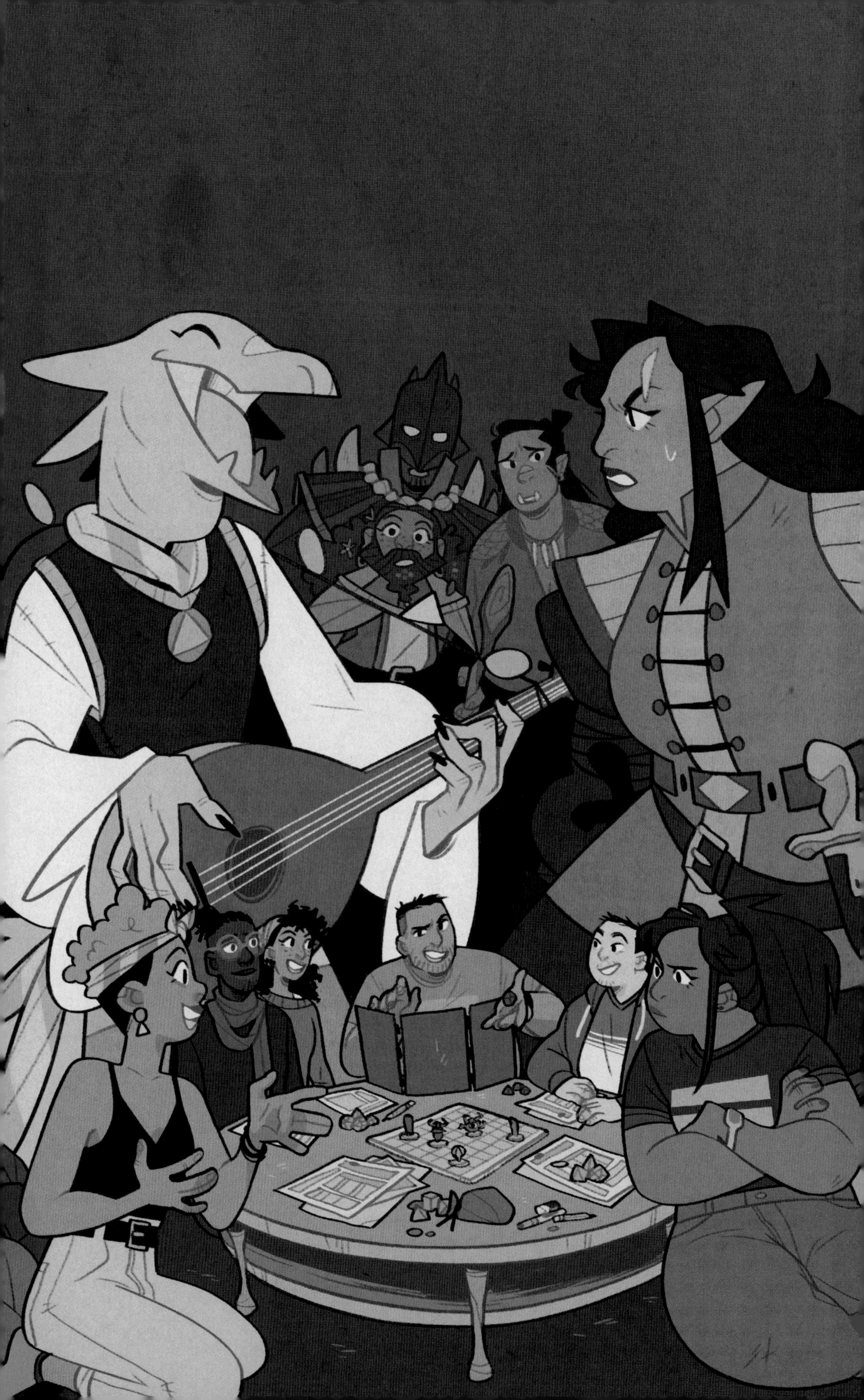

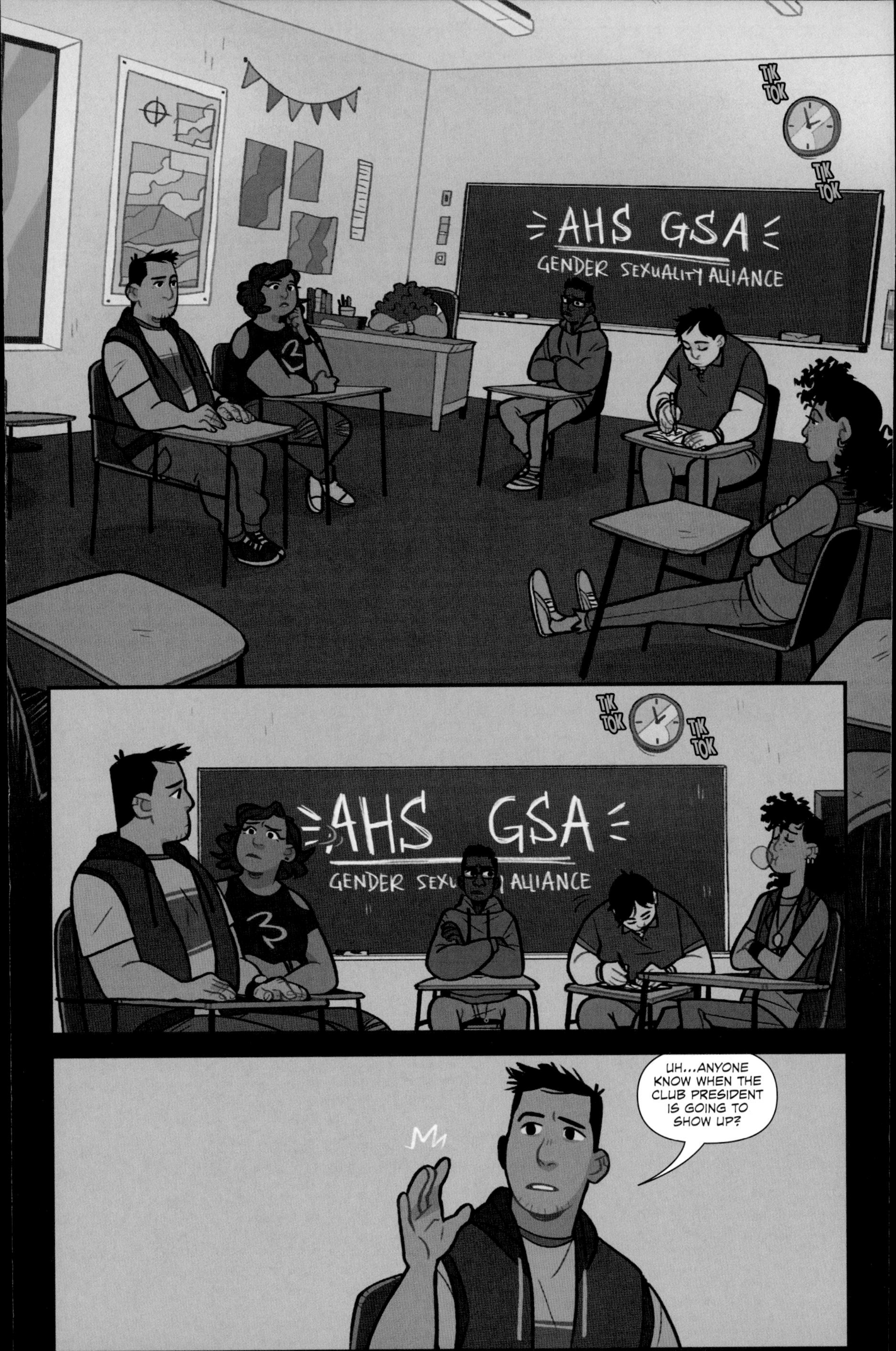
TIK TOK
TIK TOK
AHS GSA
GENDER SEXUALITY ALLIANCE
TIK TOK
TIK TOK
AHS GSA
UH...ANYONE KNOW WHEN THE CLUB PRESIDENT IS GOING TO SHOW UP?

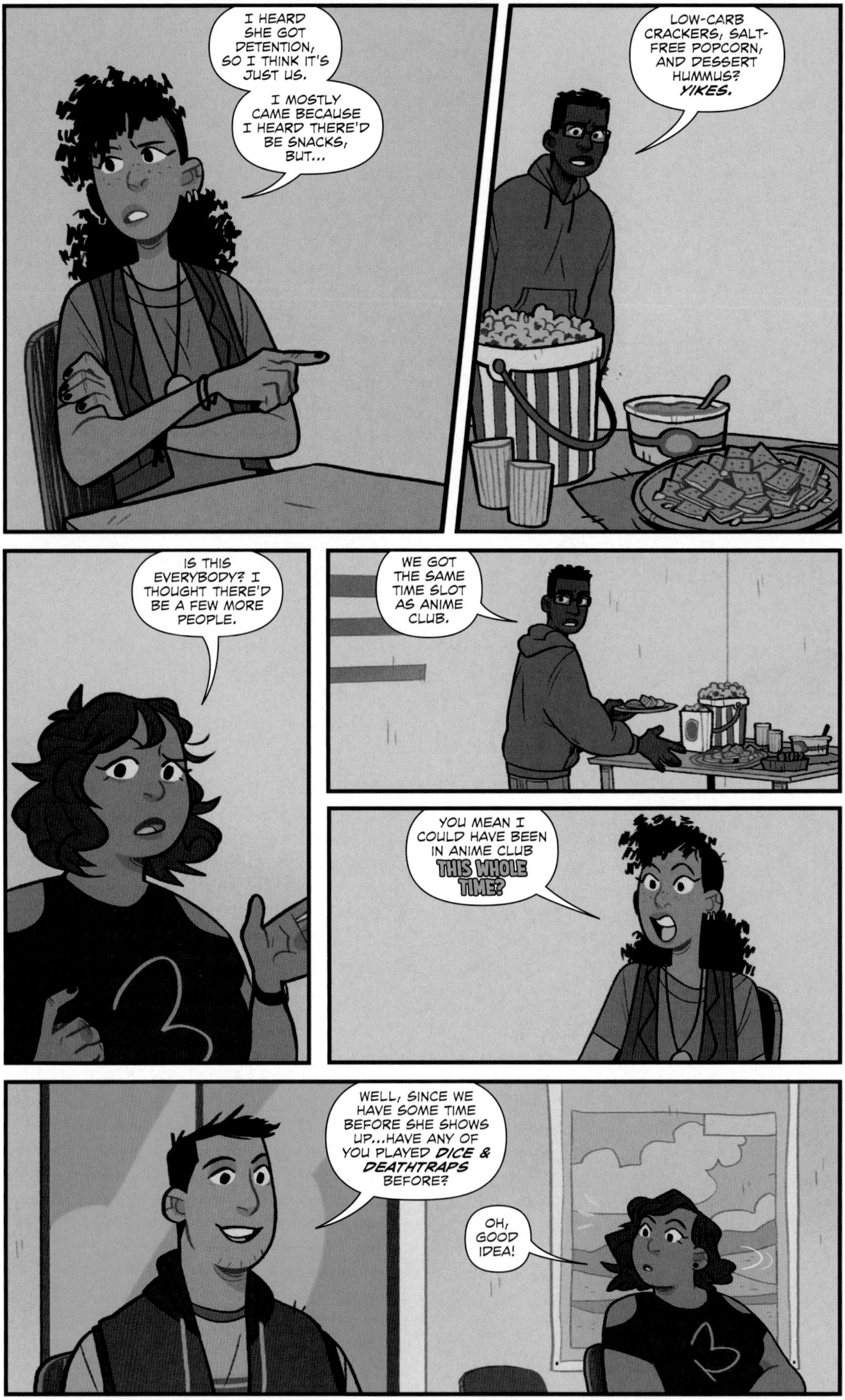
I HEARD SHE GOT DETENTION, SO I THINK IT'S JUST US.
I MOSTLY CAME BECAUSE I HEARD THERE'D BE SNACKS, BUT...
LOW-CARB CRACKERS, SALT-FREE POPCORN, AND DESSERT HUMMUS? *YIKES.*
IS THIS EVERYBODY? I THOUGHT THERE'D BE A FEW MORE PEOPLE.
WE GOT THE SAME TIME SLOT AS ANIME CLUB.
YOU MEAN I COULD HAVE BEEN IN ANIME CLUB **THIS WHOLE TIME?**
WELL, SINCE WE HAVE SOME TIME BEFORE SHE SHOWS UP...HAVE ANY OF YOU PLAYED *DICE & DEATHTRAPS* BEFORE?
OH, GOOD IDEA!

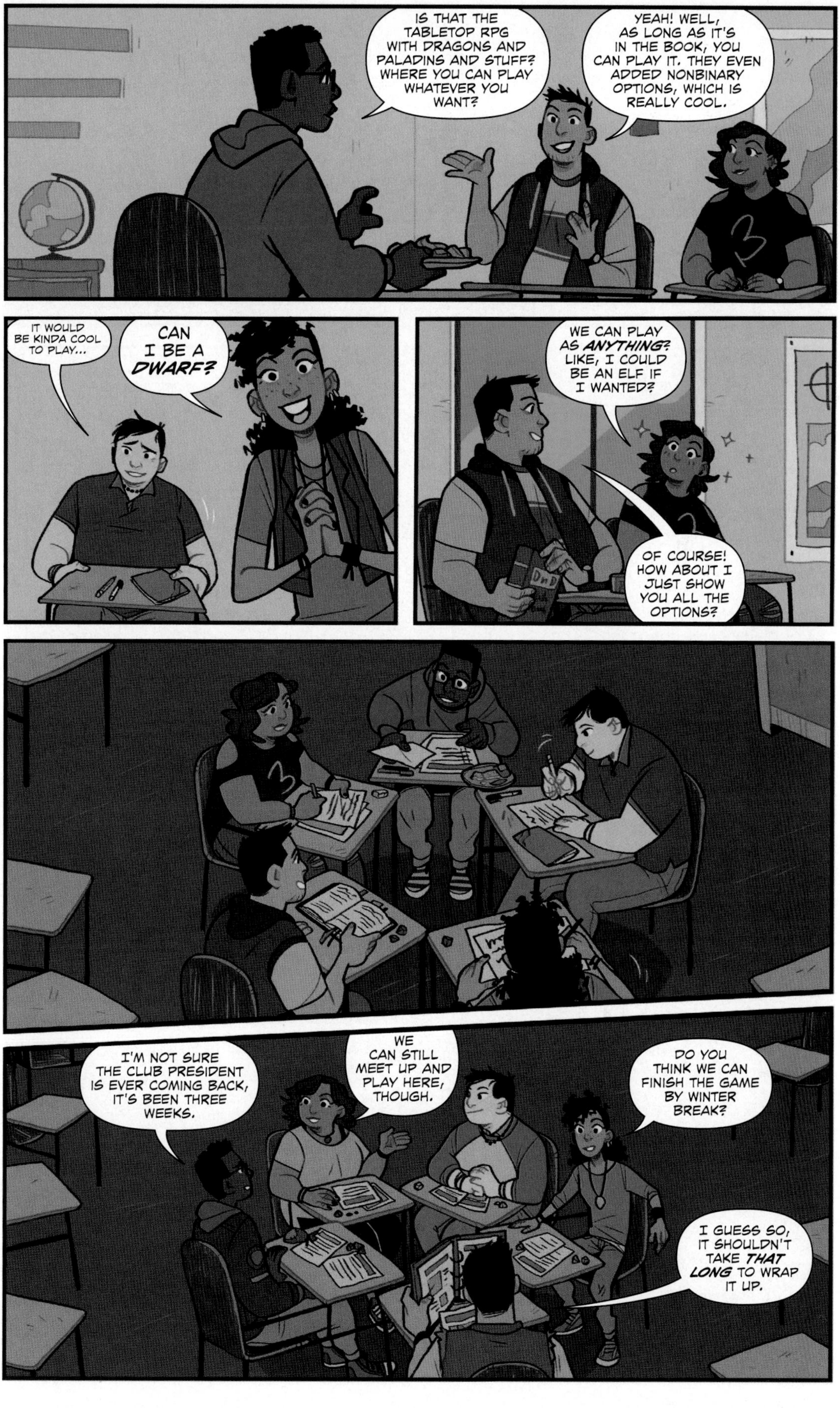
IS THAT THE TABLETOP RPG WITH DRAGONS AND PALADINS AND STUFF? WHERE YOU CAN PLAY WHATEVER YOU WANT?
YEAH! WELL, AS LONG AS IT'S IN THE BOOK, YOU CAN PLAY IT. THEY EVEN ADDED NONBINARY OPTIONS, WHICH IS REALLY COOL.
IT WOULD BE KINDA COOL TO PLAY...
CAN I BE A DWARF?
WE CAN PLAY AS ANYTHING? LIKE, I COULD BE AN ELF IF I WANTED?
OF COURSE! HOW ABOUT I JUST SHOW YOU ALL THE OPTIONS?
DnD
I'M NOT SURE THE CLUB PRESIDENT IS EVER COMING BACK, IT'S BEEN THREE WEEKS.
WE CAN STILL MEET UP AND PLAY HERE, THOUGH.
DO YOU THINK WE CAN FINISH THE GAME BY WINTER BREAK?
I GUESS SO, IT SHOULDN'T TAKE THAT LONG TO WRAP IT UP.

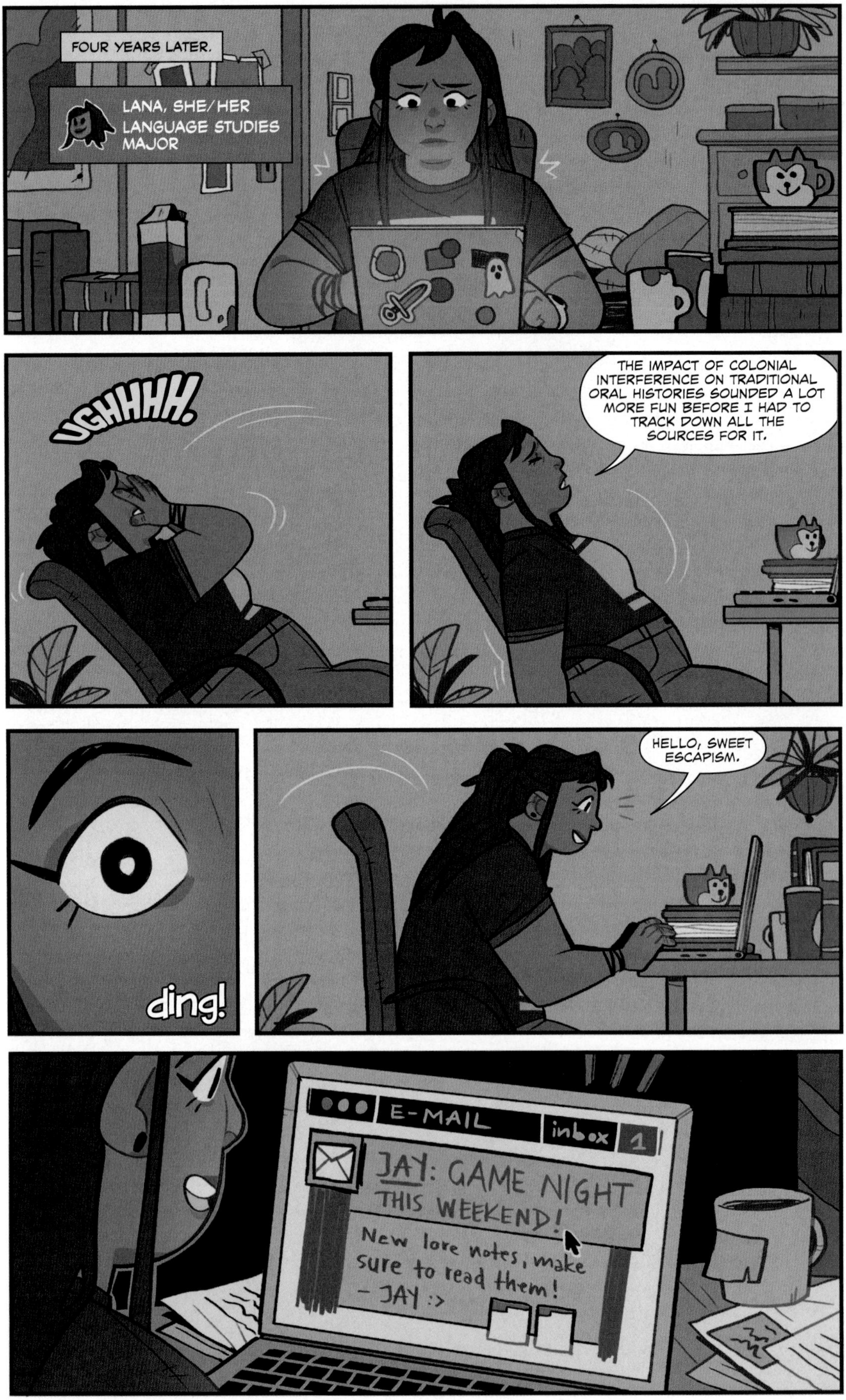
FOUR YEARS LATER.
LANA, SHE/HER
LANGUAGE STUDIES MAJOR
UGHHHH!
THE IMPACT OF COLONIAL INTERFERENCE ON TRADITIONAL ORAL HISTORIES SOUNDED A LOT MORE FUN BEFORE I HAD TO TRACK DOWN ALL THE SOURCES FOR IT.
ding!
HELLO, SWEET ESCAPISM.
E-MAIL
inbox 1
JAY: GAME NIGHT THIS WEEKEND!
New lore notes, make sure to read them!
- JAY :>

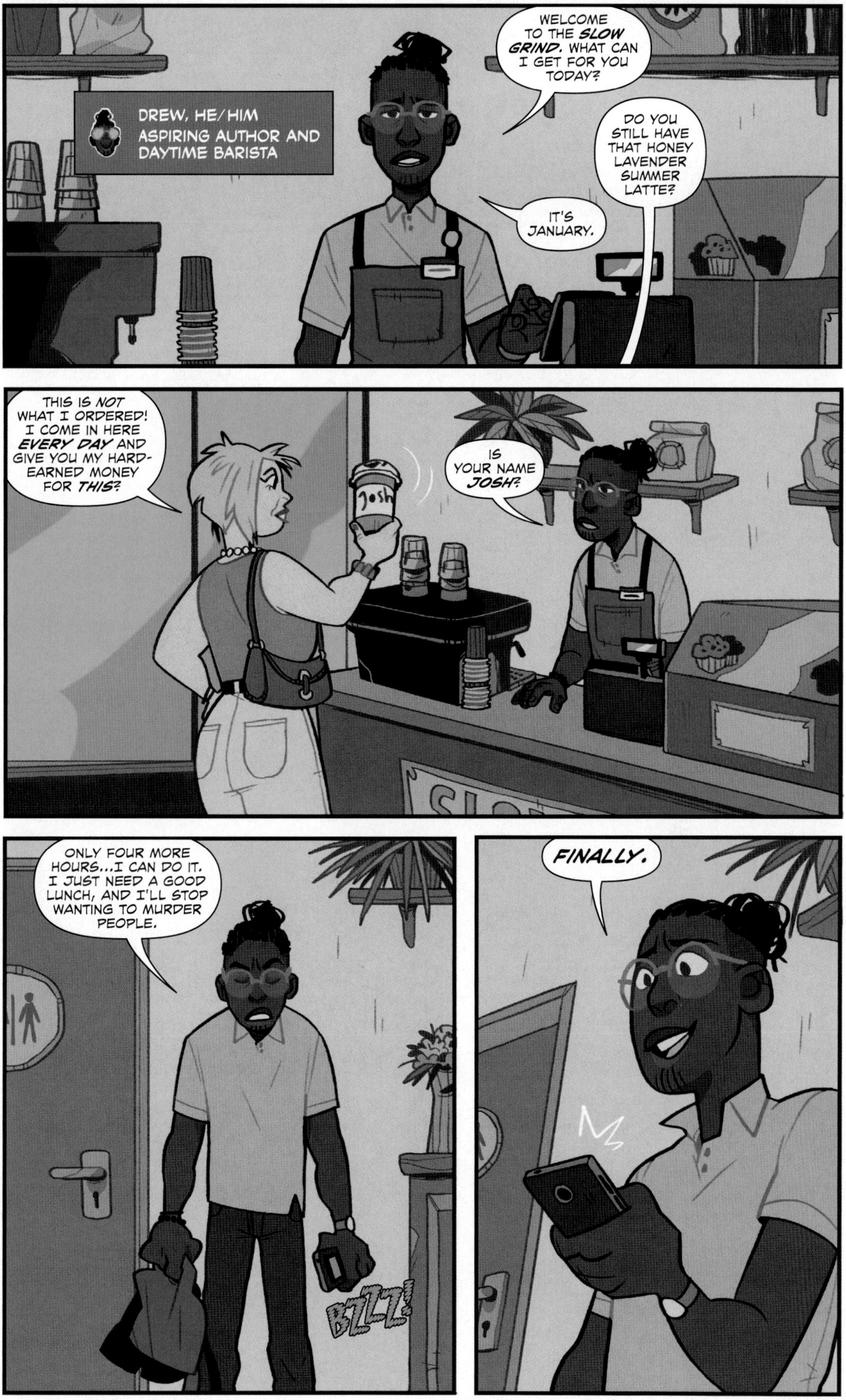
DREW, HE/HIM
ASPIRING AUTHOR AND DAYTIME BARISTA
WELCOME TO THE SLOW GRIND. WHAT CAN I GET FOR YOU TODAY?
DO YOU STILL HAVE THAT HONEY LAVENDER SUMMER LATTE?
IT'S JANUARY.
THIS IS NOT WHAT I ORDERED! I COME IN HERE EVERY DAY AND GIVE YOU MY HARD-EARNED MONEY FOR THIS?
Josh
IS YOUR NAME JOSH?
ONLY FOUR MORE HOURS...I CAN DO IT. I JUST NEED A GOOD LUNCH, AND I'LL STOP WANTING TO MURDER PEOPLE.
BZZZ!
FINALLY.

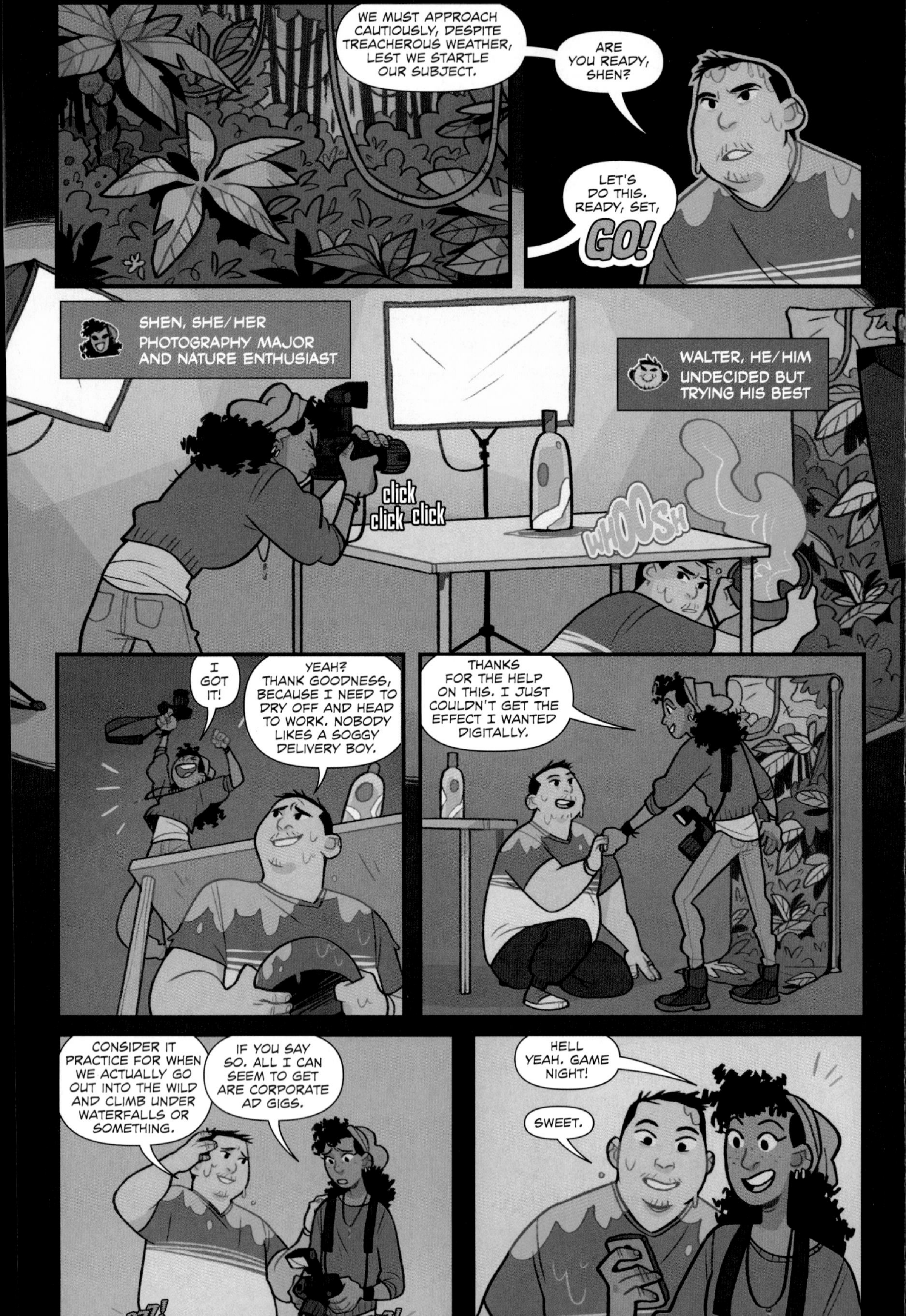

WE MUST APPROACH CAUTIOUSLY, DESPITE TREACHEROUS WEATHER, LEST WE STARTLE OUR SUBJECT.
ARE YOU READY, SHEN?
LET'S DO THIS. READY, SET, GO!
SHEN, SHE/HER
PHOTOGRAPHY MAJOR AND NATURE ENTHUSIAST
WALTER, HE/HIM
UNDECIDED BUT TRYING HIS BEST
click click click
WHOOSH
I GOT IT!
YEAH? THANK GOODNESS, BECAUSE I NEED TO DRY OFF AND HEAD TO WORK. NOBODY LIKES A SOGGY DELIVERY BOY.
THANKS FOR THE HELP ON THIS. I JUST COULDN'T GET THE EFFECT I WANTED DIGITALLY.
CONSIDER IT PRACTICE FOR WHEN WE ACTUALLY GO OUT INTO THE WILD AND CLIMB UNDER WATERFALLS OR SOMETHING.
IF YOU SAY SO. ALL I CAN SEEM TO GET ARE CORPORATE AD GIGS.
BZZZ! BZZZ!
HELL YEAH. GAME NIGHT!
SWEET.

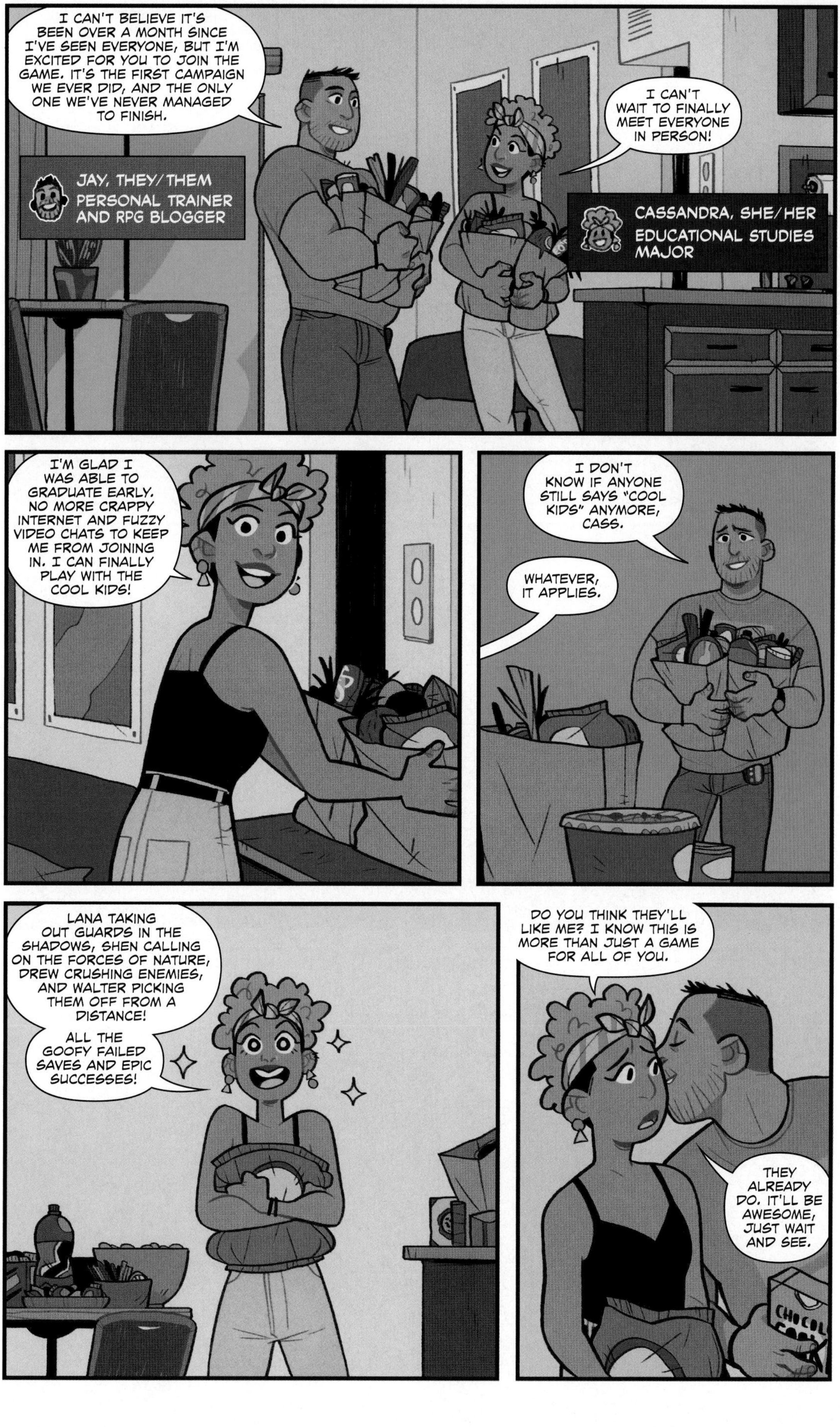
I CAN'T BELIEVE IT'S BEEN OVER A MONTH SINCE I'VE SEEN EVERYONE, BUT I'M EXCITED FOR YOU TO JOIN THE GAME. IT'S THE FIRST CAMPAIGN WE EVER DID, AND THE ONLY ONE WE'VE NEVER MANAGED TO FINISH.
I CAN'T WAIT TO FINALLY MEET EVERYONE IN PERSON!
JAY, THEY/THEM
PERSONAL TRAINER AND RPG BLOGGER
CASSANDRA, SHE/HER
EDUCATIONAL STUDIES MAJOR
I'M GLAD I WAS ABLE TO GRADUATE EARLY. NO MORE CRAPPY INTERNET AND FUZZY VIDEO CHATS TO KEEP ME FROM JOINING IN. I CAN FINALLY PLAY WITH THE COOL KIDS!
I DON'T KNOW IF ANYONE STILL SAYS "COOL KIDS" ANYMORE, CASS.
WHATEVER, IT APPLIES.
LANA TAKING OUT GUARDS IN THE SHADOWS, SHEN CALLING ON THE FORCES OF NATURE, DREW CRUSHING ENEMIES, AND WALTER PICKING THEM OFF FROM A DISTANCE!
ALL THE GOOFY FAILED SAVES AND EPIC SUCCESSES!
DO YOU THINK THEY'LL LIKE ME? I KNOW THIS IS MORE THAN JUST A GAME FOR ALL OF YOU.
THEY ALREADY DO. IT'LL BE AWESOME, JUST WAIT AND SEE.

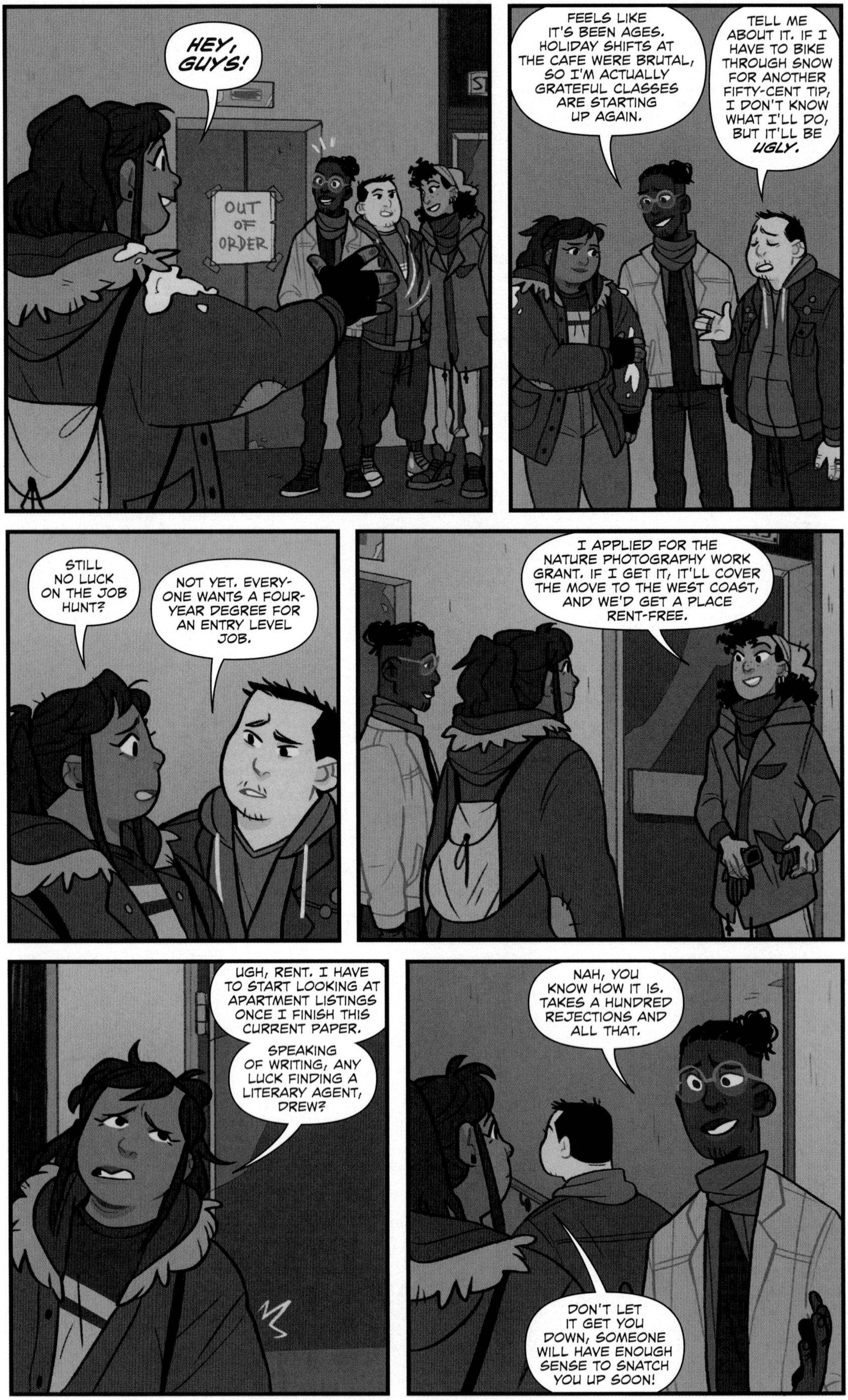
HEY, GUYS!
OUT OF ORDER
FEELS LIKE IT'S BEEN AGES. HOLIDAY SHIFTS AT THE CAFE WERE BRUTAL, SO I'M ACTUALLY GRATEFUL CLASSES ARE STARTING UP AGAIN.
TELL ME ABOUT IT. IF I HAVE TO BIKE THROUGH SNOW FOR ANOTHER FIFTY-CENT TIP, I DON'T KNOW WHAT I'LL DO, BUT IT'LL BE UGLY.
STILL NO LUCK ON THE JOB HUNT?
NOT YET. EVERY-ONE WANTS A FOUR-YEAR DEGREE FOR AN ENTRY LEVEL JOB.
I APPLIED FOR THE NATURE PHOTOGRAPHY WORK GRANT. IF I GET IT, IT'LL COVER THE MOVE TO THE WEST COAST, AND WE'D GET A PLACE RENT-FREE.
UGH, RENT. I HAVE TO START LOOKING AT APARTMENT LISTINGS ONCE I FINISH THIS CURRENT PAPER.
SPEAKING OF WRITING, ANY LUCK FINDING A LITERARY AGENT, DREW?
NAH, YOU KNOW HOW IT IS. TAKES A HUNDRED REJECTIONS AND ALL THAT.
DON'T LET IT GET YOU DOWN, SOMEONE WILL HAVE ENOUGH SENSE TO SNATCH YOU UP SOON!

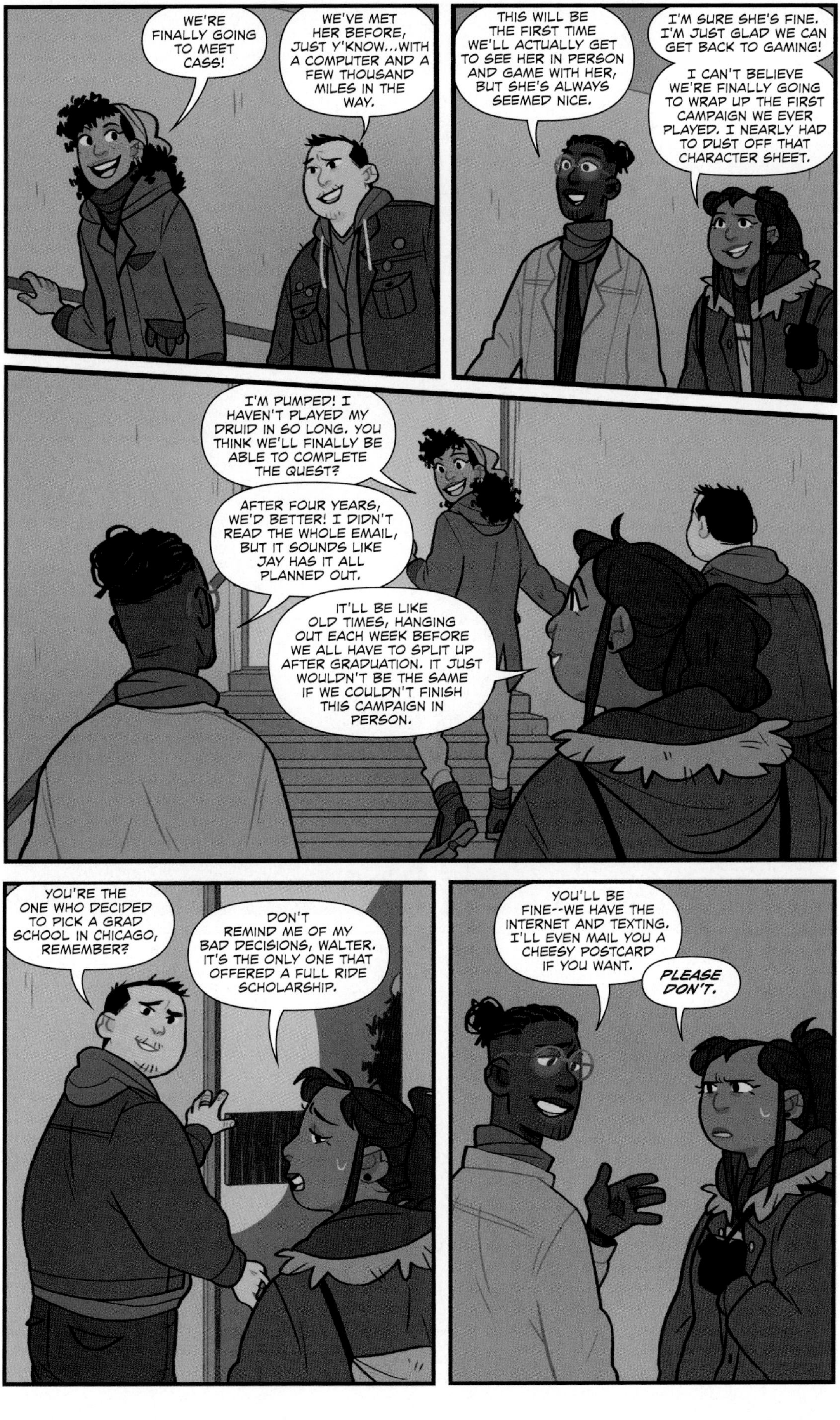
WE'RE FINALLY GOING TO MEET CASS!
WE'VE MET HER BEFORE, JUST Y'KNOW...WITH A COMPUTER AND A FEW THOUSAND MILES IN THE WAY.
THIS WILL BE THE FIRST TIME WE'LL ACTUALLY GET TO SEE HER IN PERSON AND GAME WITH HER, BUT SHE'S ALWAYS SEEMED NICE.
I'M SURE SHE'S FINE. I'M JUST GLAD WE CAN GET BACK TO GAMING!
I CAN'T BELIEVE WE'RE FINALLY GOING TO WRAP UP THE FIRST CAMPAIGN WE EVER PLAYED. I NEARLY HAD TO DUST OFF THAT CHARACTER SHEET.
I'M PUMPED! I HAVEN'T PLAYED MY DRUID IN SO LONG. YOU THINK WE'LL FINALLY BE ABLE TO COMPLETE THE QUEST?
AFTER FOUR YEARS, WE'D BETTER! I DIDN'T READ THE WHOLE EMAIL, BUT IT SOUNDS LIKE JAY HAS IT ALL PLANNED OUT.
IT'LL BE LIKE OLD TIMES, HANGING OUT EACH WEEK BEFORE WE ALL HAVE TO SPLIT UP AFTER GRADUATION. IT JUST WOULDN'T BE THE SAME IF WE COULDN'T FINISH THIS CAMPAIGN IN PERSON.
YOU'RE THE ONE WHO DECIDED TO PICK A GRAD SCHOOL IN CHICAGO, REMEMBER?
DON'T REMIND ME OF MY BAD DECISIONS, WALTER. IT'S THE ONLY ONE THAT OFFERED A FULL RIDE SCHOLARSHIP.
YOU'LL BE FINE--WE HAVE THE INTERNET AND TEXTING. I'LL EVEN MAIL YOU A CHEESY POSTCARD IF YOU WANT.
PLEASE DON'T.

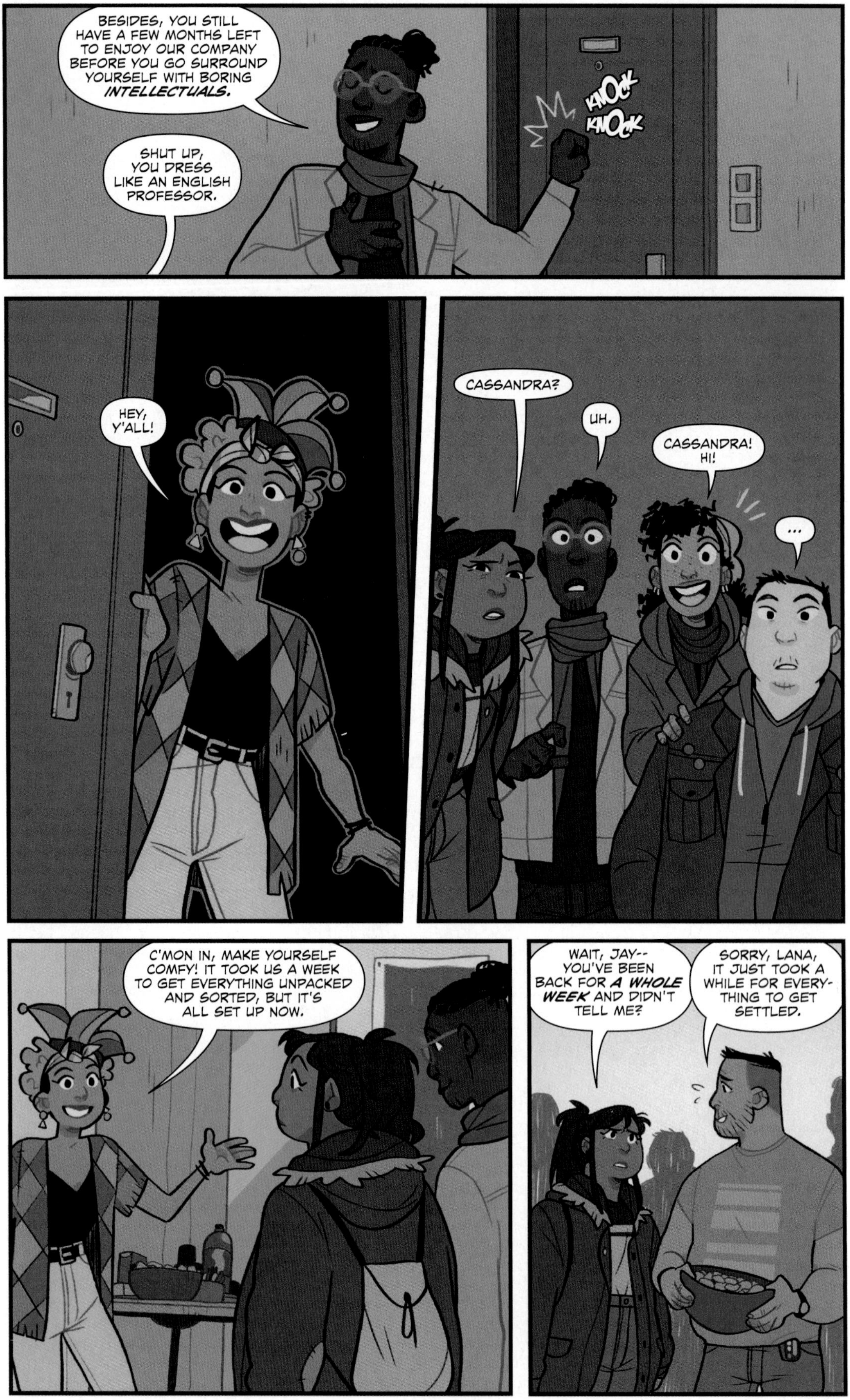
BESIDES, YOU STILL HAVE A FEW MONTHS LEFT TO ENJOY OUR COMPANY BEFORE YOU GO SURROUND YOURSELF WITH BORING *INTELLECTUALS.*
KNOCK KNOCK
SHUT UP, YOU DRESS LIKE AN ENGLISH PROFESSOR.
HEY, Y'ALL!
CASSANDRA?
UH.
CASSANDRA! HI!
...
C'MON IN, MAKE YOURSELF COMFY! IT TOOK US A WEEK TO GET EVERYTHING UNPACKED AND SORTED, BUT IT'S ALL SET UP NOW.
WAIT, JAY-- YOU'VE BEEN BACK FOR *A WHOLE WEEK* AND DIDN'T TELL ME?
SORRY, LANA, IT JUST TOOK A WHILE FOR EVERY-THING TO GET SETTLED.

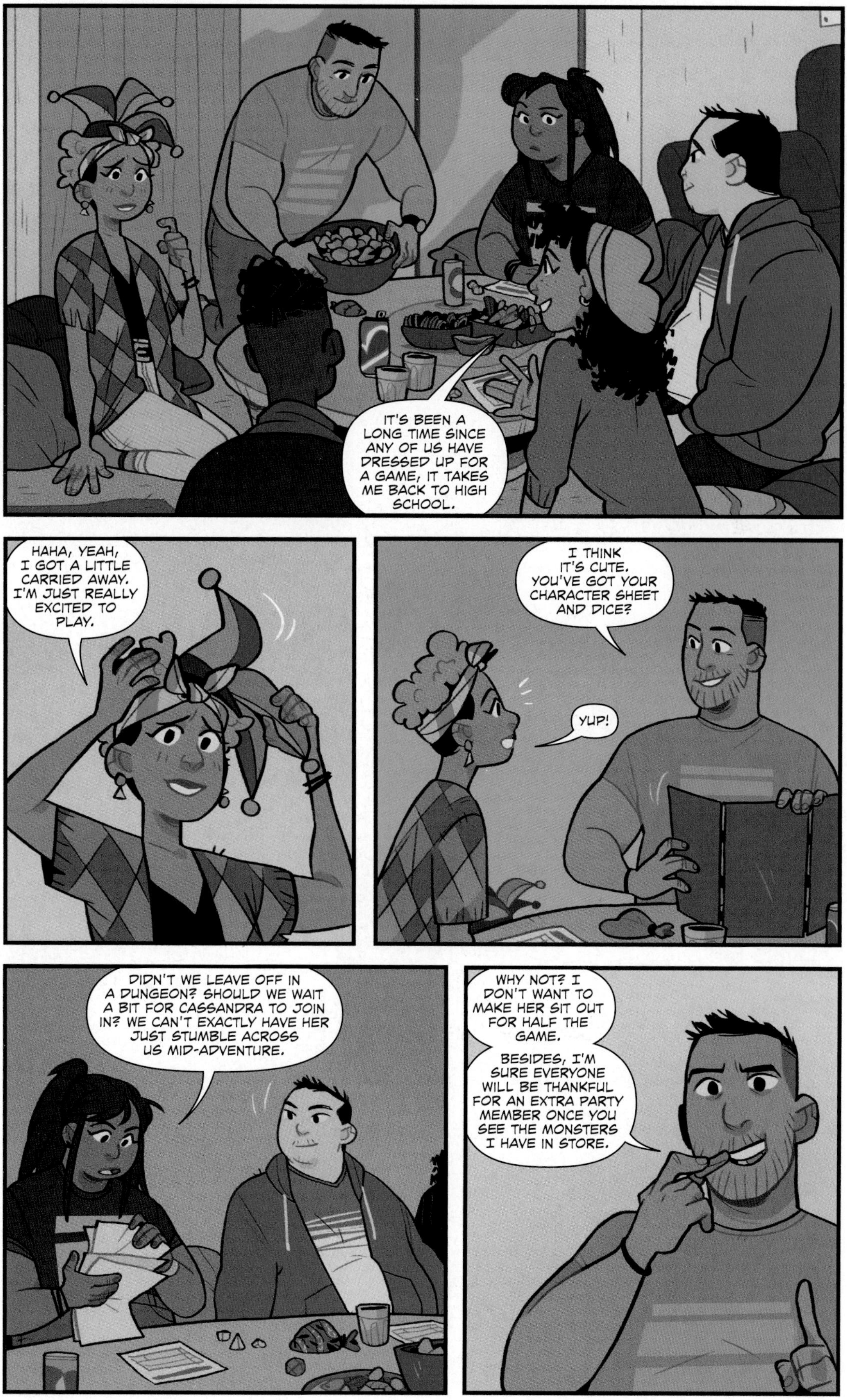
IT'S BEEN A LONG TIME SINCE ANY OF US HAVE DRESSED UP FOR A GAME, IT TAKES ME BACK TO HIGH SCHOOL.
HAHA, YEAH, I GOT A LITTLE CARRIED AWAY. I'M JUST REALLY EXCITED TO PLAY.
I THINK IT'S CUTE. YOU'VE GOT YOUR CHARACTER SHEET AND DICE?
YUP!
DIDN'T WE LEAVE OFF IN A DUNGEON? SHOULD WE WAIT A BIT FOR CASSANDRA TO JOIN IN? WE CAN'T EXACTLY HAVE HER JUST STUMBLE ACROSS US MID-ADVENTURE.
WHY NOT? I DON'T WANT TO MAKE HER SIT OUT FOR HALF THE GAME.
BESIDES, I'M SURE EVERYONE WILL BE THANKFUL FOR AN EXTRA PARTY MEMBER ONCE YOU SEE THE MONSTERS I HAVE IN STORE.

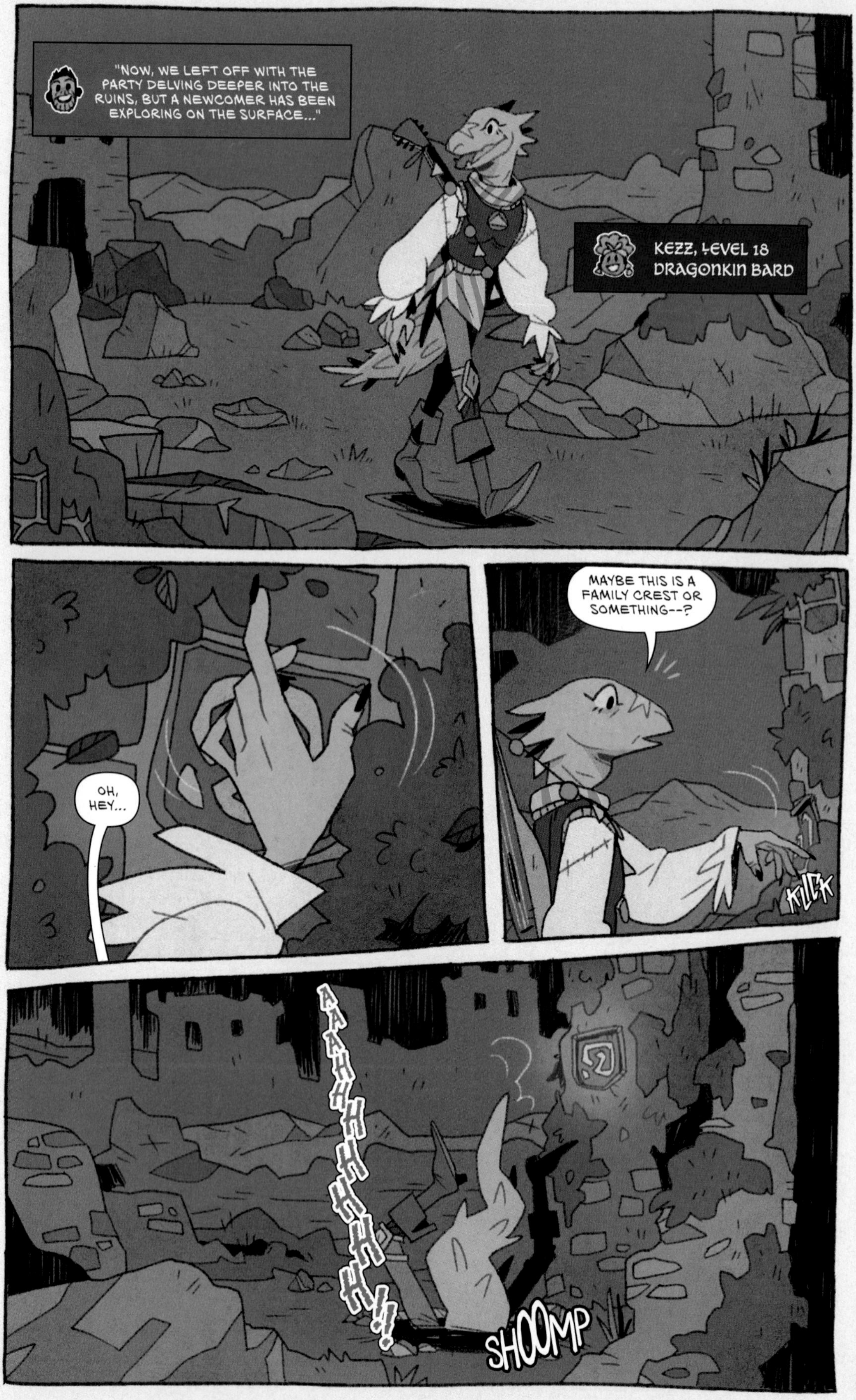
"NOW, WE LEFT OFF WITH THE PARTY DELVING DEEPER INTO THE RUINS, BUT A NEWCOMER HAS BEEN EXPLORING ON THE SURFACE..."
KEZZ, LEVEL 18 DRAGONKIN BARD
OH, HEY...
MAYBE THIS IS A FAMILY CREST OR SOMETHING--?
KLICK
AAAHHHHHHHH!!
SHOOMP

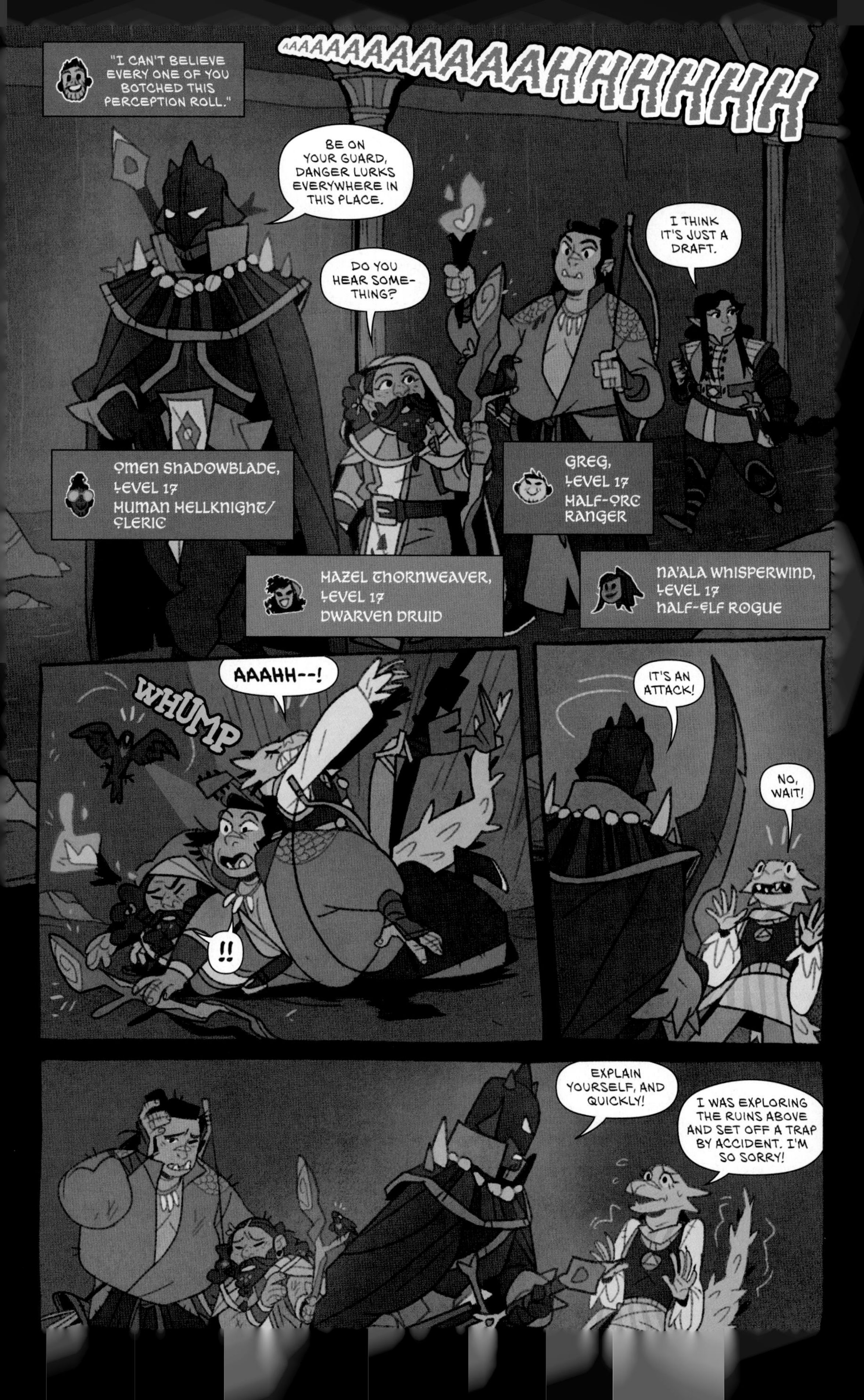
"I CAN'T BELIEVE EVERY ONE OF YOU BOTCHED THIS PERCEPTION ROLL."
AAAAAAAAAAAAAHHHHHHH
BE ON YOUR GUARD, DANGER LURKS EVERYWHERE IN THIS PLACE.
DO YOU HEAR SOME-THING?
I THINK IT'S JUST A DRAFT.
OMEN SHADOWBLADE, LEVEL 17
HUMAN HELLKNIGHT/ CLERIC
GREG, LEVEL 17
HALF-ORC RANGER
HAZEL THORNWEAVER, LEVEL 17
DWARVEN DRUID
NA'ALA WHISPERWIND, LEVEL 17
HALF-ELF ROGUE
WHUMP
AAAHH--!
!!
IT'S AN ATTACK!
NO, WAIT!
EXPLAIN YOURSELF, AND QUICKLY!
I WAS EXPLORING THE RUINS ABOVE AND SET OFF A TRAP BY ACCIDENT. I'M SO SORRY!

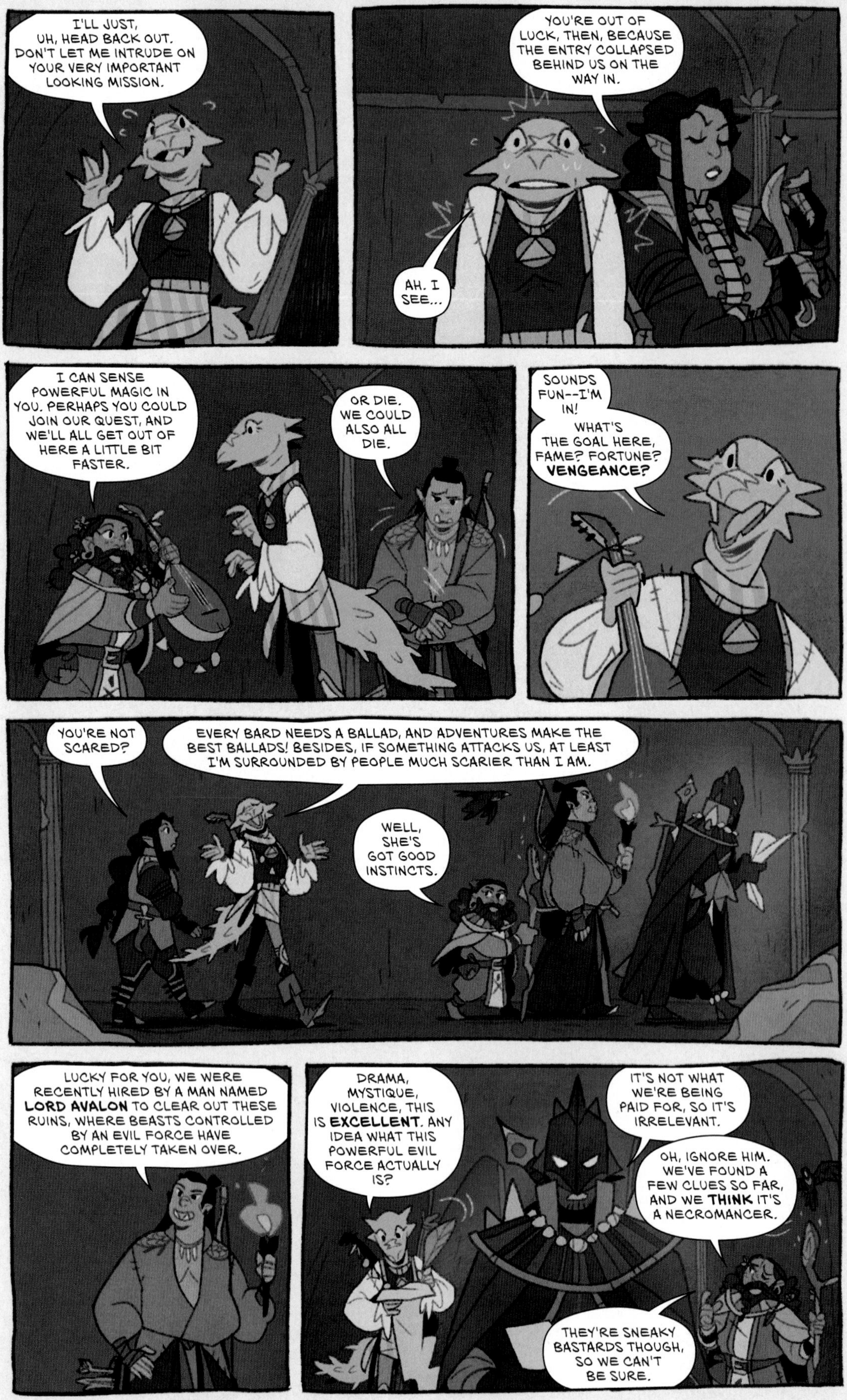
I'LL JUST, UH, HEAD BACK OUT. DON'T LET ME INTRUDE ON YOUR VERY IMPORTANT LOOKING MISSION.
YOU'RE OUT OF LUCK, THEN, BECAUSE THE ENTRY COLLAPSED BEHIND US ON THE WAY IN.
AH. I SEE...
I CAN SENSE POWERFUL MAGIC IN YOU. PERHAPS YOU COULD JOIN OUR QUEST, AND WE'LL ALL GET OUT OF HERE A LITTLE BIT FASTER.
OR DIE. WE COULD ALSO ALL DIE.
SOUNDS FUN--I'M IN!
WHAT'S THE GOAL HERE, FAME? FORTUNE? **VENGEANCE?**
YOU'RE NOT SCARED?
EVERY BARD NEEDS A BALLAD, AND ADVENTURES MAKE THE BEST BALLADS! BESIDES, IF SOMETHING ATTACKS US, AT LEAST I'M SURROUNDED BY PEOPLE MUCH SCARIER THAN I AM.
WELL, SHE'S GOT GOOD INSTINCTS.
LUCKY FOR YOU, WE WERE RECENTLY HIRED BY A MAN NAMED **LORD AVALON** TO CLEAR OUT THESE RUINS, WHERE BEASTS CONTROLLED BY AN EVIL FORCE HAVE COMPLETELY TAKEN OVER.
DRAMA, MYSTIQUE, VIOLENCE, THIS IS **EXCELLENT**. ANY IDEA WHAT THIS POWERFUL EVIL FORCE ACTUALLY IS?
IT'S NOT WHAT WE'RE BEING PAID FOR, SO IT'S IRRELEVANT.
OH, IGNORE HIM. WE'VE FOUND A FEW CLUES SO FAR, AND WE **THINK** IT'S A NECROMANCER.
THEY'RE SNEAKY BASTARDS THOUGH, SO WE CAN'T BE SURE.

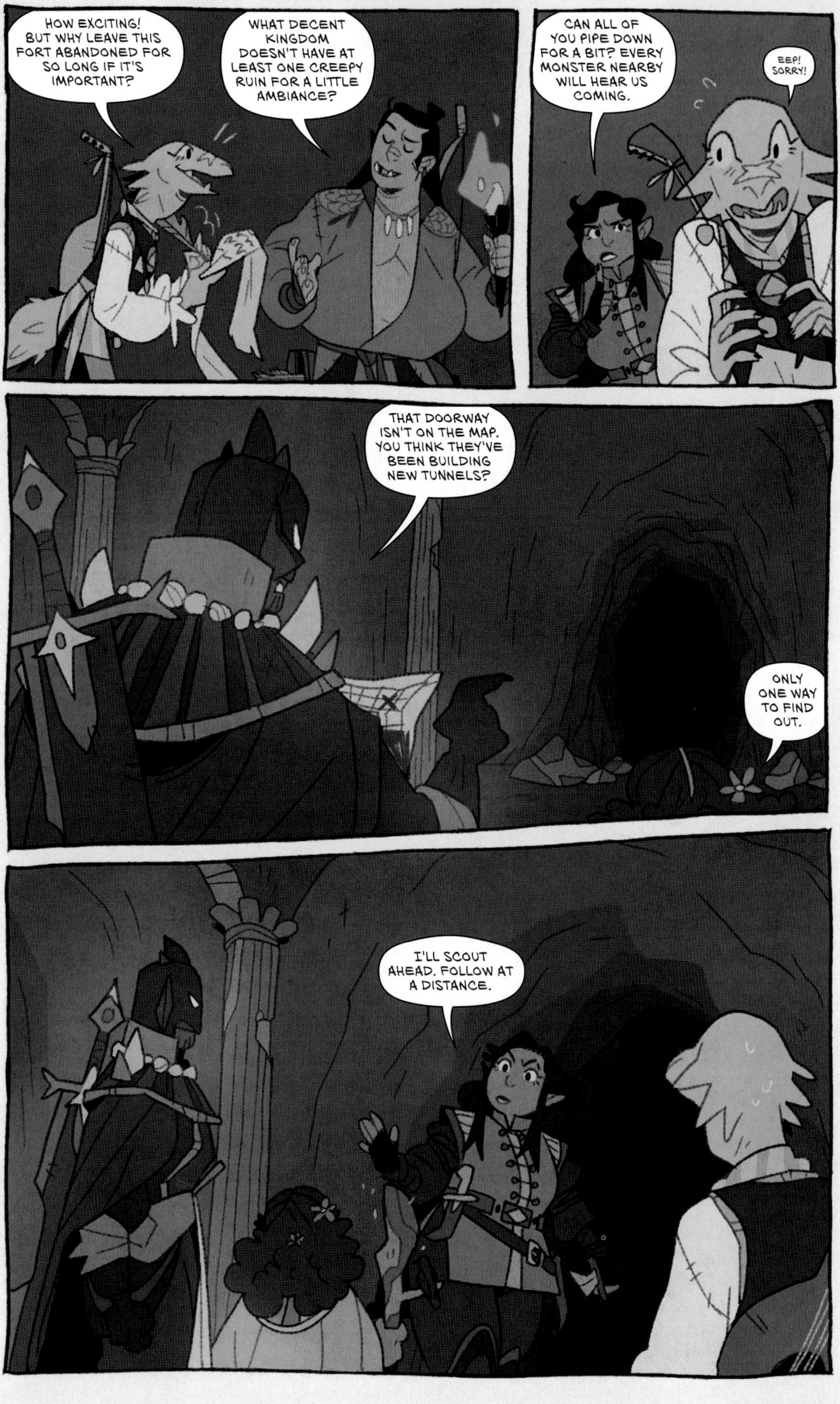
HOW EXCITING! BUT WHY LEAVE THIS FORT ABANDONED FOR SO LONG IF IT'S IMPORTANT?
WHAT DECENT KINGDOM DOESN'T HAVE AT LEAST ONE CREEPY RUIN FOR A LITTLE AMBIANCE?
CAN ALL OF YOU PIPE DOWN FOR A BIT? EVERY MONSTER NEARBY WILL HEAR US COMING.
EEP! SORRY!
THAT DOORWAY ISN'T ON THE MAP. YOU THINK THEY'VE BEEN BUILDING NEW TUNNELS?
ONLY ONE WAY TO FIND OUT.
I'LL SCOUT AHEAD. FOLLOW AT A DISTANCE.

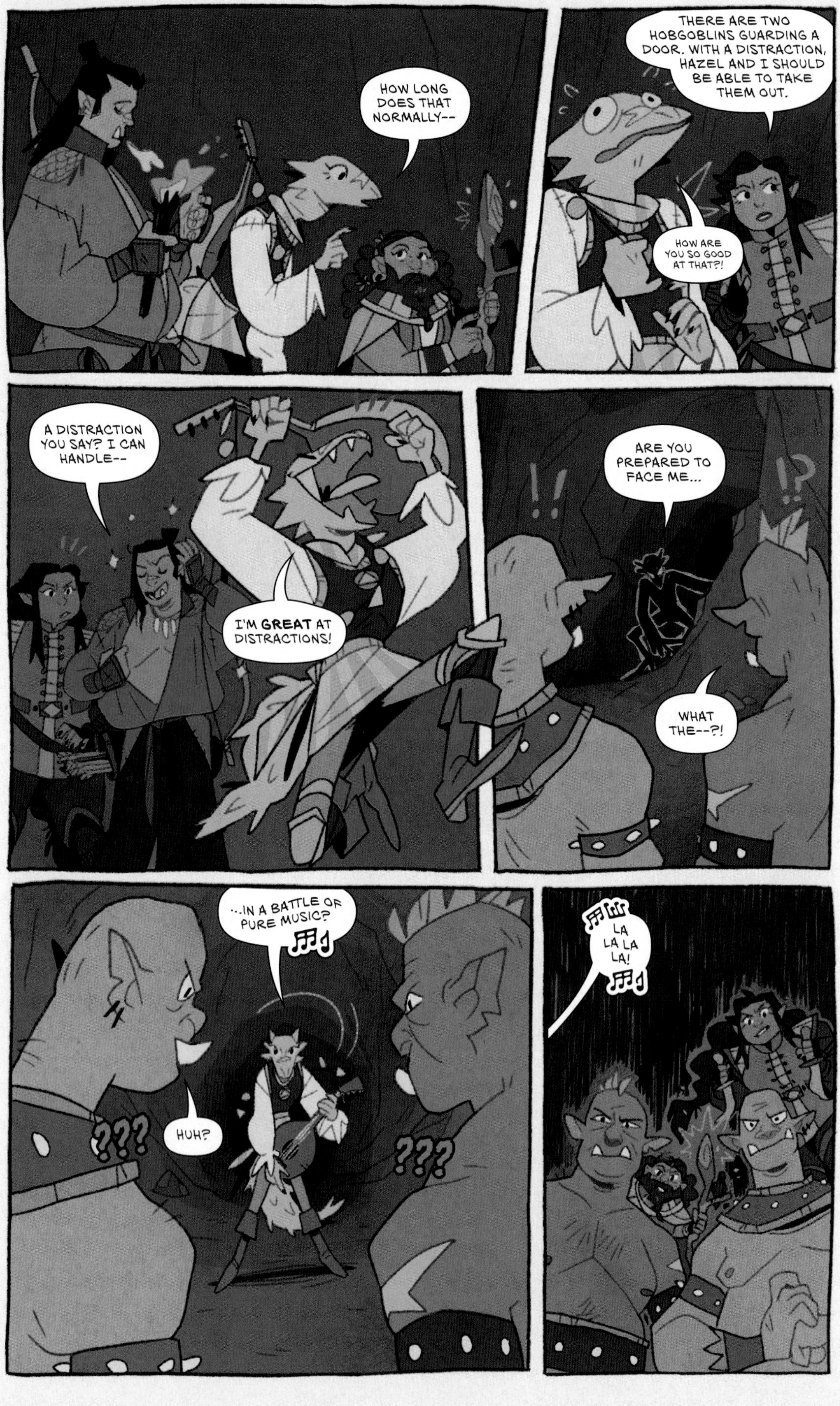
HOW LONG DOES THAT NORMALLY--
THERE ARE TWO HOBGOBLINS GUARDING A DOOR. WITH A DISTRACTION, HAZEL AND I SHOULD BE ABLE TO TAKE THEM OUT.
HOW ARE YOU SO GOOD AT THAT?!
A DISTRACTION YOU SAY? I CAN HANDLE--
I'M **GREAT** AT DISTRACTIONS!
!!
!?
ARE YOU PREPARED TO FACE ME...
WHAT THE--?!
...IN A BATTLE OF PURE MUSIC?
???
HUH?
???
LA LA LA LA!

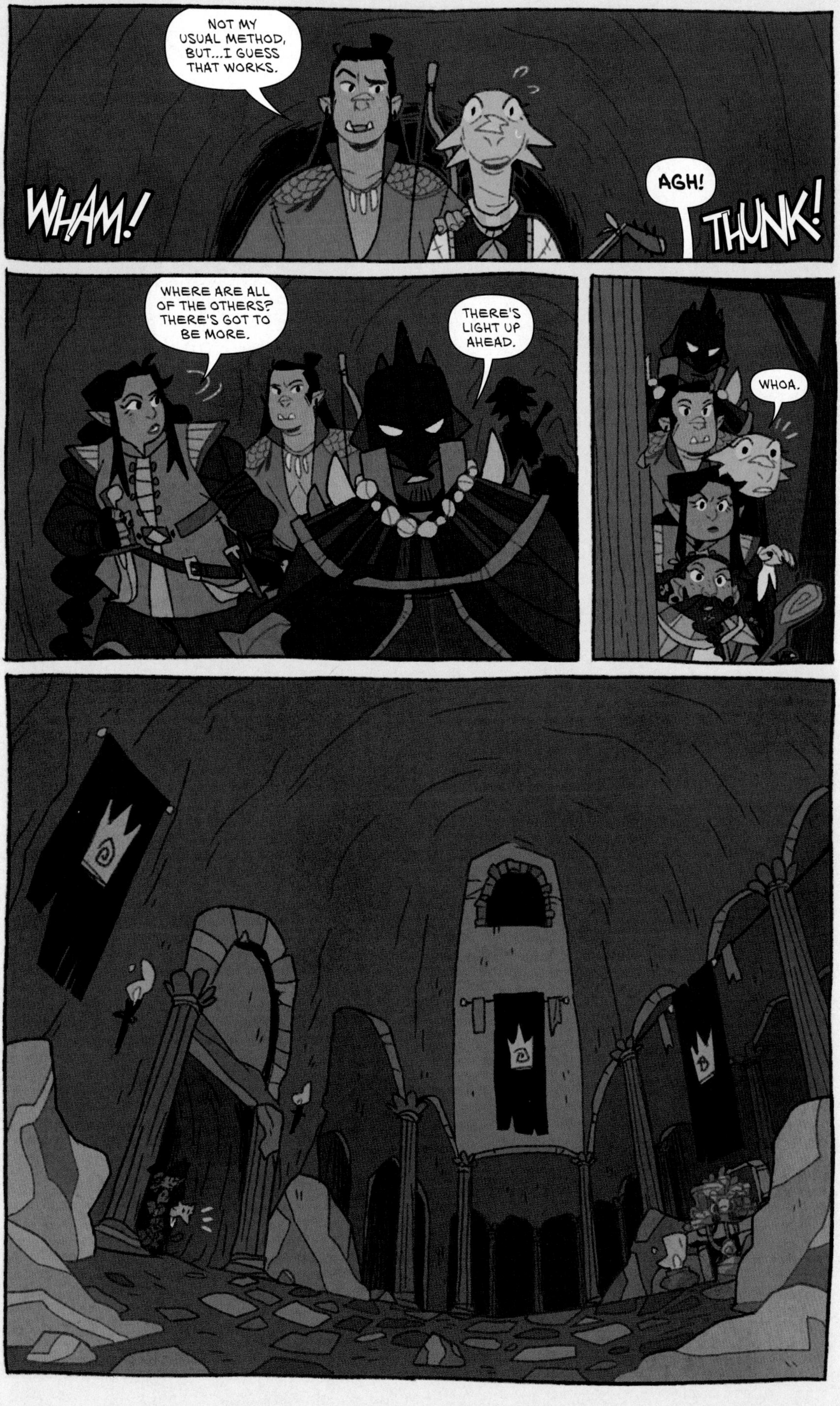
NOT MY USUAL METHOD, BUT...I GUESS THAT WORKS.
WHAM!
AGH!
THUNK!
WHERE ARE ALL OF THE OTHERS? THERE'S GOT TO BE MORE.
THERE'S LIGHT UP AHEAD.
WHOA.

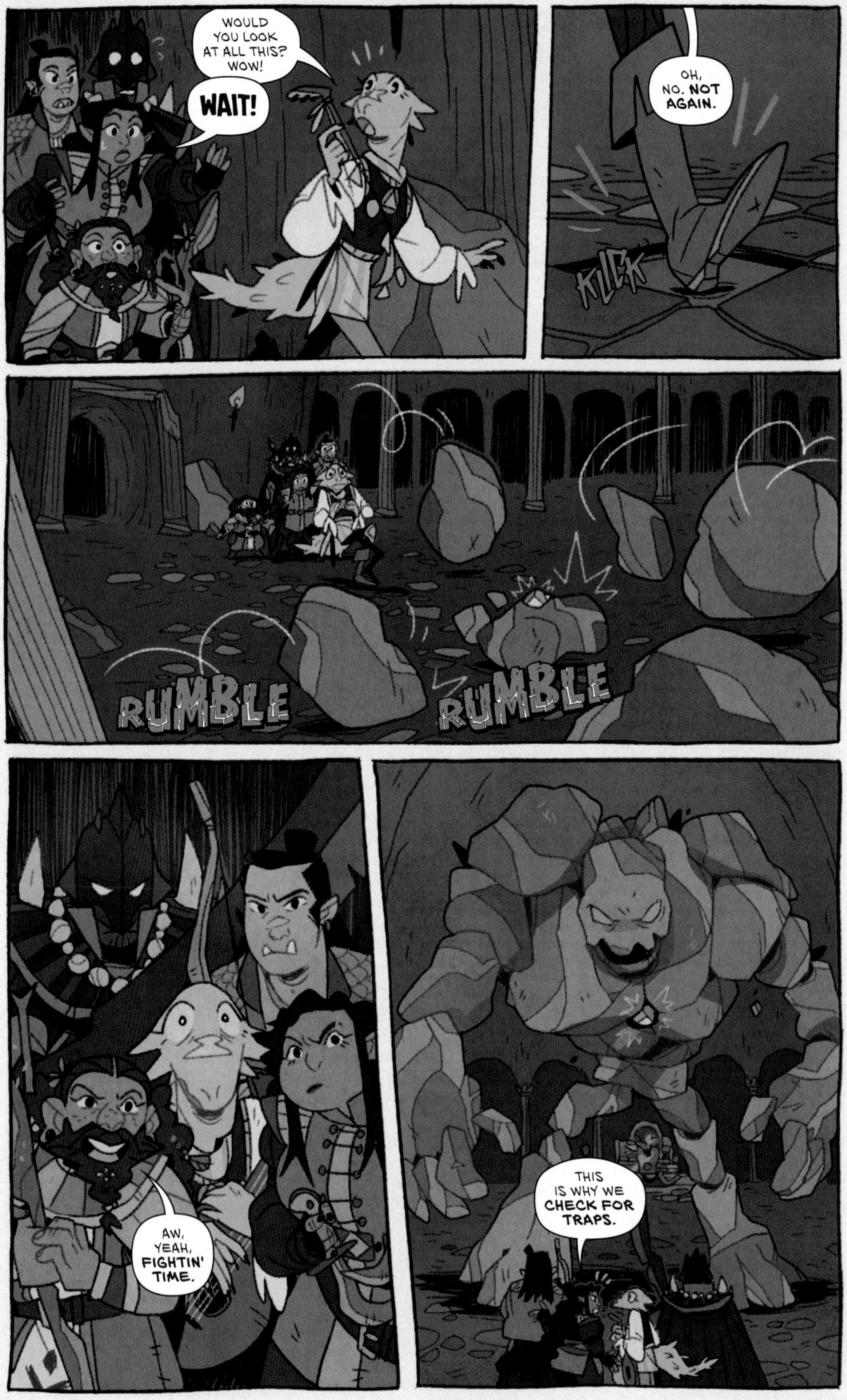
WOULD YOU LOOK AT ALL THIS? WOW!
WAIT!
OH, NO. NOT AGAIN.
KLICK
RUMBLE
RUMBLE
AW, YEAH, FIGHTIN' TIME.
THIS IS WHY WE CHECK FOR TRAPS.

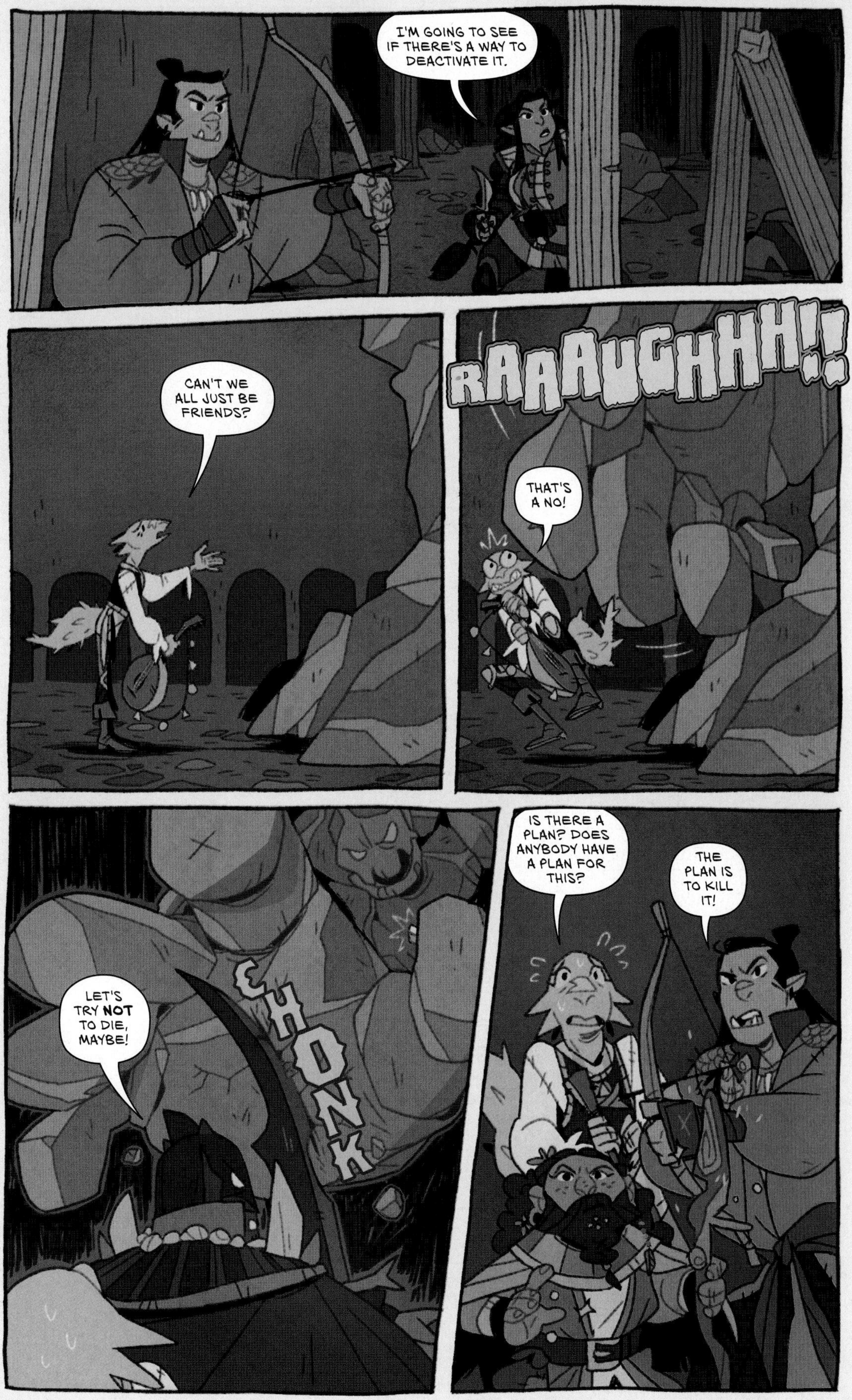
I'M GOING TO SEE IF THERE'S A WAY TO DEACTIVATE IT.
CAN'T WE ALL JUST BE FRIENDS?
RAAAUGHHH!!
THAT'S A NO!
LET'S TRY **NOT** TO DIE, MAYBE!
CHONK
IS THERE A PLAN? DOES ANYBODY HAVE A PLAN FOR THIS?
THE PLAN IS TO KILL IT!

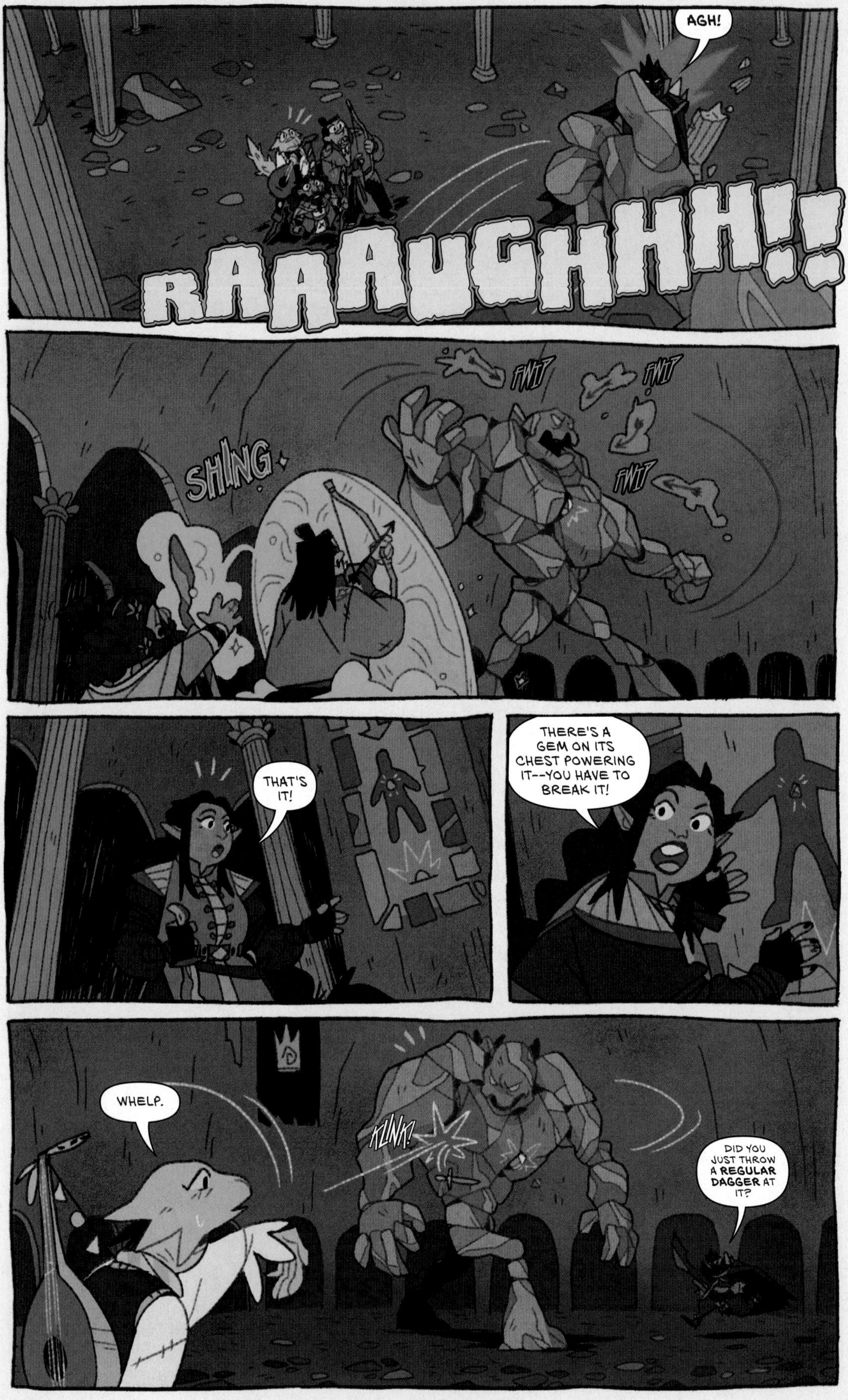
AGH!
RAAAUGHHH!!
FWIP
FWIP
SHING
FWIP
THAT'S IT!
THERE'S A GEM ON ITS CHEST POWERING IT--YOU HAVE TO BREAK IT!
WHELP.
KLINK!
DID YOU JUST THROW A **REGULAR DAGGER** AT IT?

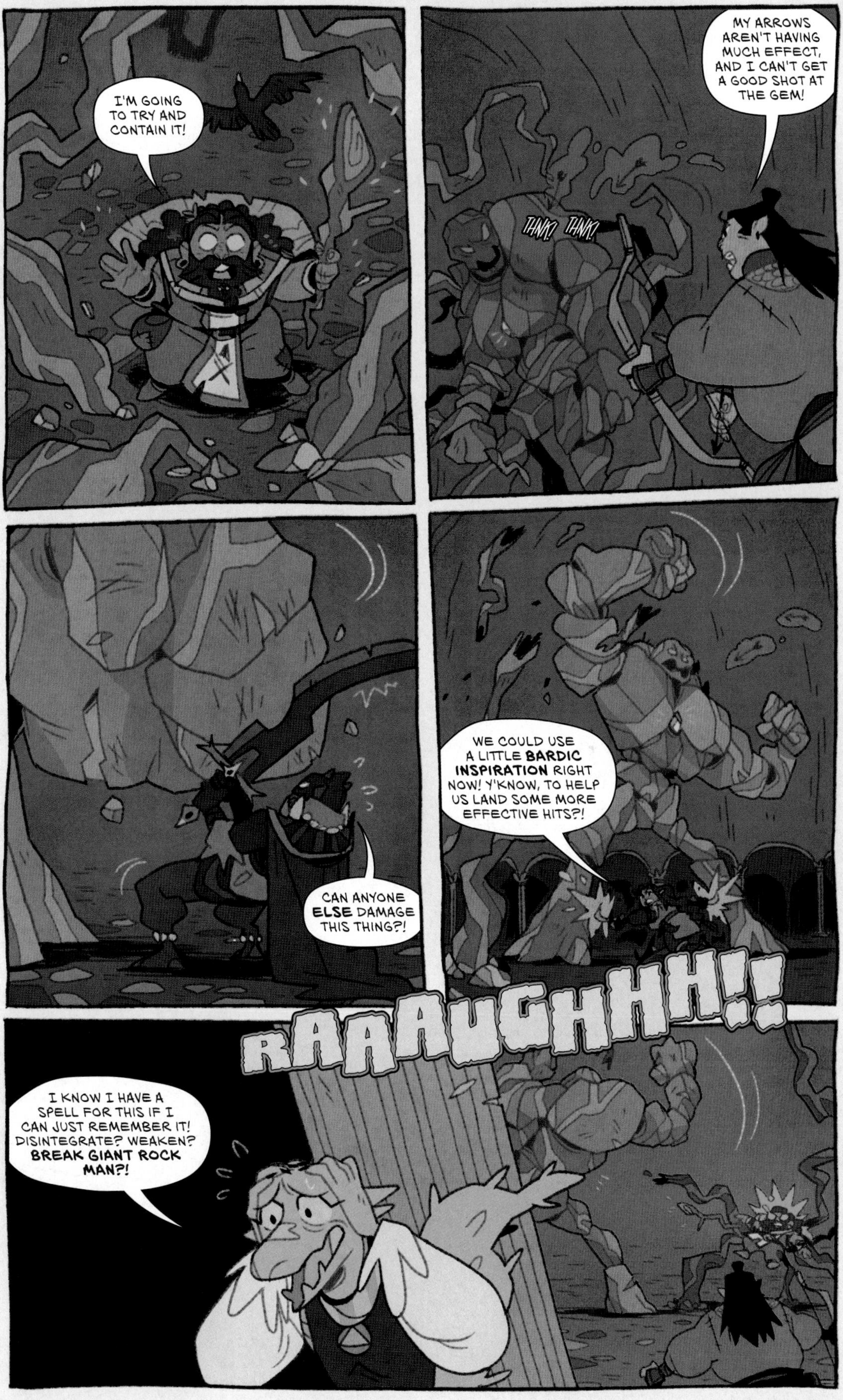
I'M GOING TO TRY AND CONTAIN IT!
MY ARROWS AREN'T HAVING MUCH EFFECT, AND I CAN'T GET A GOOD SHOT AT THE GEM!
THNK! THNK!
CAN ANYONE ELSE DAMAGE THIS THING?!
WE COULD USE A LITTLE BARDIC INSPIRATION RIGHT NOW! Y'KNOW, TO HELP US LAND SOME MORE EFFECTIVE HITS?!
RAAAUGHHH!!
I KNOW I HAVE A SPELL FOR THIS IF I CAN JUST REMEMBER IT! DISINTEGRATE? WEAKEN? BREAK GIANT ROCK MAN?!

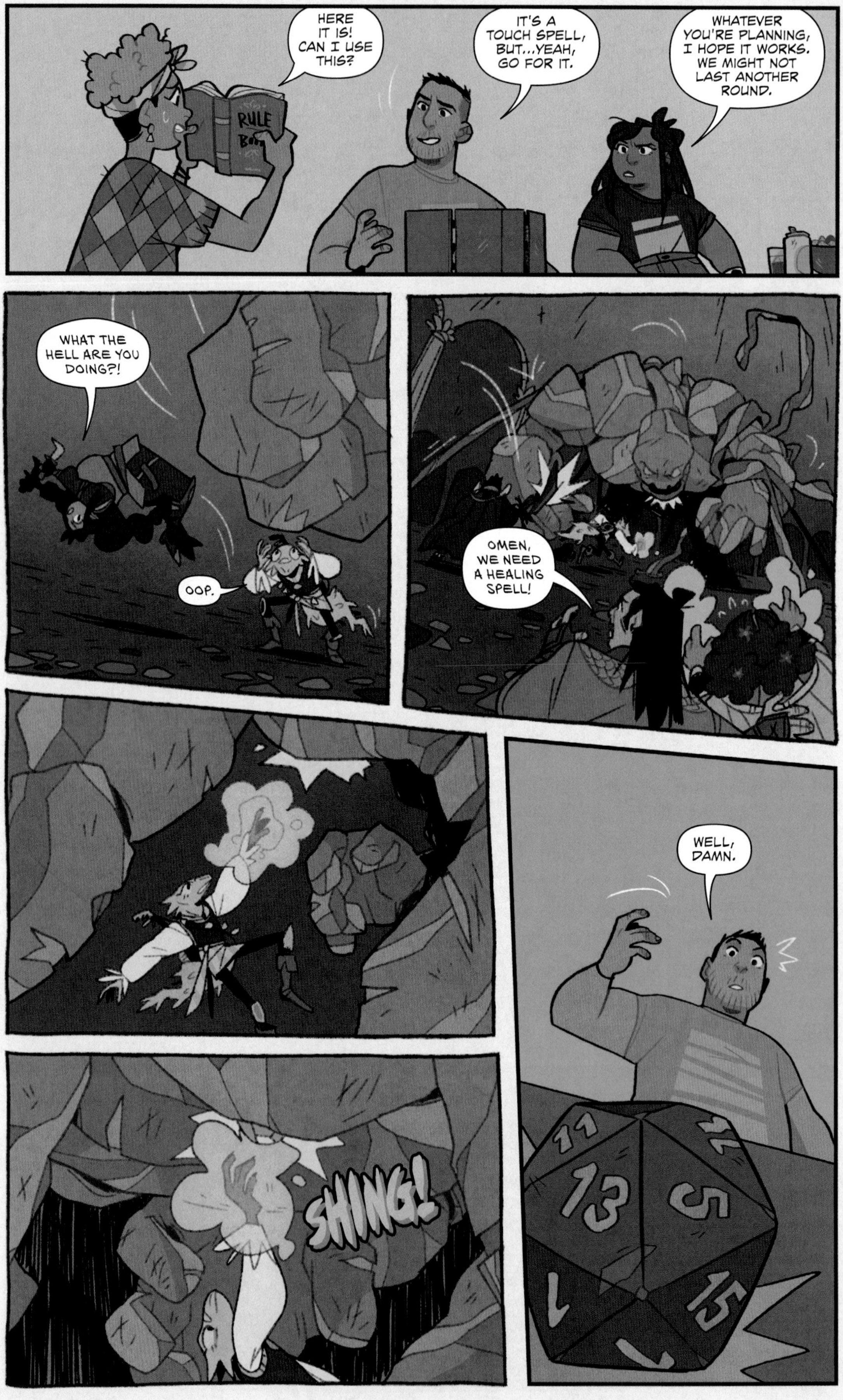
HERE IT IS! CAN I USE THIS?
RULE Book
IT'S A TOUCH SPELL, BUT...YEAH, GO FOR IT.
WHATEVER YOU'RE PLANNING, I HOPE IT WORKS. WE MIGHT NOT LAST ANOTHER ROUND.
WHAT THE HELL ARE YOU DOING?!
OOP.
OMEN, WE NEED A HEALING SPELL!
SHING!
WELL, DAMN.
13
5
15

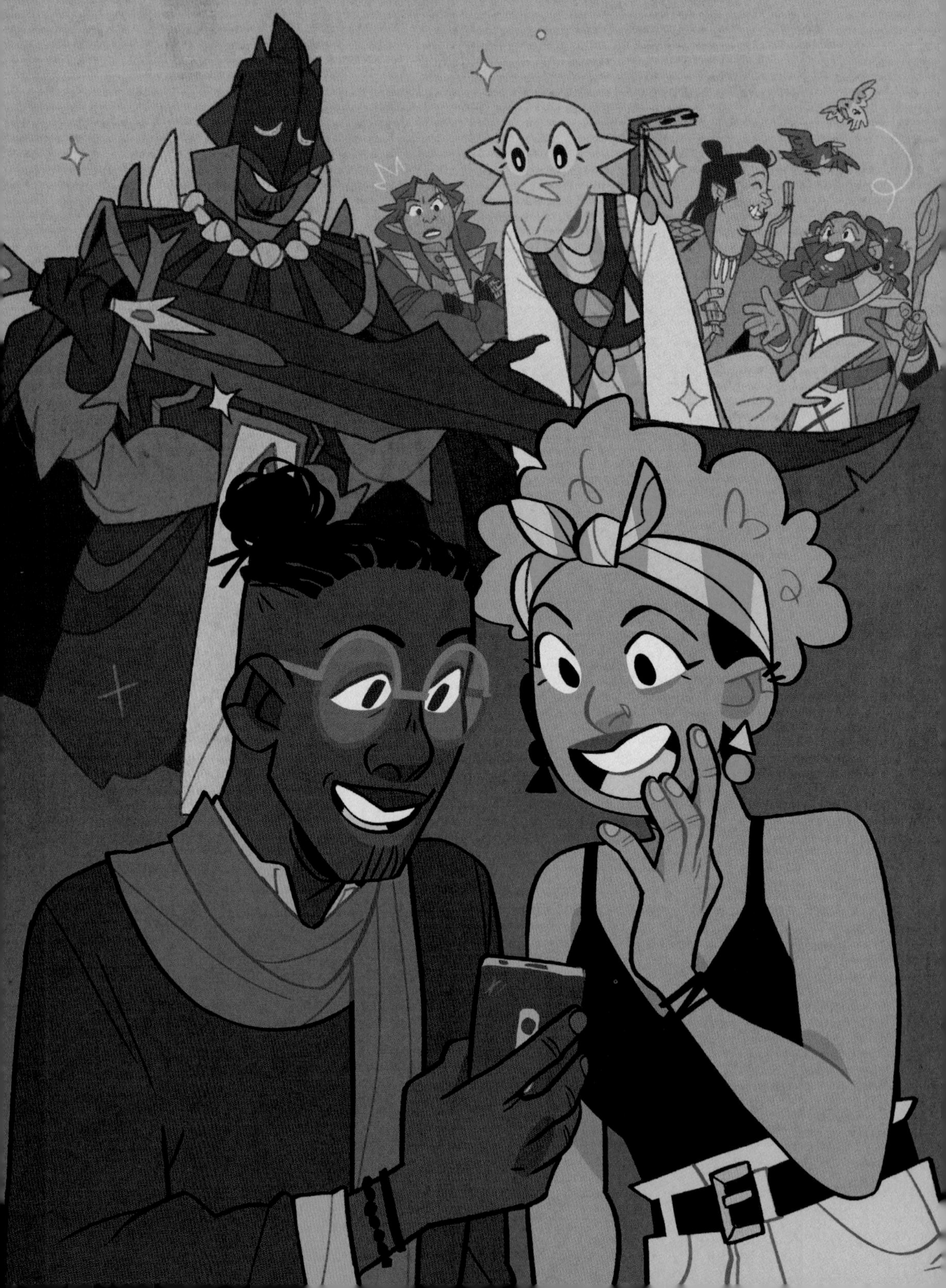

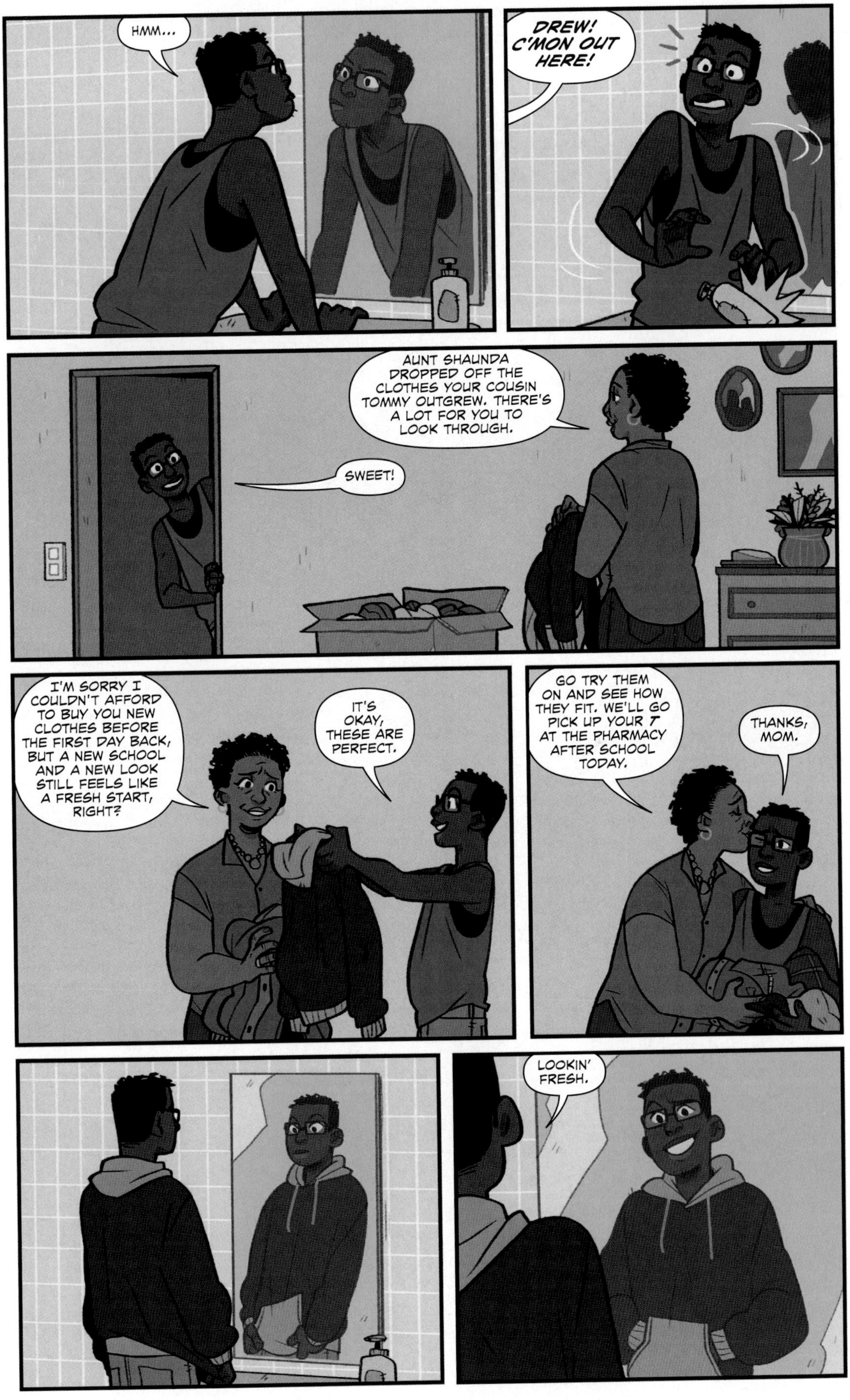
HMM...
DREW! C'MON OUT HERE!
AUNT SHAUNDA DROPPED OFF THE CLOTHES YOUR COUSIN TOMMY OUTGREW. THERE'S A LOT FOR YOU TO LOOK THROUGH.
SWEET!
I'M SORRY I COULDN'T AFFORD TO BUY YOU NEW CLOTHES BEFORE THE FIRST DAY BACK, BUT A NEW SCHOOL AND A NEW LOOK STILL FEELS LIKE A FRESH START, RIGHT?
IT'S OKAY, THESE ARE PERFECT.
GO TRY THEM ON AND SEE HOW THEY FIT. WE'LL GO PICK UP YOUR T AT THE PHARMACY AFTER SCHOOL TODAY.
THANKS, MOM.
LOOKIN' FRESH.

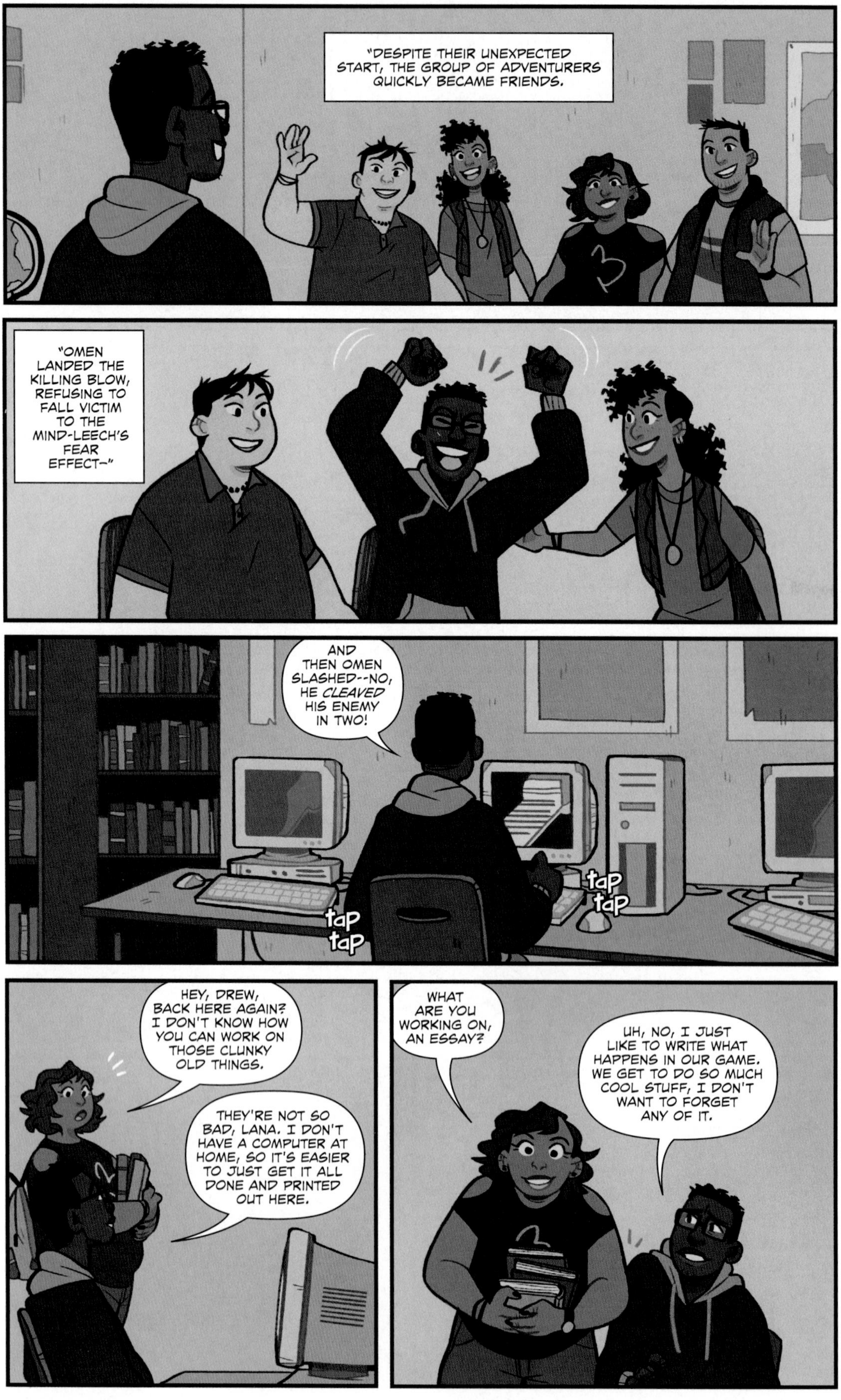
"DESPITE THEIR UNEXPECTED START, THE GROUP OF ADVENTURERS QUICKLY BECAME FRIENDS.
"OMEN LANDED THE KILLING BLOW, REFUSING TO FALL VICTIM TO THE MIND-LEECH'S FEAR EFFECT–"
AND THEN OMEN SLASHED--NO, HE *CLEAVED* HIS ENEMY IN TWO!
tap tap
tap tap
HEY, DREW, BACK HERE AGAIN? I DON'T KNOW HOW YOU CAN WORK ON THOSE CLUNKY OLD THINGS.
THEY'RE NOT SO BAD, LANA. I DON'T HAVE A COMPUTER AT HOME, SO IT'S EASIER TO JUST GET IT ALL DONE AND PRINTED OUT HERE.
WHAT ARE YOU WORKING ON, AN ESSAY?
UH, NO, I JUST LIKE TO WRITE WHAT HAPPENS IN OUR GAME. WE GET TO DO SO MUCH COOL STUFF, I DON'T WANT TO FORGET ANY OF IT.

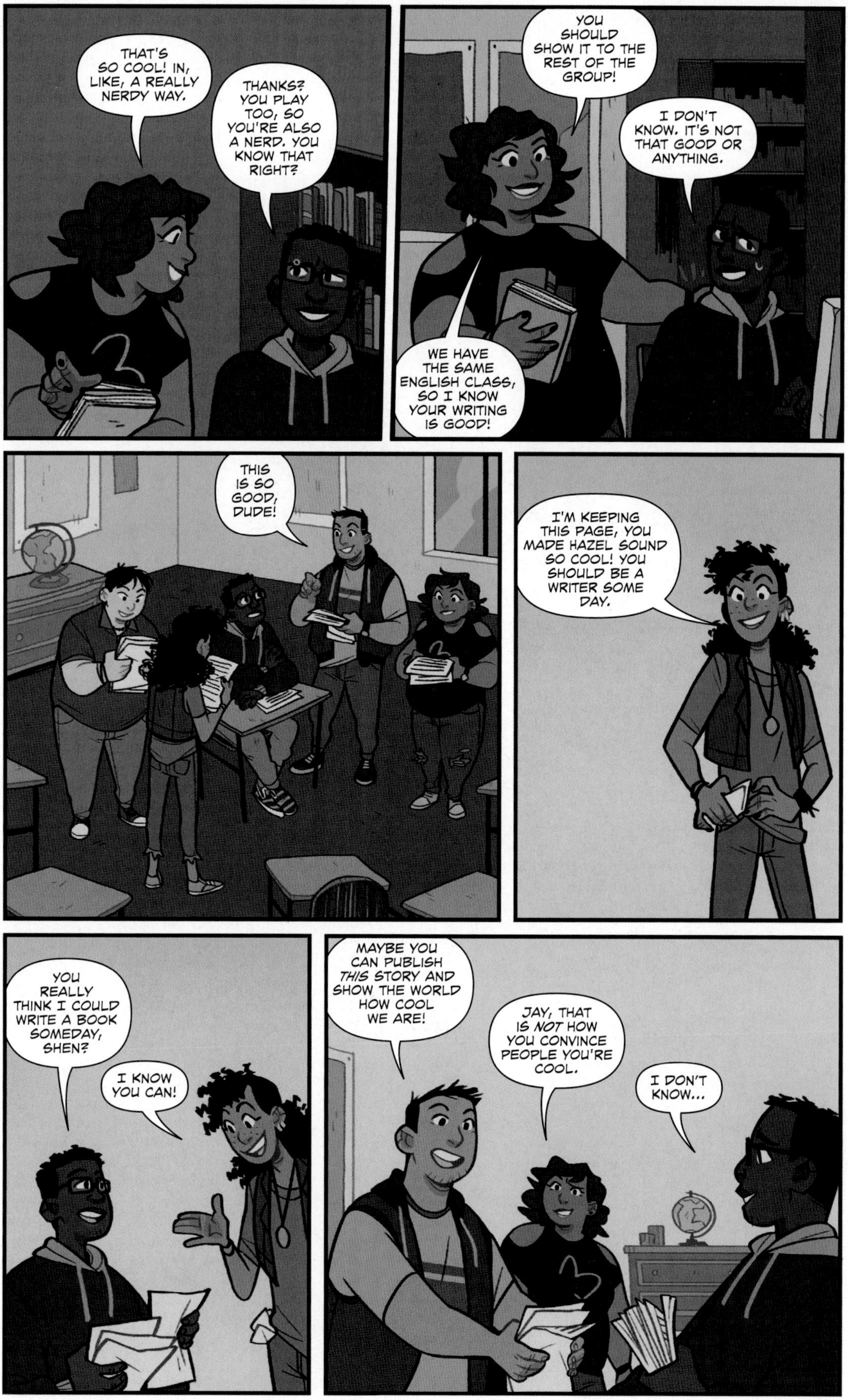
THAT'S SO COOL! IN, LIKE, A REALLY NERDY WAY.
THANKS? YOU PLAY TOO, SO YOU'RE ALSO A NERD. YOU KNOW THAT RIGHT?
YOU SHOULD SHOW IT TO THE REST OF THE GROUP!
I DON'T KNOW. IT'S NOT THAT GOOD OR ANYTHING.
WE HAVE THE SAME ENGLISH CLASS, SO I KNOW YOUR WRITING IS GOOD!
THIS IS SO GOOD, DUDE!
I'M KEEPING THIS PAGE, YOU MADE HAZEL SOUND SO COOL! YOU SHOULD BE A WRITER SOME DAY.
YOU REALLY THINK I COULD WRITE A BOOK SOMEDAY, SHEN?
I KNOW YOU CAN!
MAYBE YOU CAN PUBLISH *THIS* STORY AND SHOW THE WORLD HOW COOL WE ARE!
JAY, THAT IS *NOT* HOW YOU CONVINCE PEOPLE YOU'RE COOL.
I DON'T KNOW...

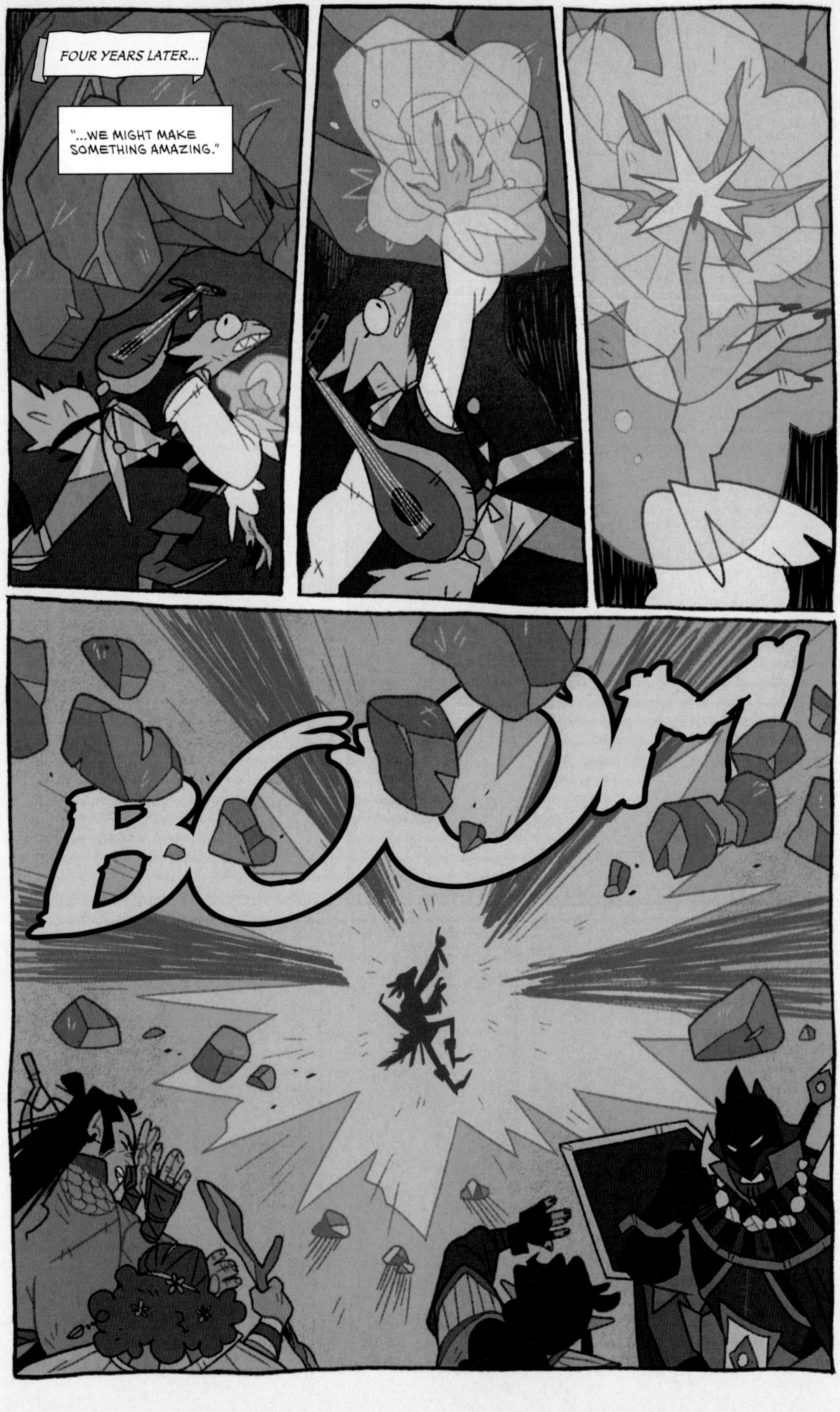
FOUR YEARS LATER...
"...WE MIGHT MAKE SOMETHING AMAZING."
BOOM

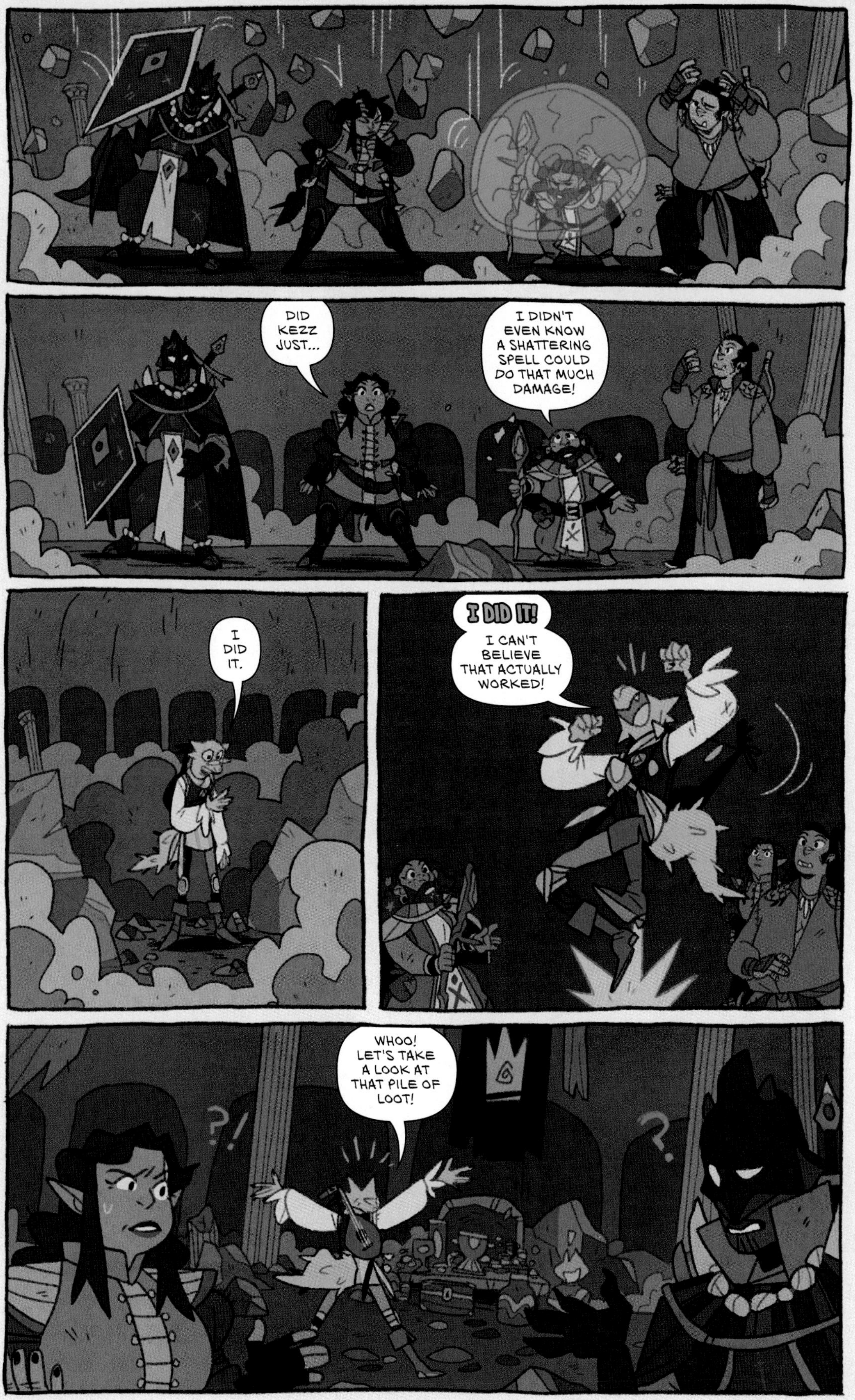
DID KEZZ JUST...
I DIDN'T EVEN KNOW A SHATTERING SPELL COULD DO THAT MUCH DAMAGE!
I DID IT.
I DID IT!
I CAN'T BELIEVE THAT ACTUALLY WORKED!
WHOO! LET'S TAKE A LOOK AT THAT PILE OF LOOT!
?!
?

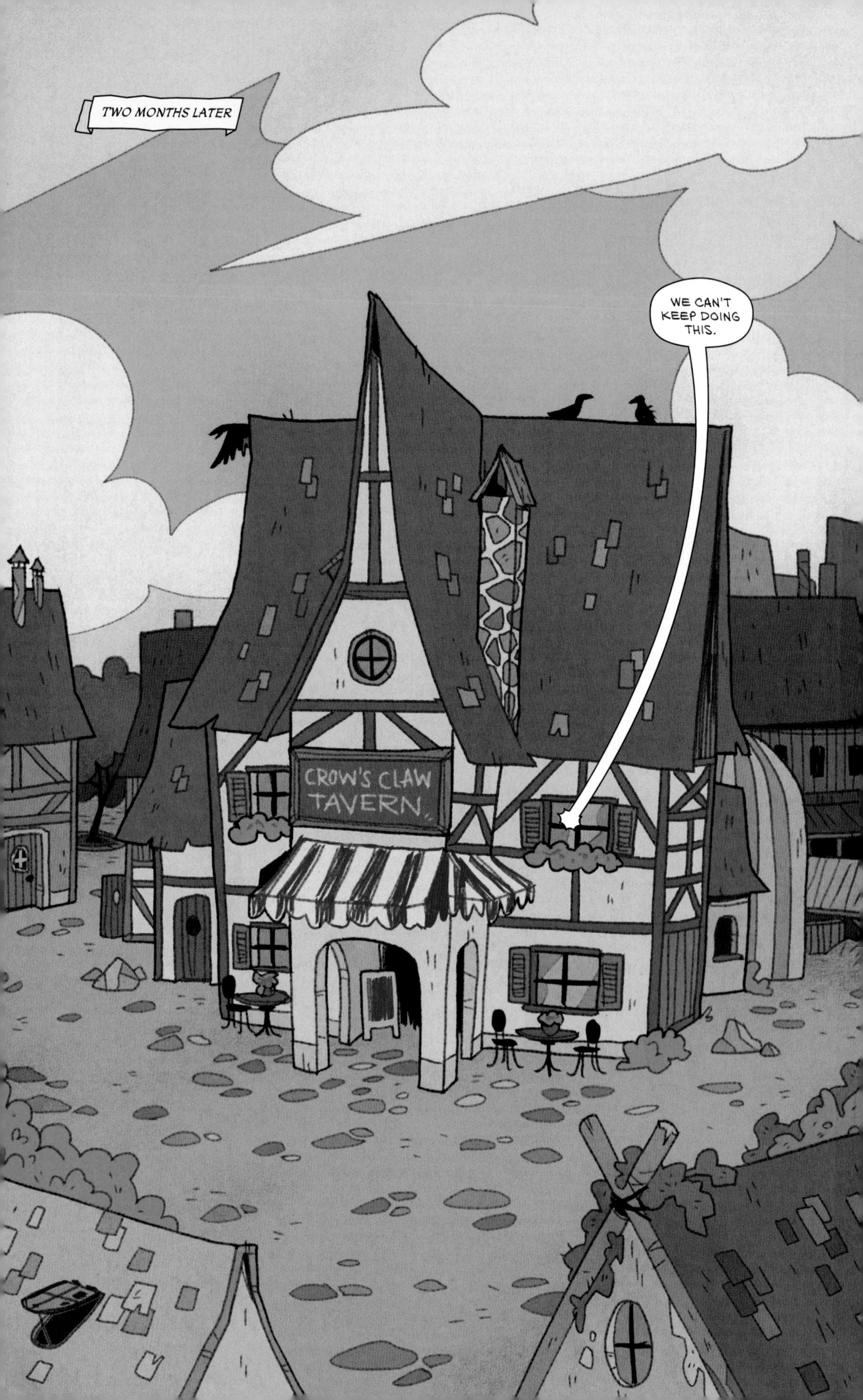
TWO MONTHS LATER
WE CAN'T KEEP DOING THIS.
CROW'S CLAW TAVERN

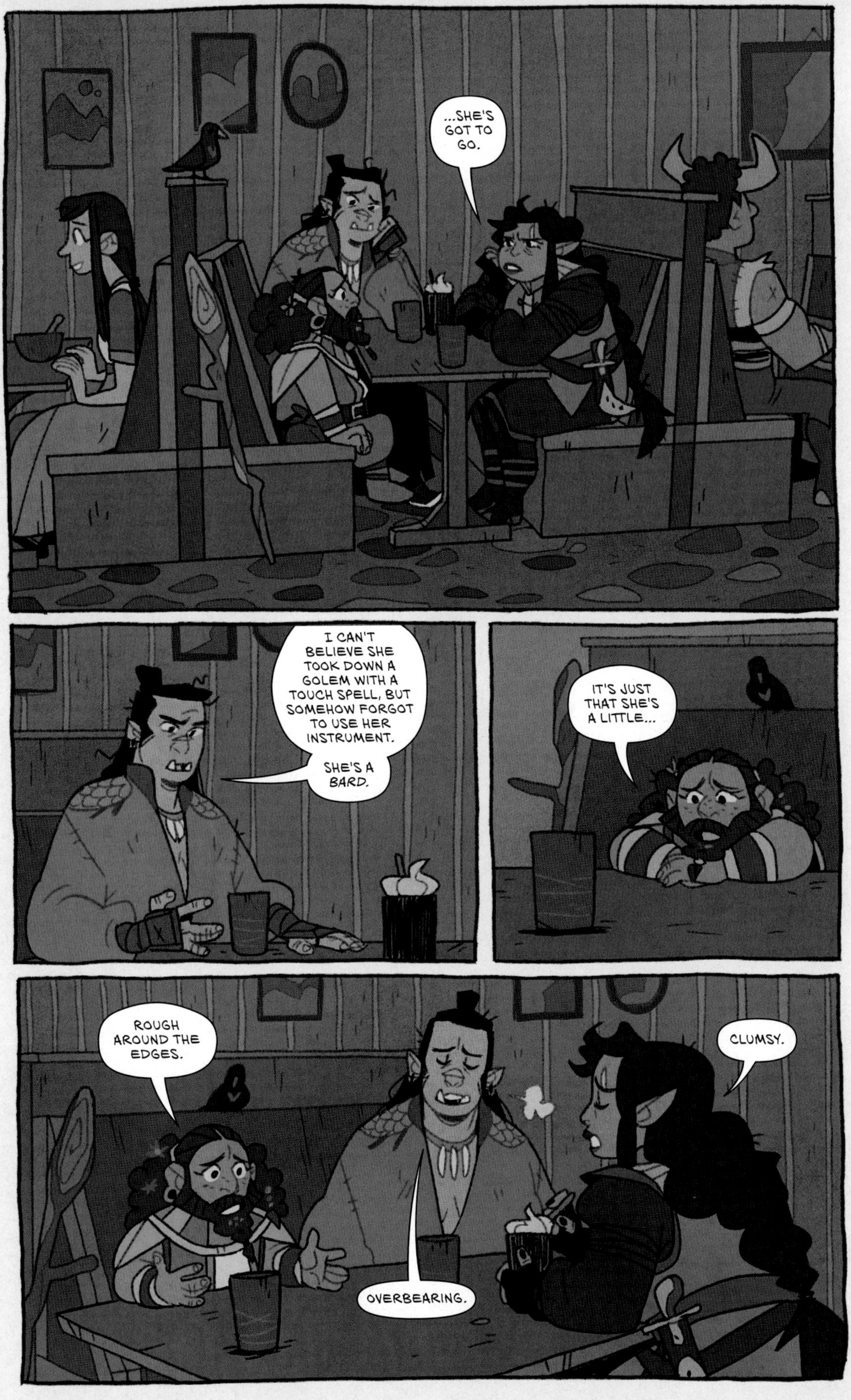
...SHE'S GOT TO GO.
I CAN'T BELIEVE SHE TOOK DOWN A GOLEM WITH A TOUCH SPELL, BUT SOMEHOW FORGOT TO USE HER INSTRUMENT.
SHE'S A BARD.
IT'S JUST THAT SHE'S A LITTLE...
ROUGH AROUND THE EDGES.
OVERBEARING.
CLUMSY.

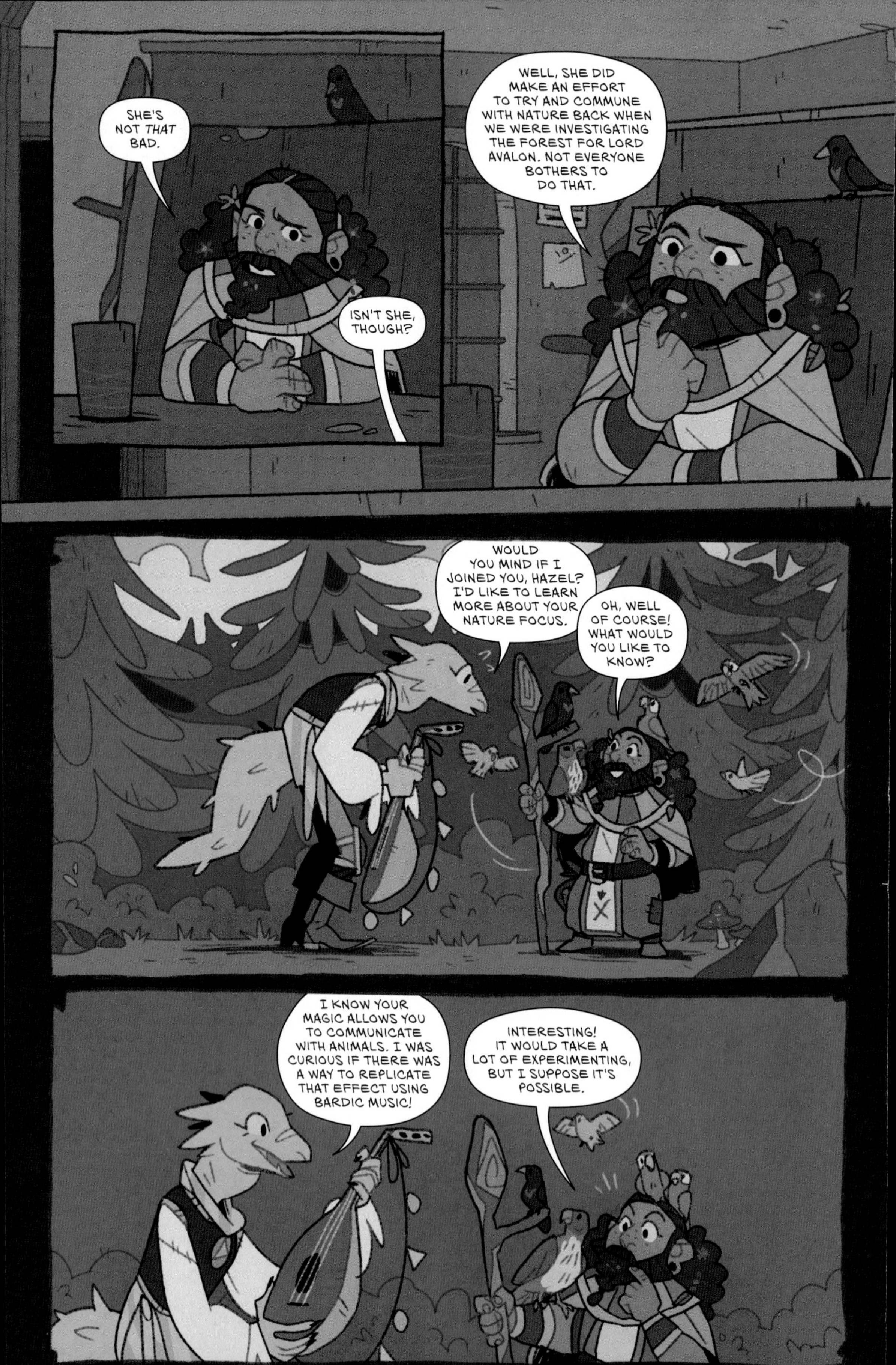
SHE'S NOT *THAT* BAD.
ISN'T SHE, THOUGH?
WELL, SHE DID MAKE AN EFFORT TO TRY AND COMMUNE WITH NATURE BACK WHEN WE WERE INVESTIGATING THE FOREST FOR LORD AVALON. NOT EVERYONE BOTHERS TO DO THAT.
WOULD YOU MIND IF I JOINED YOU, HAZEL? I'D LIKE TO LEARN MORE ABOUT YOUR NATURE FOCUS.
OH, WELL OF COURSE! WHAT WOULD YOU LIKE TO KNOW?
I KNOW YOUR MAGIC ALLOWS YOU TO COMMUNICATE WITH ANIMALS. I WAS CURIOUS IF THERE WAS A WAY TO REPLICATE THAT EFFECT USING BARDIC MUSIC!
INTERESTING! IT WOULD TAKE A LOT OF EXPERIMENTING, BUT I SUPPOSE IT'S POSSIBLE.

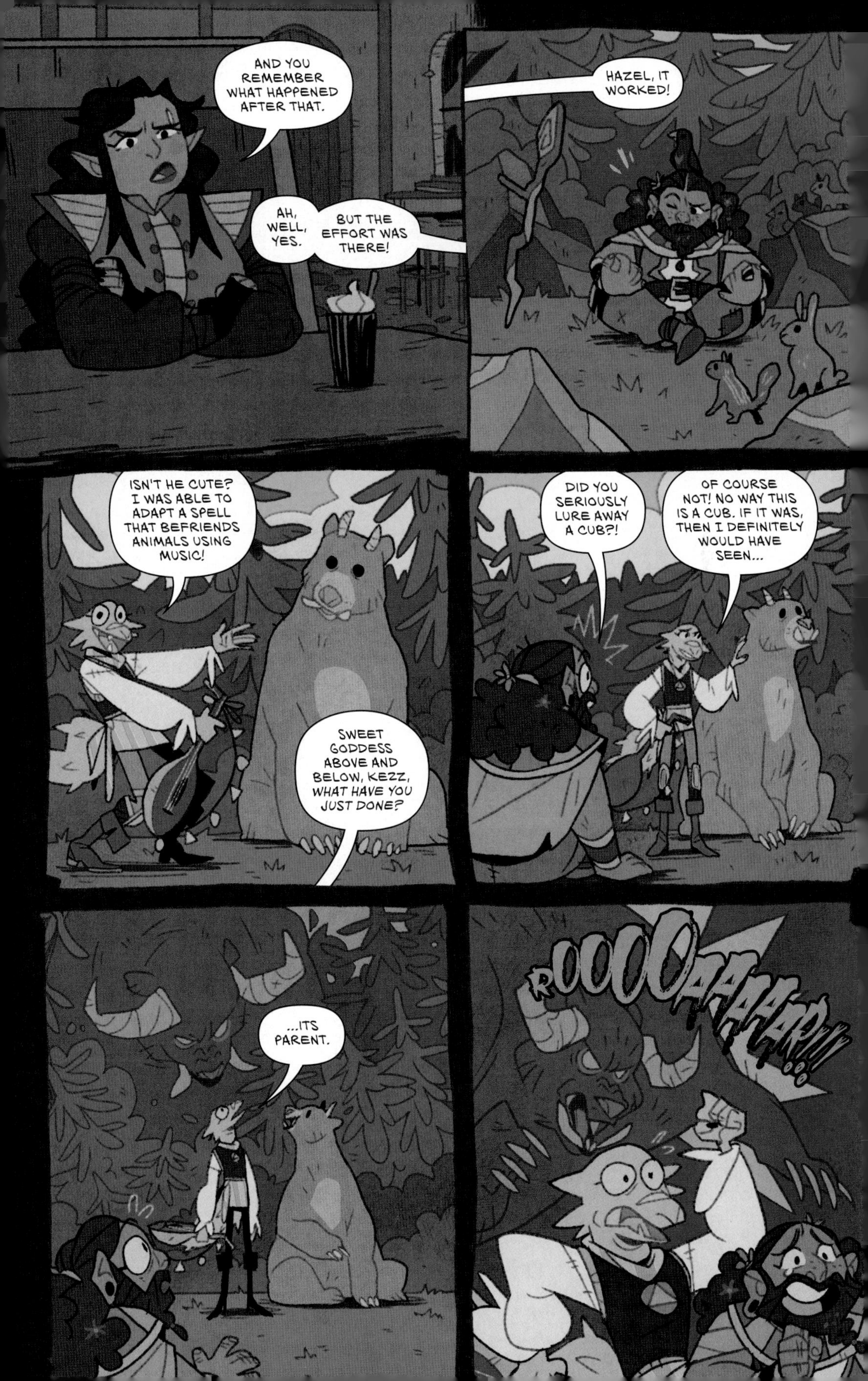

AND YOU REMEMBER WHAT HAPPENED AFTER THAT.
AH, WELL, YES.
BUT THE EFFORT WAS THERE!
HAZEL, IT WORKED!
ISN'T HE CUTE? I WAS ABLE TO ADAPT A SPELL THAT BEFRIENDS ANIMALS USING MUSIC!
SWEET GODDESS ABOVE AND BELOW, KEZZ, WHAT HAVE YOU JUST DONE?
DID YOU SERIOUSLY LURE AWAY A CUB?!
OF COURSE NOT! NO WAY THIS IS A CUB. IF IT WAS, THEN I DEFINITELY WOULD HAVE SEEN...
...ITS PARENT.
ROOOOAAAAARR!!!

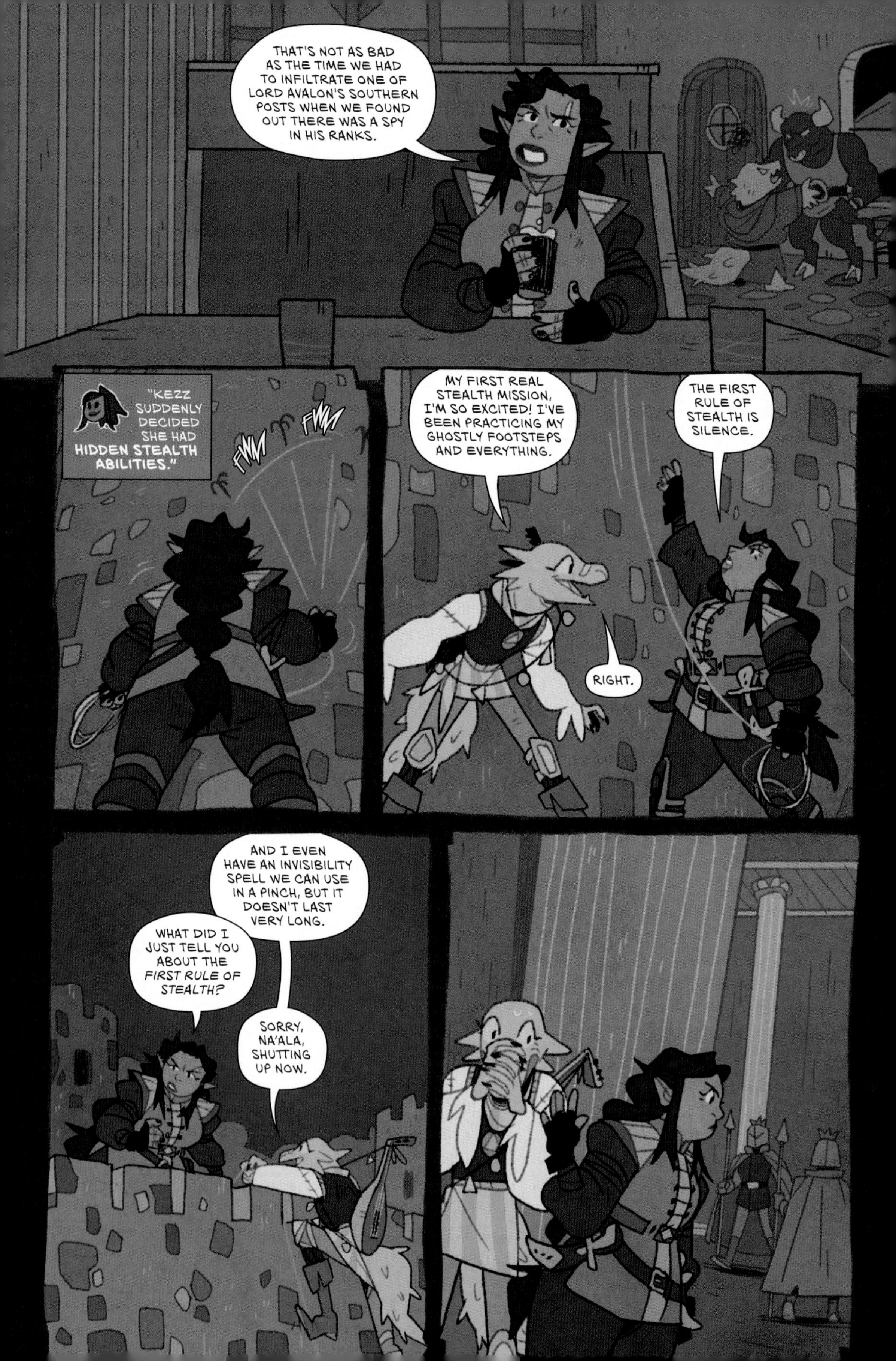
THAT'S NOT AS BAD AS THE TIME WE HAD TO INFILTRATE ONE OF LORD AVALON'S SOUTHERN POSTS WHEN WE FOUND OUT THERE WAS A SPY IN HIS RANKS.
"KEZZ SUDDENLY DECIDED SHE HAD HIDDEN STEALTH ABILITIES."
FWM
FWM
MY FIRST REAL STEALTH MISSION, I'M SO EXCITED! I'VE BEEN PRACTICING MY GHOSTLY FOOTSTEPS AND EVERYTHING.
THE FIRST RULE OF STEALTH IS SILENCE.
RIGHT.
AND I EVEN HAVE AN INVISIBILITY SPELL WE CAN USE IN A PINCH, BUT IT DOESN'T LAST VERY LONG.
WHAT DID I JUST TELL YOU ABOUT THE FIRST RULE OF STEALTH?
SORRY, NA'ALA, SHUTTING UP NOW.

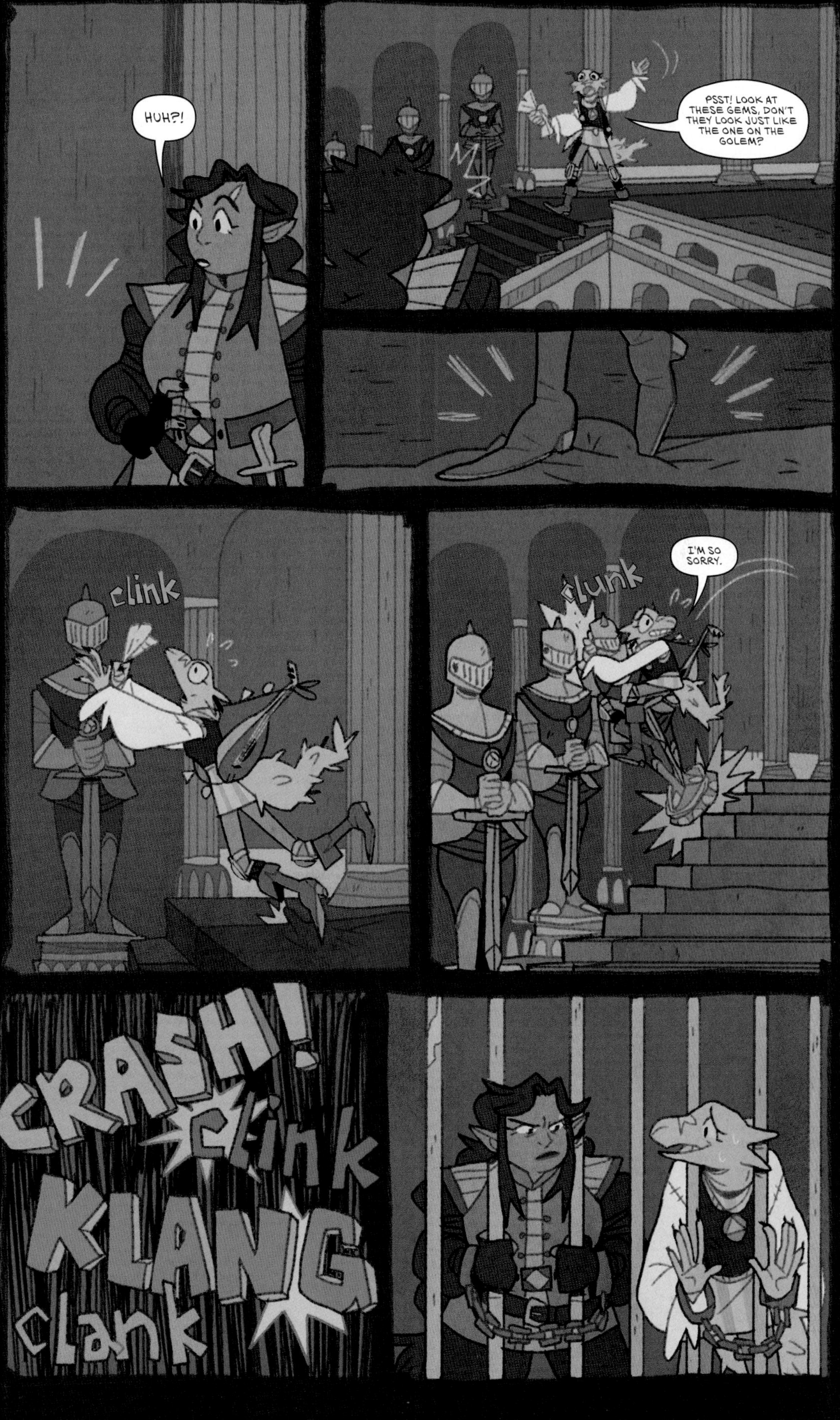
HUH?!
PSST! LOOK AT THESE GEMS, DON'T THEY LOOK JUST LIKE THE ONE ON THE GOLEM?
clink
clunk
I'M SO SORRY.
CRASH!
clink
KLANG
clank

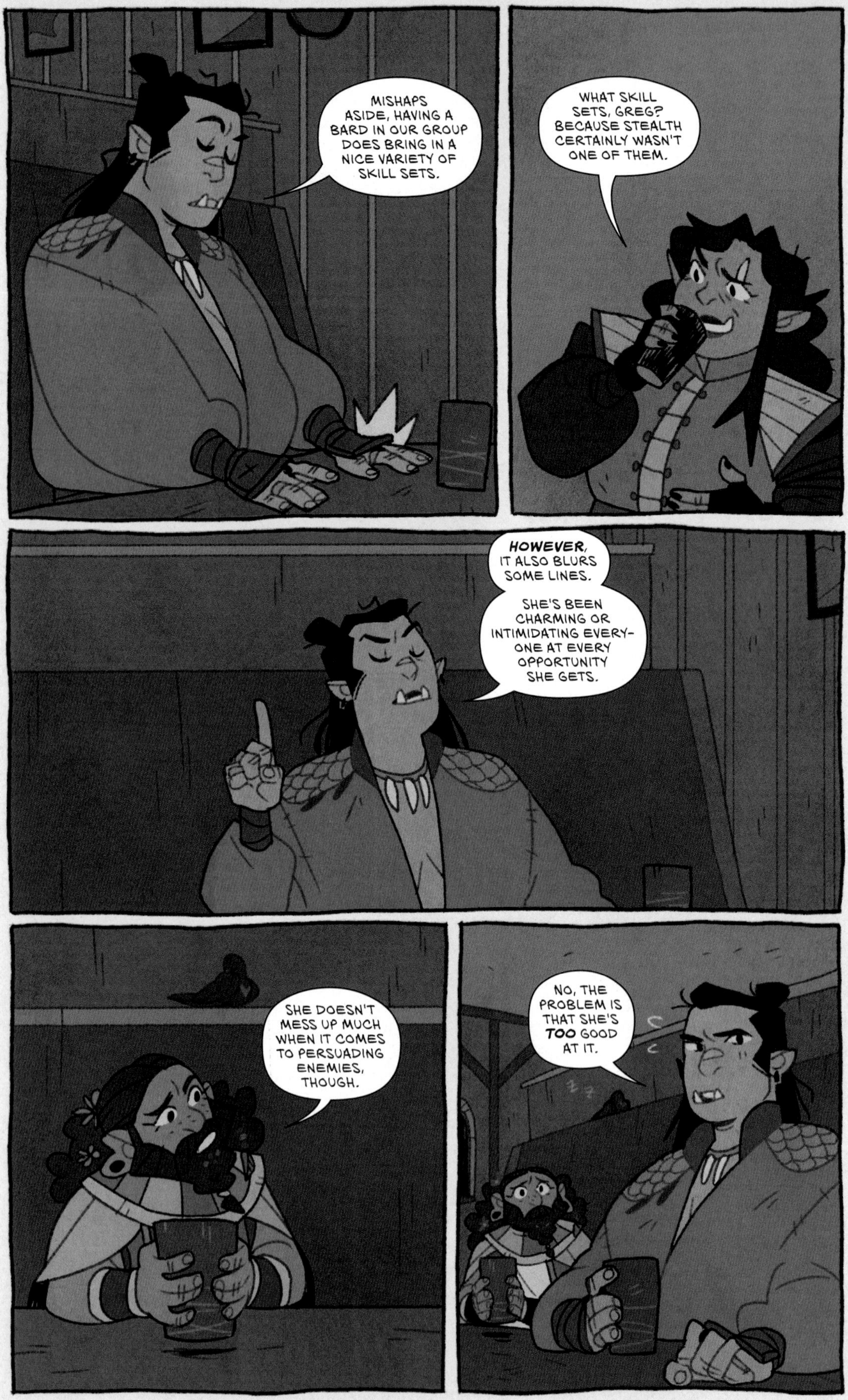
MISHAPS ASIDE, HAVING A BARD IN OUR GROUP DOES BRING IN A NICE VARIETY OF SKILL SETS.
WHAT SKILL SETS, GREG? BECAUSE STEALTH CERTAINLY WASN'T ONE OF THEM.
HOWEVER, IT ALSO BLURS SOME LINES.
SHE'S BEEN CHARMING OR INTIMIDATING EVERY-ONE AT EVERY OPPORTUNITY SHE GETS.
SHE DOESN'T MESS UP MUCH WHEN IT COMES TO PERSUADING ENEMIES, THOUGH.
NO, THE PROBLEM IS THAT SHE'S TOO GOOD AT IT.

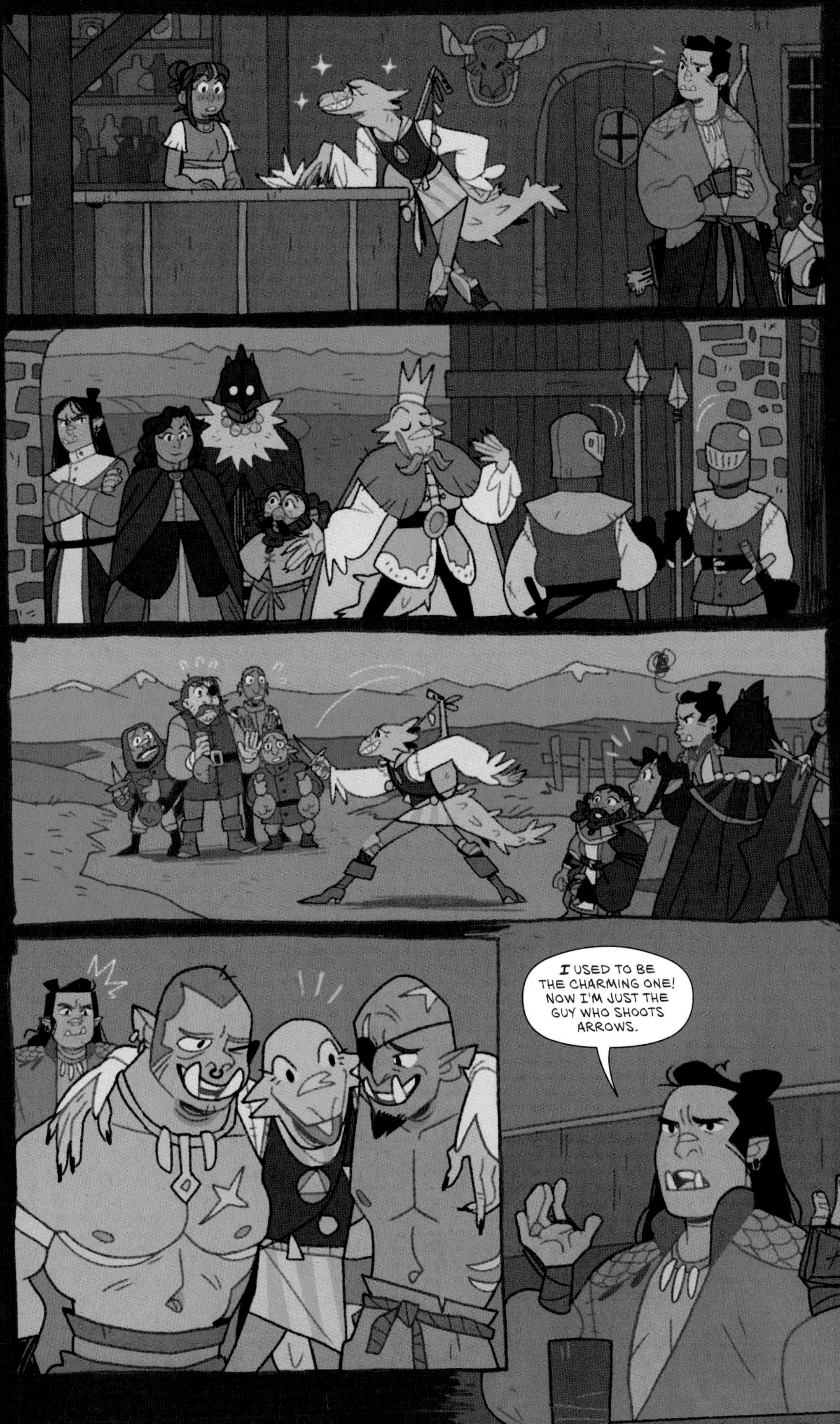
I USED TO BE THE CHARMING ONE! NOW I'M JUST THE GUY WHO SHOOTS ARROWS.

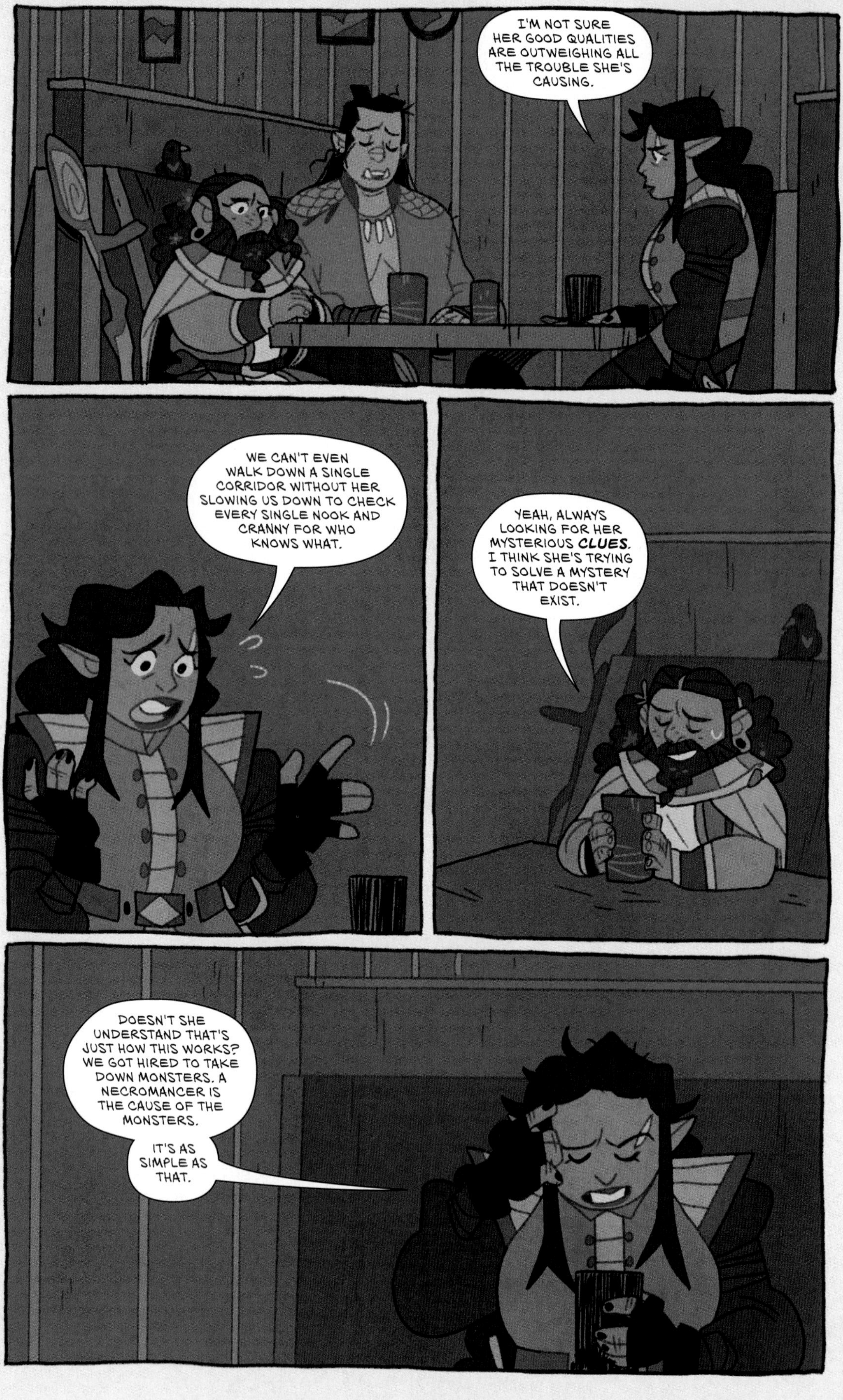
I'M NOT SURE HER GOOD QUALITIES ARE OUTWEIGHING ALL THE TROUBLE SHE'S CAUSING.
WE CAN'T EVEN WALK DOWN A SINGLE CORRIDOR WITHOUT HER SLOWING US DOWN TO CHECK EVERY SINGLE NOOK AND CRANNY FOR WHO KNOWS WHAT.
YEAH, ALWAYS LOOKING FOR HER MYSTERIOUS ***CLUES.*** I THINK SHE'S TRYING TO SOLVE A MYSTERY THAT DOESN'T EXIST.
DOESN'T SHE UNDERSTAND THAT'S JUST HOW THIS WORKS? WE GOT HIRED TO TAKE DOWN MONSTERS. A NECROMANCER IS THE CAUSE OF THE MONSTERS.
IT'S AS SIMPLE AS THAT.

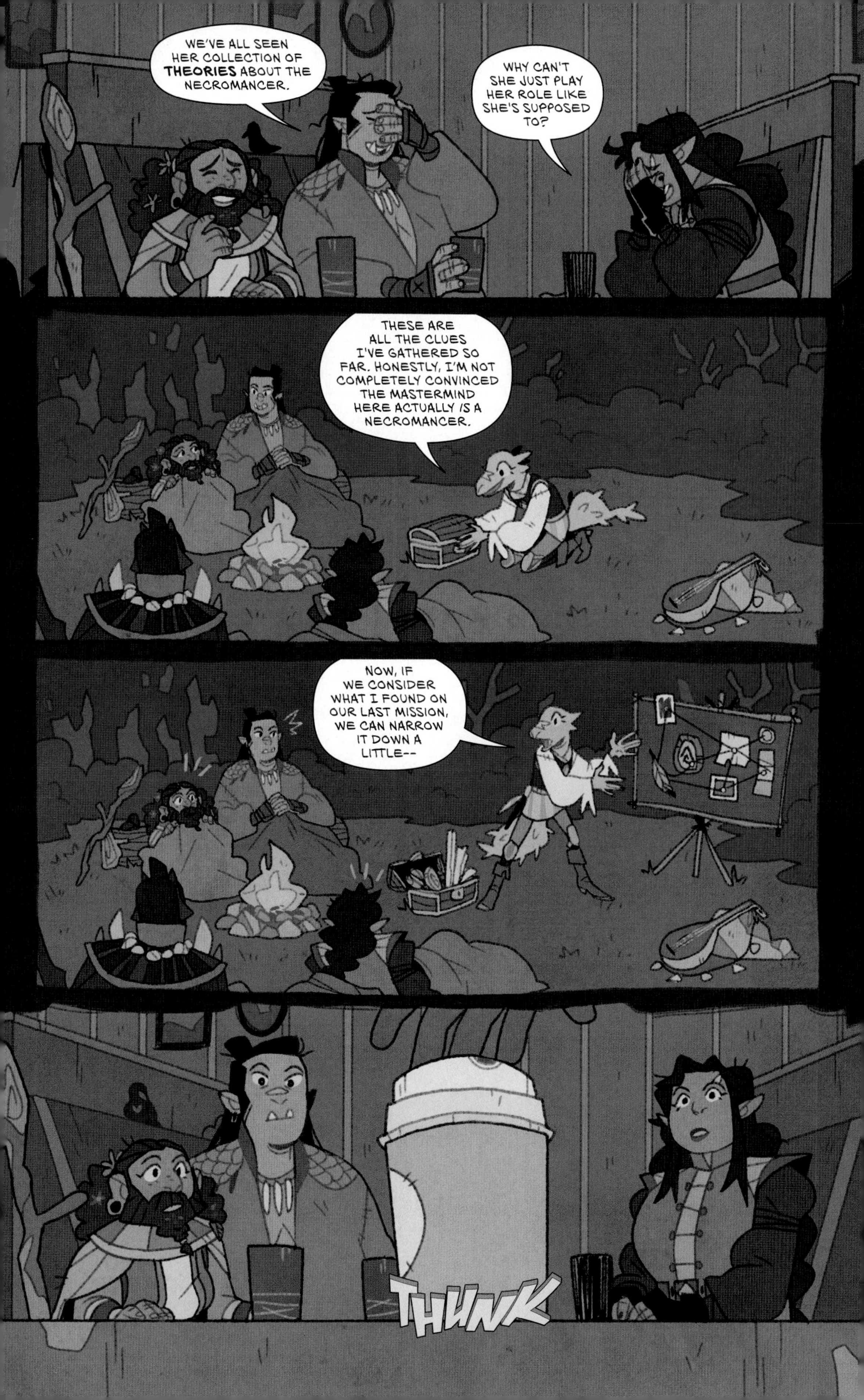
WE'VE ALL SEEN HER COLLECTION OF **THEORIES** ABOUT THE NECROMANCER.
WHY CAN'T SHE JUST PLAY HER ROLE LIKE SHE'S SUPPOSED TO?
THESE ARE ALL THE CLUES I'VE GATHERED SO FAR. HONESTLY, I'M NOT COMPLETELY CONVINCED THE MASTERMIND HERE ACTUALLY *IS* A NECROMANCER.
NOW, IF WE CONSIDER WHAT I FOUND ON OUR LAST MISSION, WE CAN NARROW IT DOWN A LITTLE--
THUNK

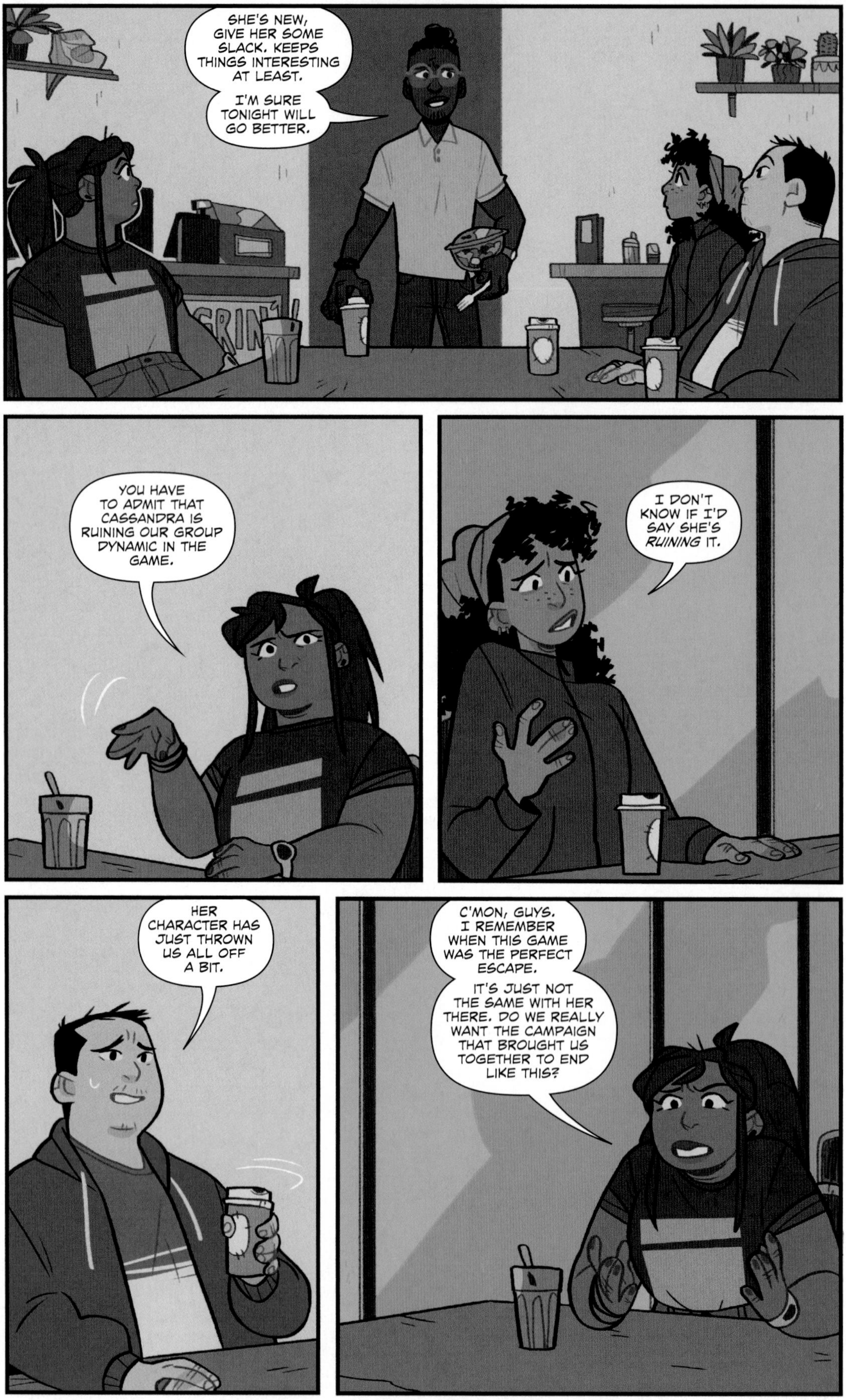
SHE'S NEW, GIVE HER SOME SLACK. KEEPS THINGS INTERESTING AT LEAST.
I'M SURE TONIGHT WILL GO BETTER.
YOU HAVE TO ADMIT THAT CASSANDRA IS RUINING OUR GROUP DYNAMIC IN THE GAME.
I DON'T KNOW IF I'D SAY SHE'S *RUINING* IT.
HER CHARACTER HAS JUST THROWN US ALL OFF A BIT.
C'MON, GUYS. I REMEMBER WHEN THIS GAME WAS THE PERFECT ESCAPE.
IT'S JUST NOT THE SAME WITH HER THERE. DO WE REALLY WANT THE CAMPAIGN THAT BROUGHT US TOGETHER TO END LIKE THIS?

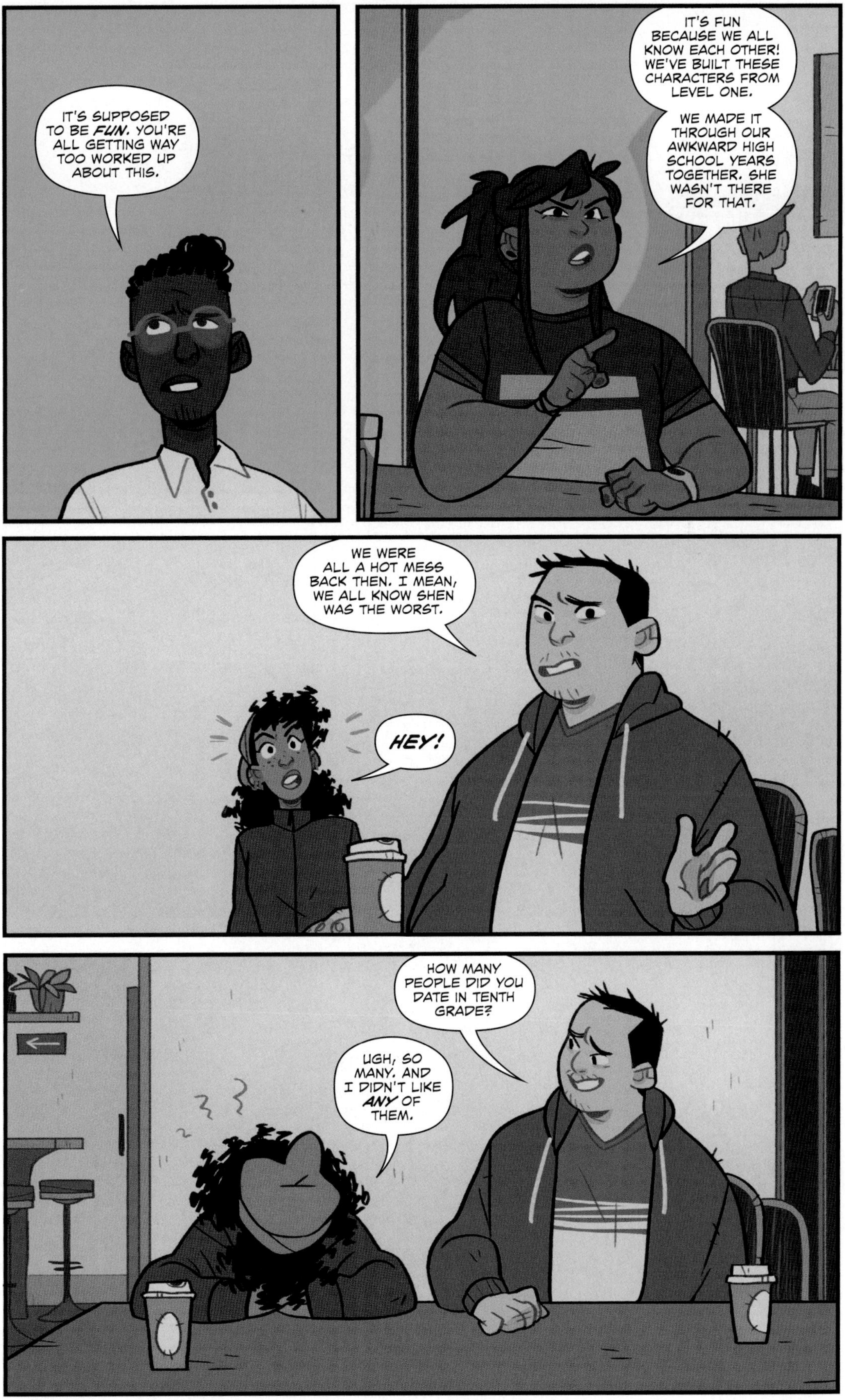
IT'S SUPPOSED TO BE *FUN*. YOU'RE ALL GETTING WAY TOO WORKED UP ABOUT THIS.
IT'S FUN BECAUSE WE ALL KNOW EACH OTHER! WE'VE BUILT THESE CHARACTERS FROM LEVEL ONE.
WE MADE IT THROUGH OUR AWKWARD HIGH SCHOOL YEARS TOGETHER. SHE WASN'T THERE FOR THAT.
WE WERE ALL A HOT MESS BACK THEN. I MEAN, WE ALL KNOW SHEN WAS THE WORST.
HEY!
HOW MANY PEOPLE DID YOU DATE IN TENTH GRADE?
UGH, SO MANY. AND I DIDN'T LIKE *ANY* OF THEM.

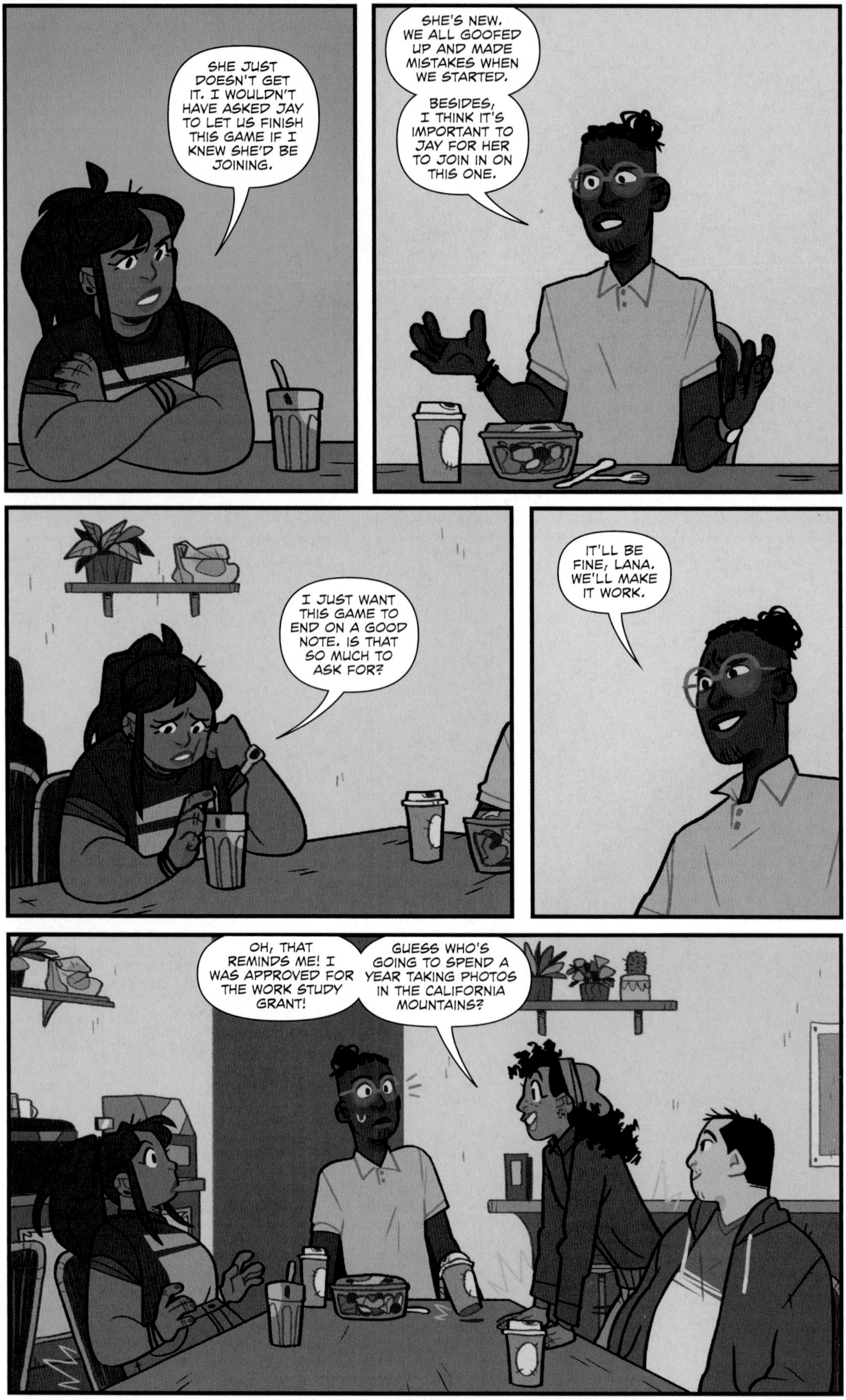
SHE JUST DOESN'T GET IT. I WOULDN'T HAVE ASKED JAY TO LET US FINISH THIS GAME IF I KNEW SHE'D BE JOINING.
SHE'S NEW. WE ALL GOOFED UP AND MADE MISTAKES WHEN WE STARTED.
BESIDES, I THINK IT'S IMPORTANT TO JAY FOR HER TO JOIN IN ON THIS ONE.
I JUST WANT THIS GAME TO END ON A GOOD NOTE. IS THAT SO MUCH TO ASK FOR?
IT'LL BE FINE, LANA. WE'LL MAKE IT WORK.
OH, THAT REMINDS ME! I WAS APPROVED FOR THE WORK STUDY GRANT!
GUESS WHO'S GOING TO SPEND A YEAR TAKING PHOTOS IN THE CALIFORNIA MOUNTAINS?

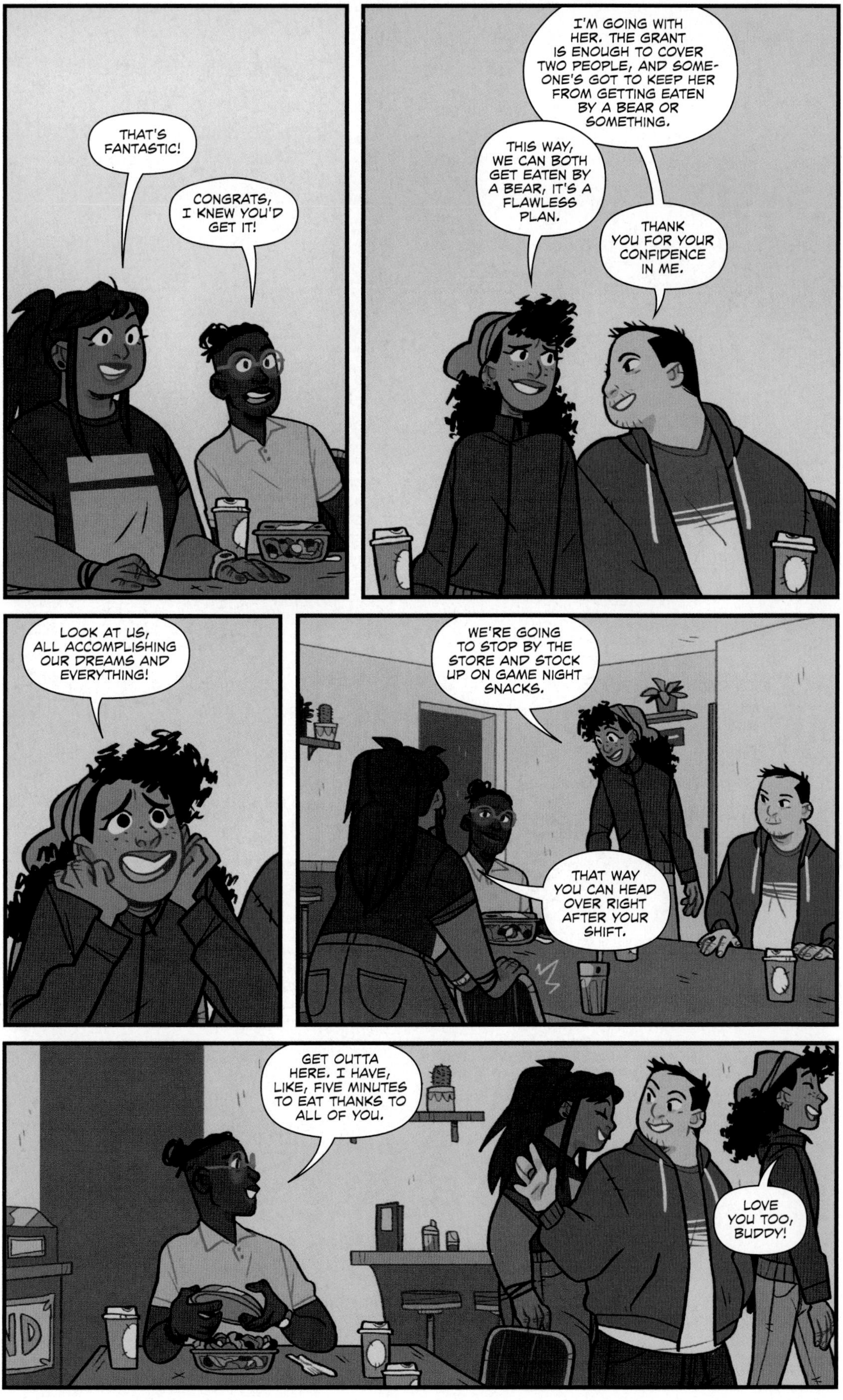
THAT'S FANTASTIC!
CONGRATS, I KNEW YOU'D GET IT!
I'M GOING WITH HER. THE GRANT IS ENOUGH TO COVER TWO PEOPLE, AND SOME-ONE'S GOT TO KEEP HER FROM GETTING EATEN BY A BEAR OR SOMETHING.
THIS WAY, WE CAN BOTH GET EATEN BY A BEAR, IT'S A FLAWLESS PLAN.
THANK YOU FOR YOUR CONFIDENCE IN ME.
LOOK AT US, ALL ACCOMPLISHING OUR DREAMS AND EVERYTHING!
WE'RE GOING TO STOP BY THE STORE AND STOCK UP ON GAME NIGHT SNACKS.
THAT WAY YOU CAN HEAD OVER RIGHT AFTER YOUR SHIFT.
GET OUTTA HERE. I HAVE, LIKE, FIVE MINUTES TO EAT THANKS TO ALL OF YOU.
LOVE YOU TOO, BUDDY!

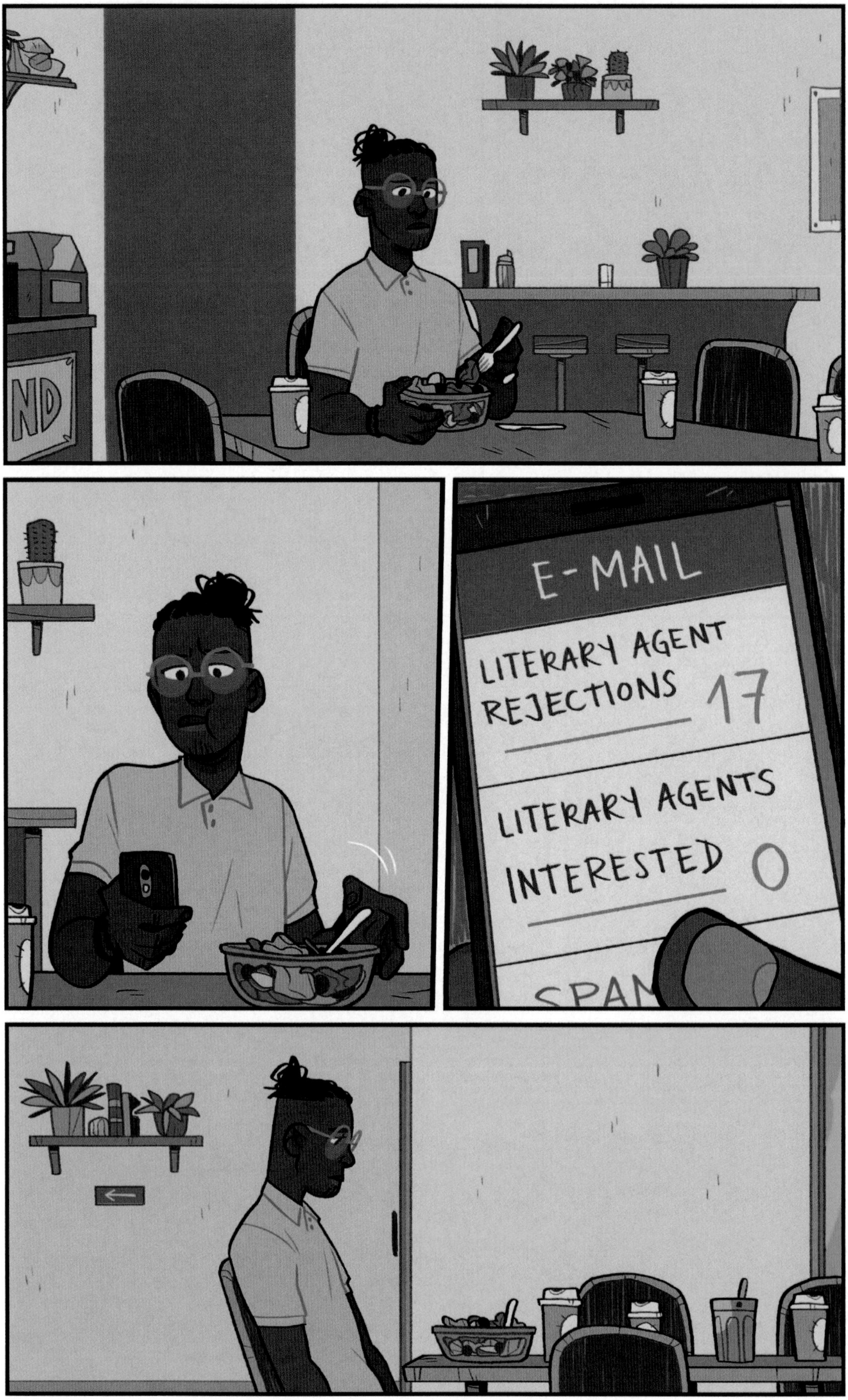
ND
E-MAIL
LITERARY AGENT REJECTIONS 17
LITERARY AGENTS INTERESTED 0

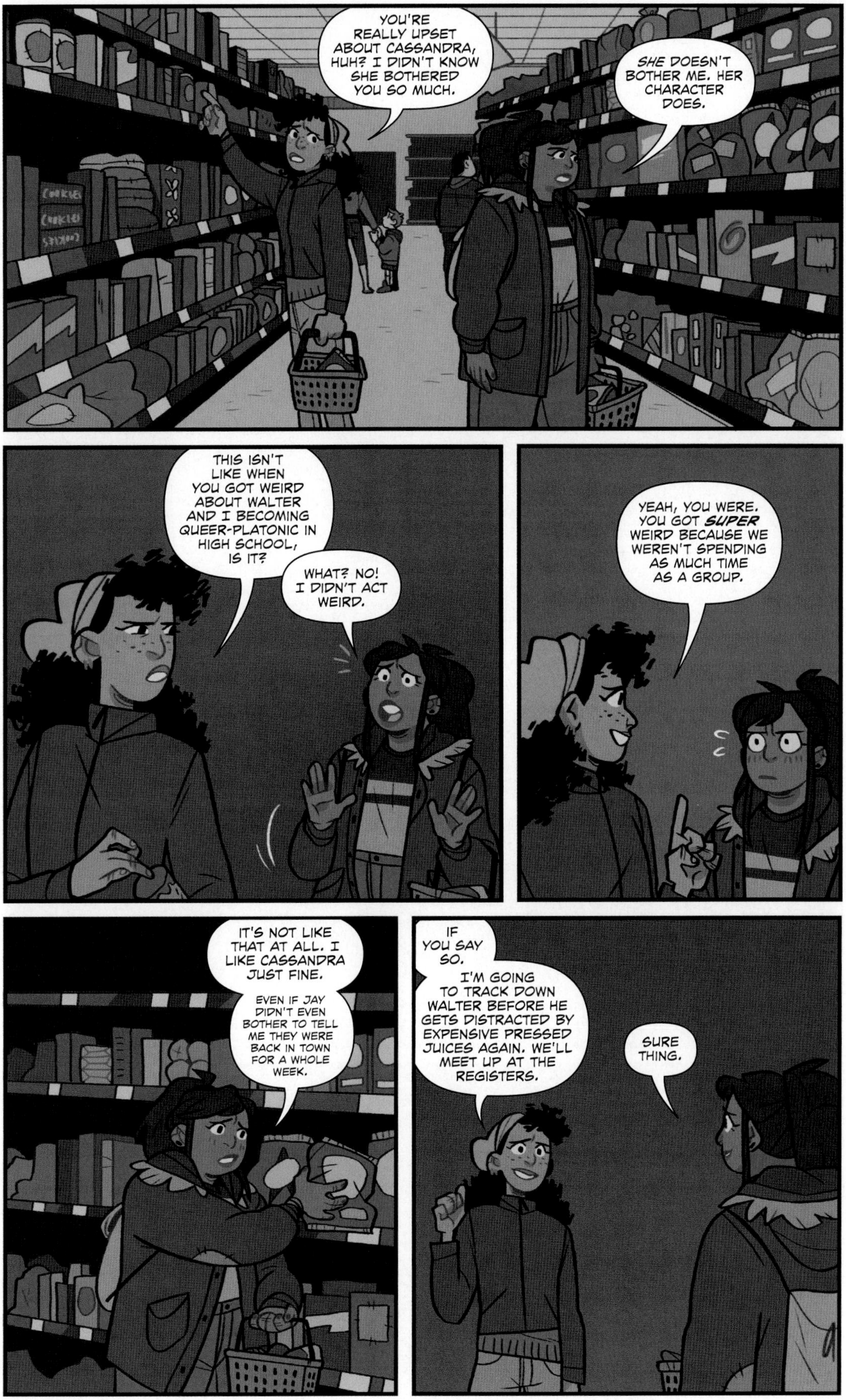
YOU'RE REALLY UPSET ABOUT CASSANDRA, HUH? I DIDN'T KNOW SHE BOTHERED YOU SO MUCH.
SHE DOESN'T BOTHER ME. HER CHARACTER DOES.
THIS ISN'T LIKE WHEN YOU GOT WEIRD ABOUT WALTER AND I BECOMING QUEER-PLATONIC IN HIGH SCHOOL, IS IT?
WHAT? NO! I DIDN'T ACT WEIRD.
YEAH, YOU WERE. YOU GOT ***SUPER*** WEIRD BECAUSE WE WEREN'T SPENDING AS MUCH TIME AS A GROUP.
IT'S NOT LIKE THAT AT ALL. I LIKE CASSANDRA JUST FINE.
EVEN IF JAY DIDN'T EVEN BOTHER TO TELL ME THEY WERE BACK IN TOWN FOR A WHOLE WEEK.
IF YOU SAY SO.
I'M GOING TO TRACK DOWN WALTER BEFORE HE GETS DISTRACTED BY EXPENSIVE PRESSED JUICES AGAIN. WE'LL MEET UP AT THE REGISTERS.
SURE THING.

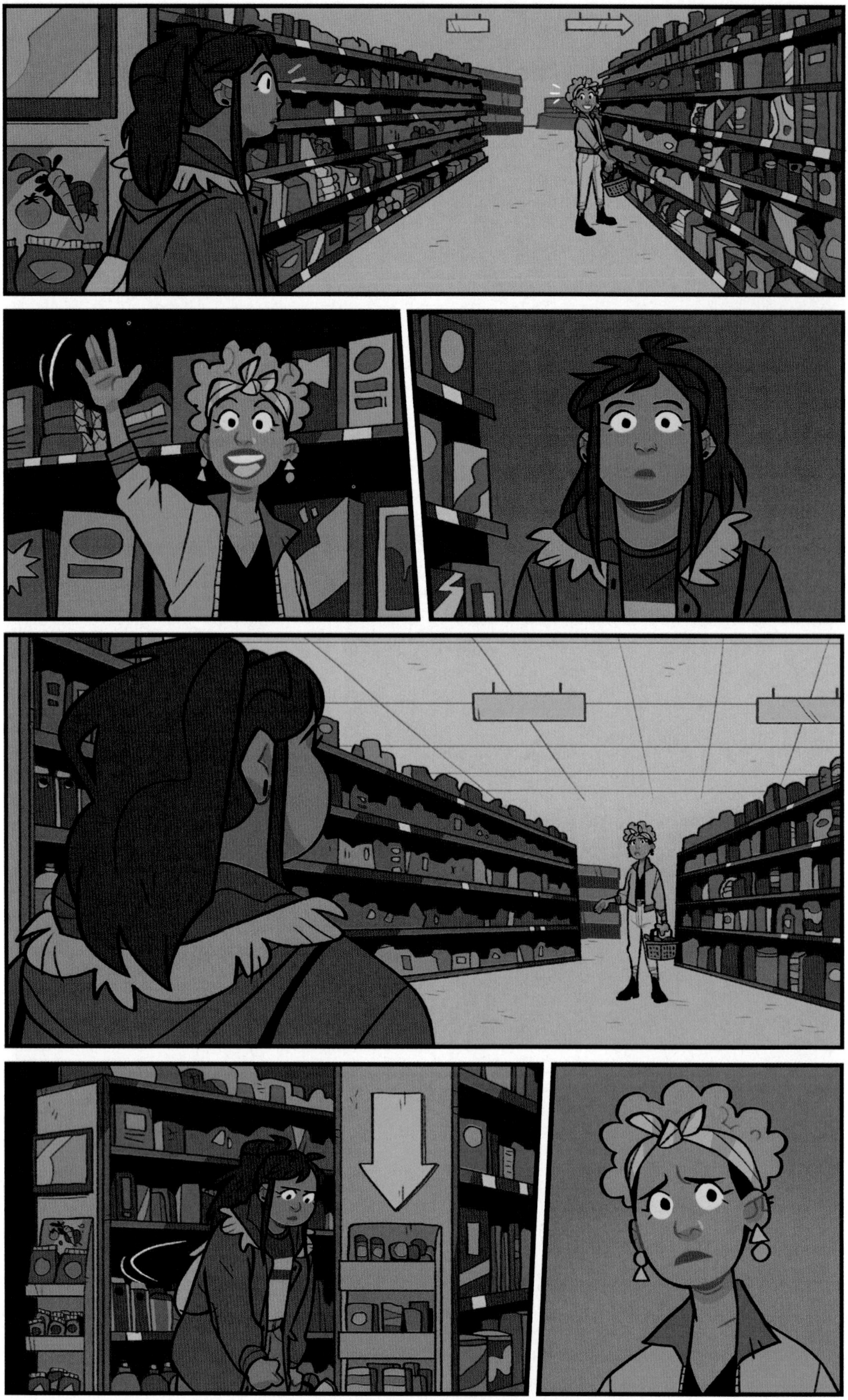

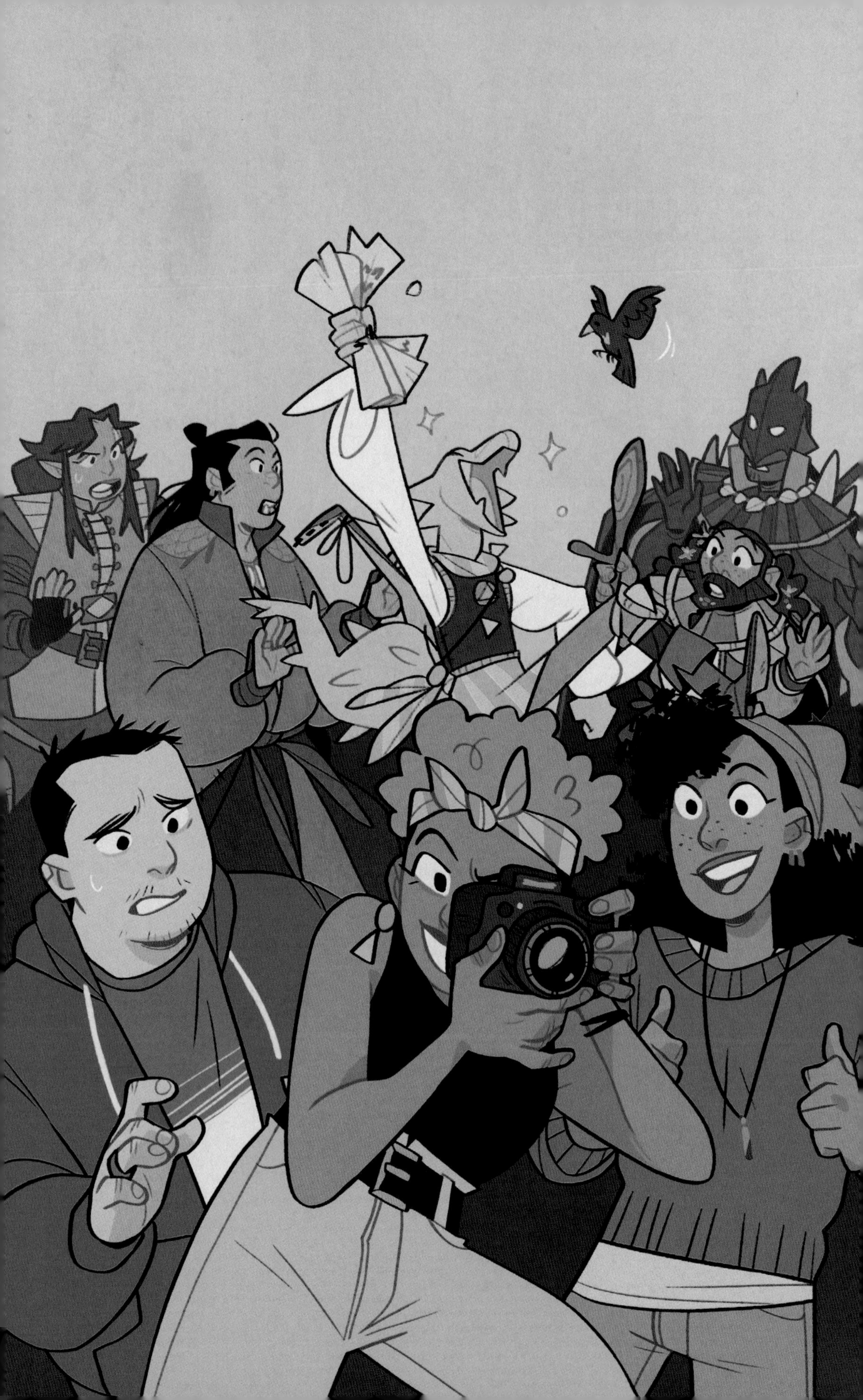

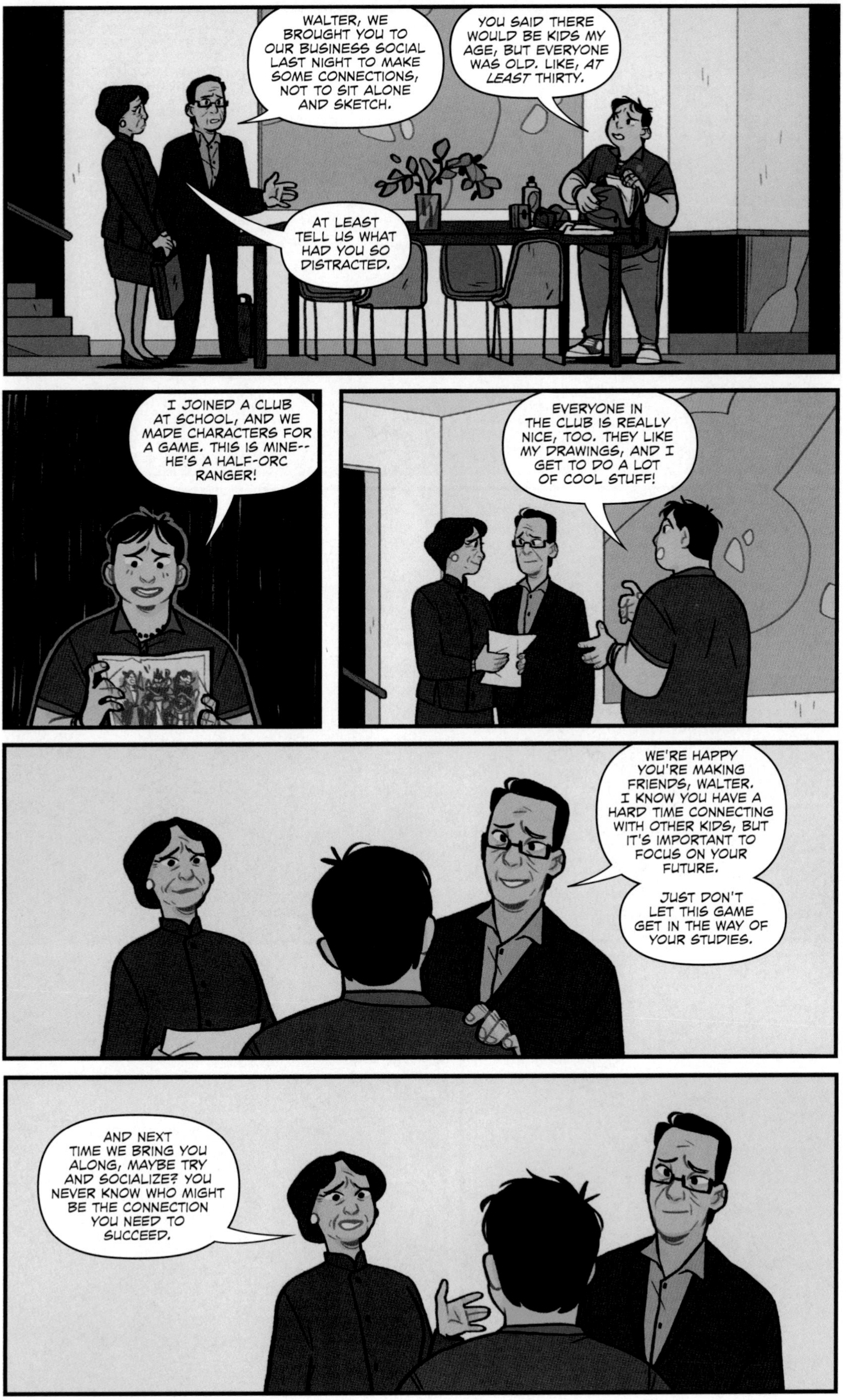
WALTER, WE BROUGHT YOU TO OUR BUSINESS SOCIAL LAST NIGHT TO MAKE SOME CONNECTIONS, NOT TO SIT ALONE AND SKETCH.
YOU SAID THERE WOULD BE KIDS MY AGE, BUT EVERYONE WAS OLD. LIKE, *AT LEAST* THIRTY.
AT LEAST TELL US WHAT HAD YOU SO DISTRACTED.
I JOINED A CLUB AT SCHOOL, AND WE MADE CHARACTERS FOR A GAME. THIS IS MINE-- HE'S A HALF-ORC RANGER!
EVERYONE IN THE CLUB IS REALLY NICE, TOO. THEY LIKE MY DRAWINGS, AND I GET TO DO A LOT OF COOL STUFF!
WE'RE HAPPY YOU'RE MAKING FRIENDS, WALTER. I KNOW YOU HAVE A HARD TIME CONNECTING WITH OTHER KIDS, BUT IT'S IMPORTANT TO FOCUS ON YOUR FUTURE.
JUST DON'T LET THIS GAME GET IN THE WAY OF YOUR STUDIES.
AND NEXT TIME WE BRING YOU ALONG, MAYBE TRY AND SOCIALIZE? YOU NEVER KNOW WHO MIGHT BE THE CONNECTION YOU NEED TO SUCCEED.

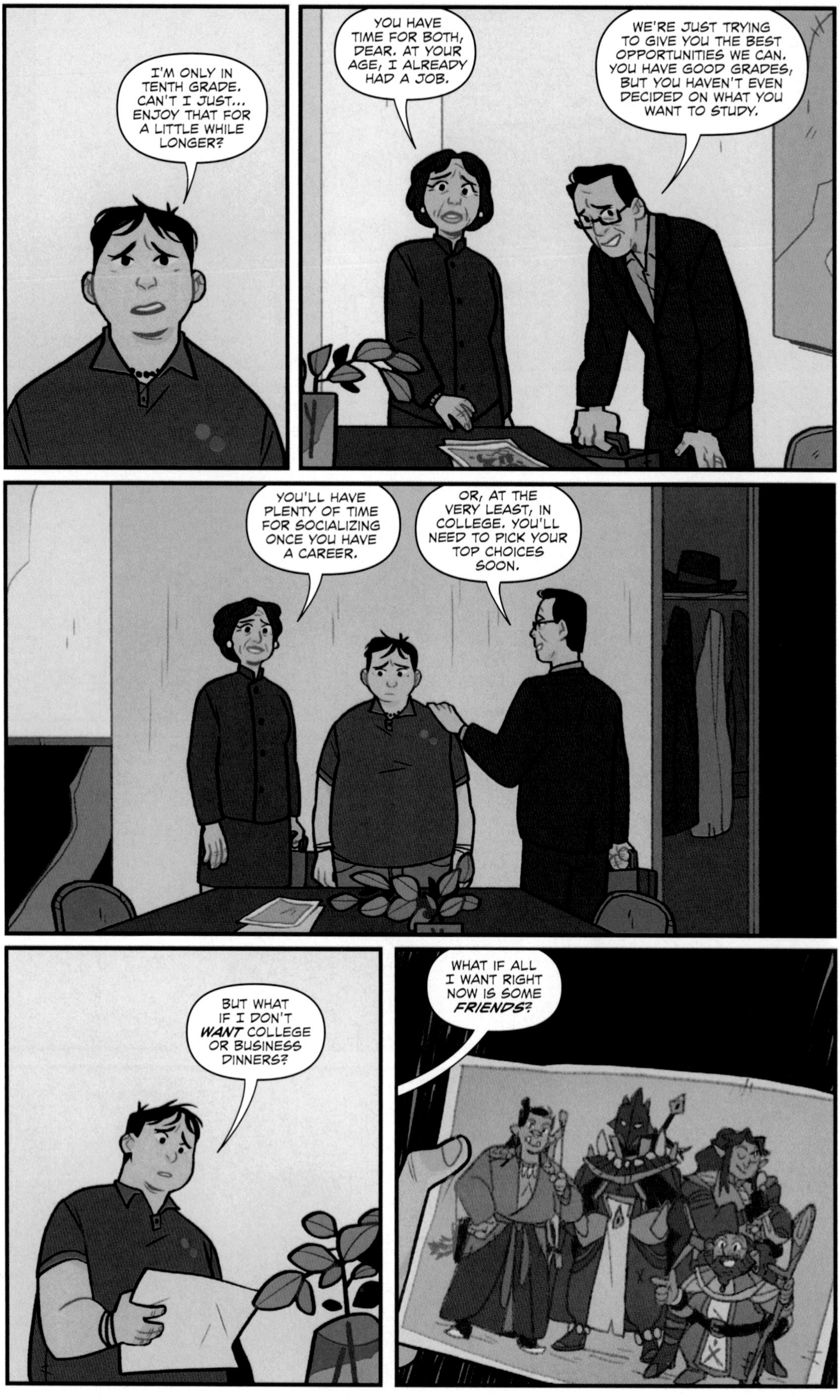
I'M ONLY IN TENTH GRADE. CAN'T I JUST... ENJOY THAT FOR A LITTLE WHILE LONGER?
YOU HAVE TIME FOR BOTH, DEAR. AT YOUR AGE, I ALREADY HAD A JOB.
WE'RE JUST TRYING TO GIVE YOU THE BEST OPPORTUNITIES WE CAN. YOU HAVE GOOD GRADES, BUT YOU HAVEN'T EVEN DECIDED ON WHAT YOU WANT TO STUDY.
YOU'LL HAVE PLENTY OF TIME FOR SOCIALIZING ONCE YOU HAVE A CAREER.
OR, AT THE VERY LEAST, IN COLLEGE. YOU'LL NEED TO PICK YOUR TOP CHOICES SOON.
BUT WHAT IF I DON'T *WANT* COLLEGE OR BUSINESS DINNERS?
WHAT IF ALL I WANT RIGHT NOW IS SOME *FRIENDS*?

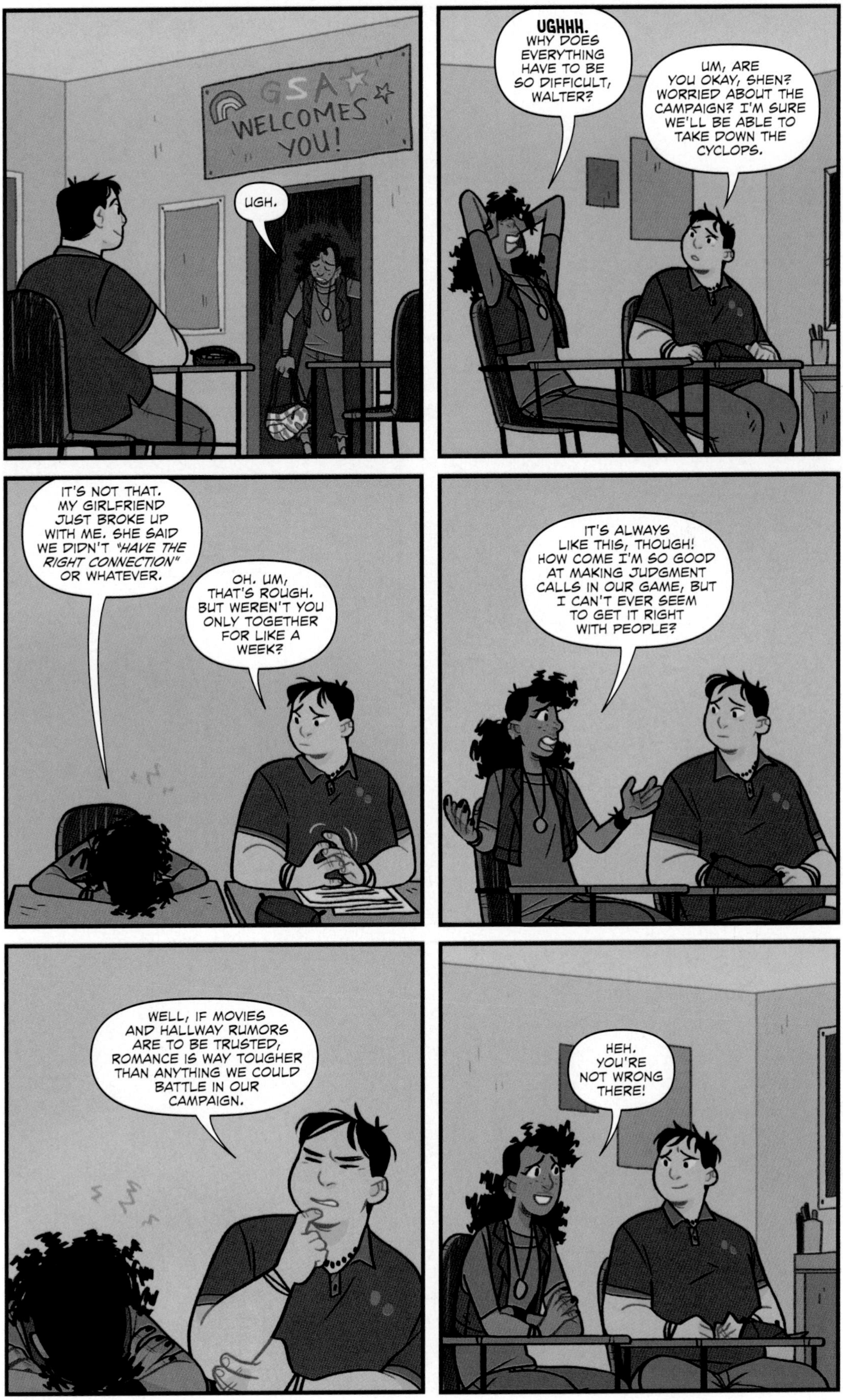
GSA WELCOMES YOU!
UGH.
UGHHH. WHY DOES EVERYTHING HAVE TO BE SO DIFFICULT, WALTER?
UM, ARE YOU OKAY, SHEN? WORRIED ABOUT THE CAMPAIGN? I'M SURE WE'LL BE ABLE TO TAKE DOWN THE CYCLOPS.
IT'S NOT THAT. MY GIRLFRIEND JUST BROKE UP WITH ME. SHE SAID WE DIDN'T "HAVE THE RIGHT CONNECTION" OR WHATEVER.
OH. UM, THAT'S ROUGH. BUT WEREN'T YOU ONLY TOGETHER FOR LIKE A WEEK?
IT'S ALWAYS LIKE THIS, THOUGH! HOW COME I'M SO GOOD AT MAKING JUDGMENT CALLS IN OUR GAME, BUT I CAN'T EVER SEEM TO GET IT RIGHT WITH PEOPLE?
WELL, IF MOVIES AND HALLWAY RUMORS ARE TO BE TRUSTED, ROMANCE IS WAY TOUGHER THAN ANYTHING WE COULD BATTLE IN OUR CAMPAIGN.
HEH. YOU'RE NOT WRONG THERE!

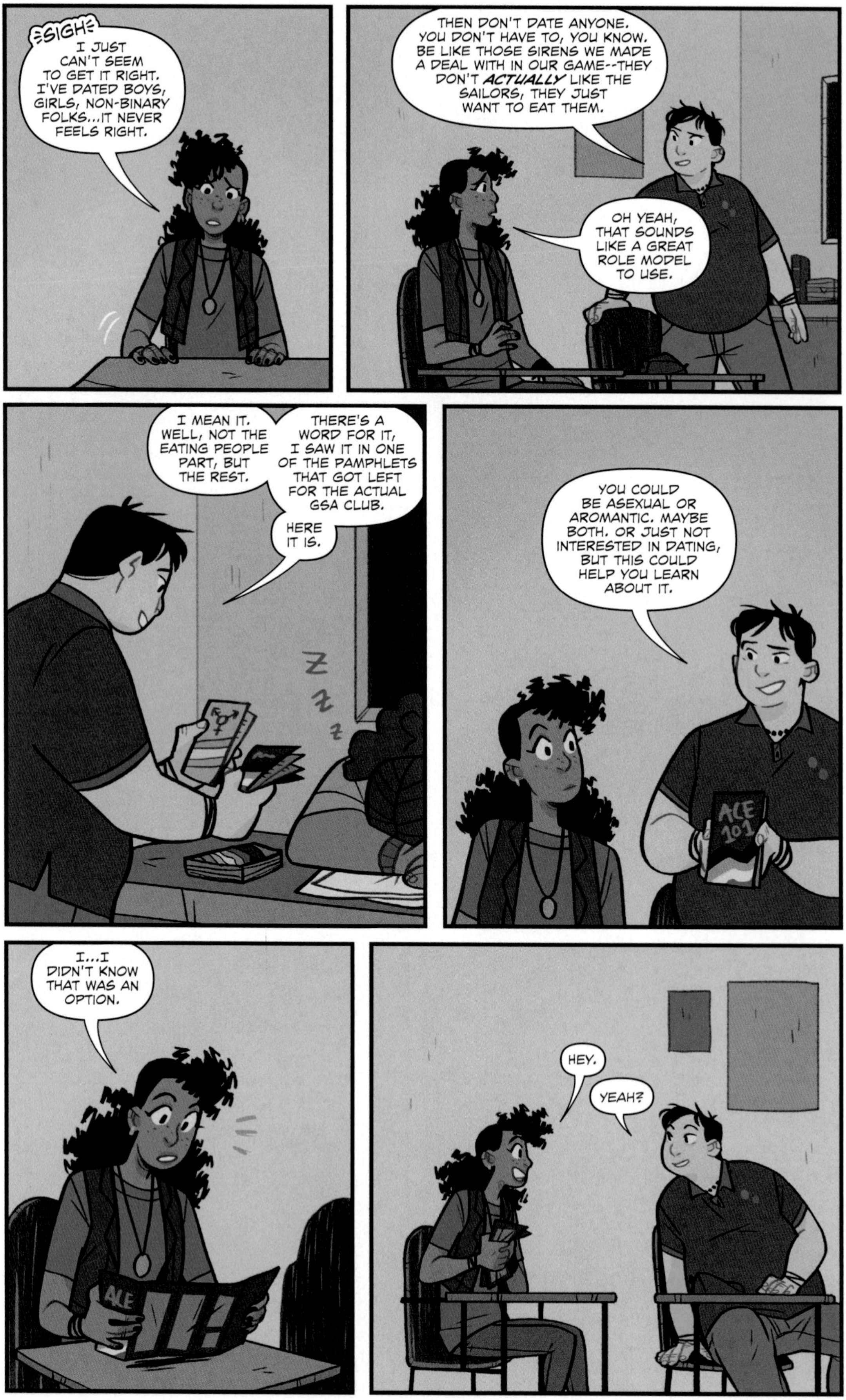
SIGH
I JUST CAN'T SEEM TO GET IT RIGHT. I'VE DATED BOYS, GIRLS, NON-BINARY FOLKS...IT NEVER FEELS RIGHT.
THEN DON'T DATE ANYONE. YOU DON'T HAVE TO, YOU KNOW. BE LIKE THOSE SIRENS WE MADE A DEAL WITH IN OUR GAME--THEY DON'T ACTUALLY LIKE THE SAILORS, THEY JUST WANT TO EAT THEM.
OH YEAH, THAT SOUNDS LIKE A GREAT ROLE MODEL TO USE.
I MEAN IT. WELL, NOT THE EATING PEOPLE PART, BUT THE REST.
THERE'S A WORD FOR IT, I SAW IT IN ONE OF THE PAMPHLETS THAT GOT LEFT FOR THE ACTUAL GSA CLUB.
HERE IT IS.
Z Z Z
YOU COULD BE ASEXUAL OR AROMANTIC. MAYBE BOTH. OR JUST NOT INTERESTED IN DATING, BUT THIS COULD HELP YOU LEARN ABOUT IT.
ACE 101
I...I DIDN'T KNOW THAT WAS AN OPTION.
ACE
HEY.
YEAH?

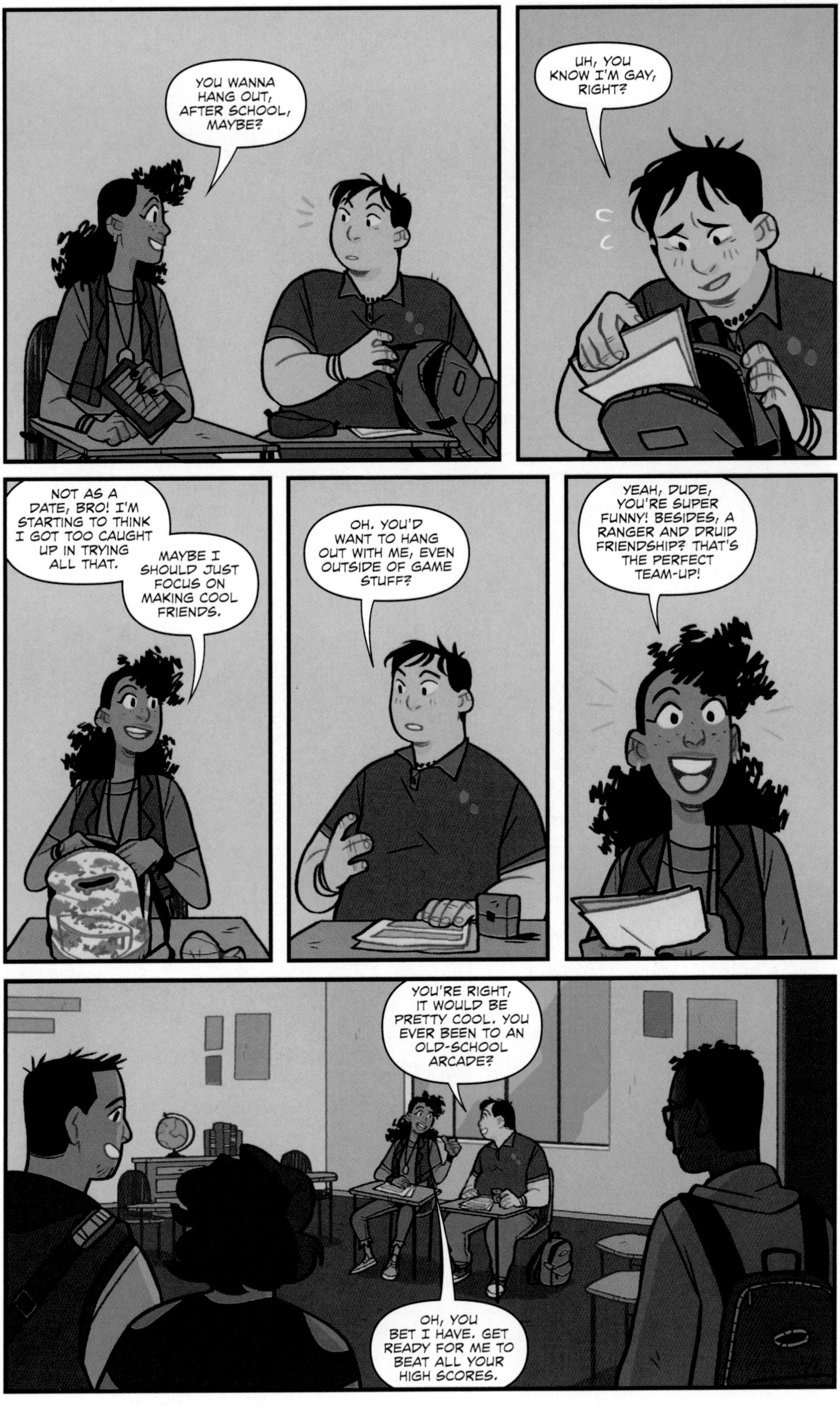
YOU WANNA HANG OUT, AFTER SCHOOL, MAYBE?
UH, YOU KNOW I'M GAY, RIGHT?
NOT AS A DATE, BRO! I'M STARTING TO THINK I GOT TOO CAUGHT UP IN TRYING ALL THAT.
MAYBE I SHOULD JUST FOCUS ON MAKING COOL FRIENDS.
OH. YOU'D WANT TO HANG OUT WITH ME, EVEN OUTSIDE OF GAME STUFF?
YEAH, DUDE, YOU'RE SUPER FUNNY! BESIDES, A RANGER AND DRUID FRIENDSHIP? THAT'S THE PERFECT TEAM-UP!
YOU'RE RIGHT, IT WOULD BE PRETTY COOL. YOU EVER BEEN TO AN OLD-SCHOOL ARCADE?
OH, YOU BET I HAVE. GET READY FOR ME TO BEAT ALL YOUR HIGH SCORES.

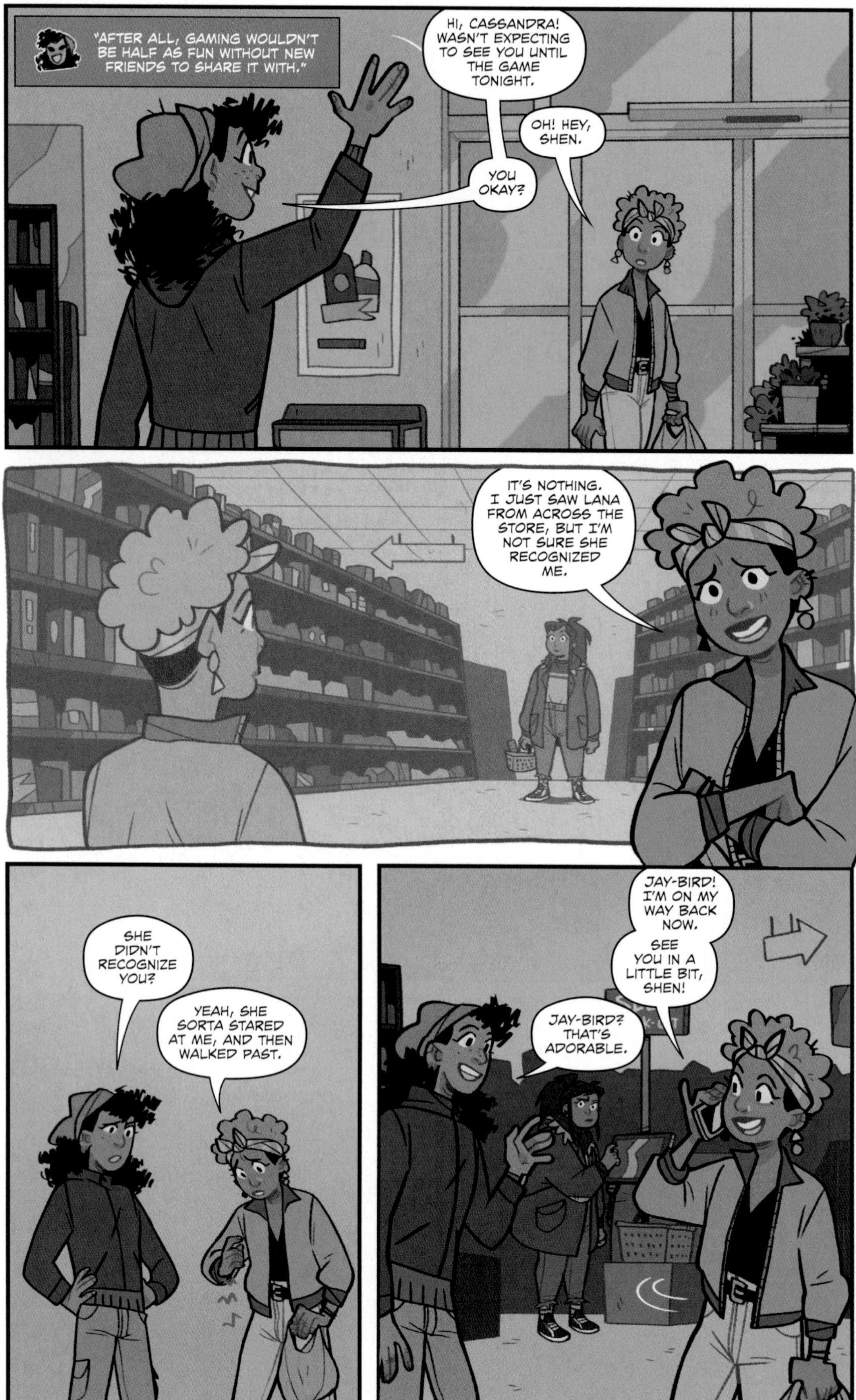
"AFTER ALL, GAMING WOULDN'T BE HALF AS FUN WITHOUT NEW FRIENDS TO SHARE IT WITH."
HI, CASSANDRA! WASN'T EXPECTING TO SEE YOU UNTIL THE GAME TONIGHT.
YOU OKAY?
OH! HEY, SHEN.
IT'S NOTHING. I JUST SAW LANA FROM ACROSS THE STORE, BUT I'M NOT SURE SHE RECOGNIZED ME.
SHE DIDN'T RECOGNIZE YOU?
YEAH, SHE SORTA STARED AT ME, AND THEN WALKED PAST.
JAY-BIRD! I'M ON MY WAY BACK NOW.
SEE YOU IN A LITTLE BIT, SHEN!
JAY-BIRD? THAT'S ADORABLE.

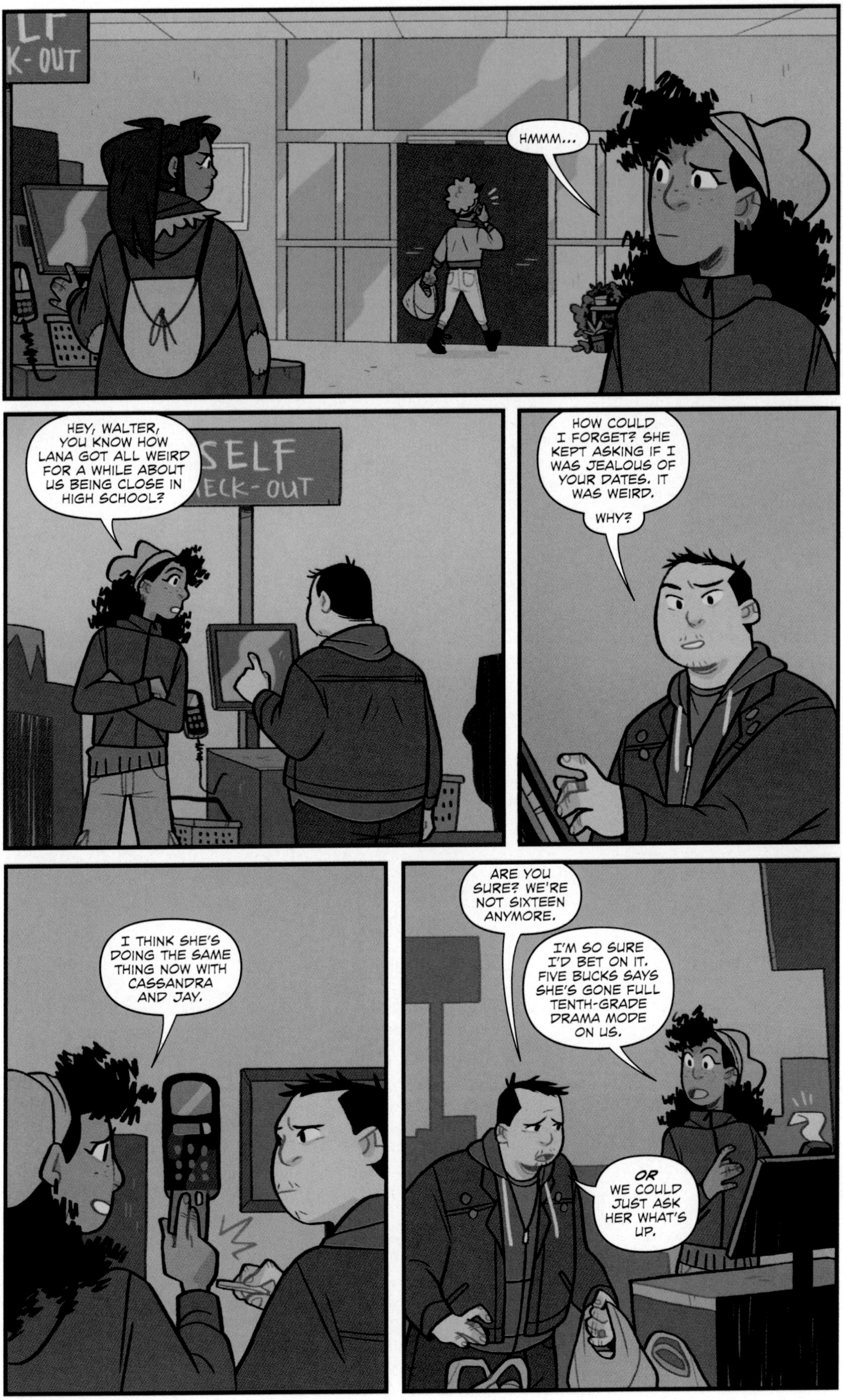
LF
K-OUT
HMMM...
SELF
ECK-OUT
HEY, WALTER, YOU KNOW HOW LANA GOT ALL WEIRD FOR A WHILE ABOUT US BEING CLOSE IN HIGH SCHOOL?
HOW COULD I FORGET? SHE KEPT ASKING IF I WAS JEALOUS OF YOUR DATES. IT WAS WEIRD.
WHY?
I THINK SHE'S DOING THE SAME THING NOW WITH CASSANDRA AND JAY.
ARE YOU SURE? WE'RE NOT SIXTEEN ANYMORE.
I'M SO SURE I'D BET ON IT. FIVE BUCKS SAYS SHE'S GONE FULL TENTH-GRADE DRAMA MODE ON US.
OR WE COULD JUST ASK HER WHAT'S UP.

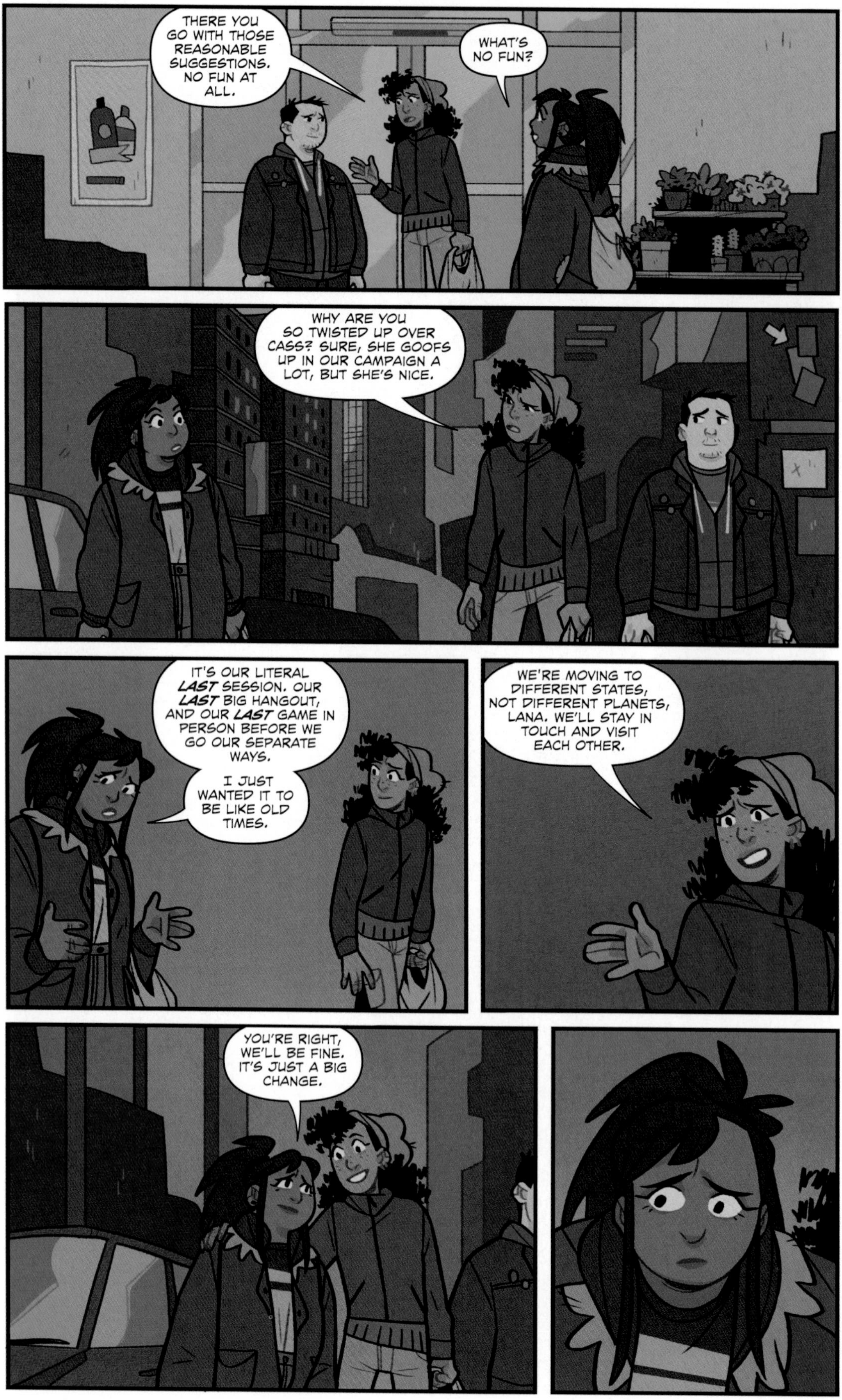
THERE YOU GO WITH THOSE REASONABLE SUGGESTIONS. NO FUN AT ALL.
WHAT'S NO FUN?
WHY ARE YOU SO TWISTED UP OVER CASS? SURE, SHE GOOFS UP IN OUR CAMPAIGN A LOT, BUT SHE'S NICE.
IT'S OUR LITERAL *LAST* SESSION. OUR *LAST* BIG HANGOUT, AND OUR *LAST* GAME IN PERSON BEFORE WE GO OUR SEPARATE WAYS.
I JUST WANTED IT TO BE LIKE OLD TIMES.
WE'RE MOVING TO DIFFERENT STATES, NOT DIFFERENT PLANETS, LANA. WE'LL STAY IN TOUCH AND VISIT EACH OTHER.
YOU'RE RIGHT, WE'LL BE FINE. IT'S JUST A BIG CHANGE.

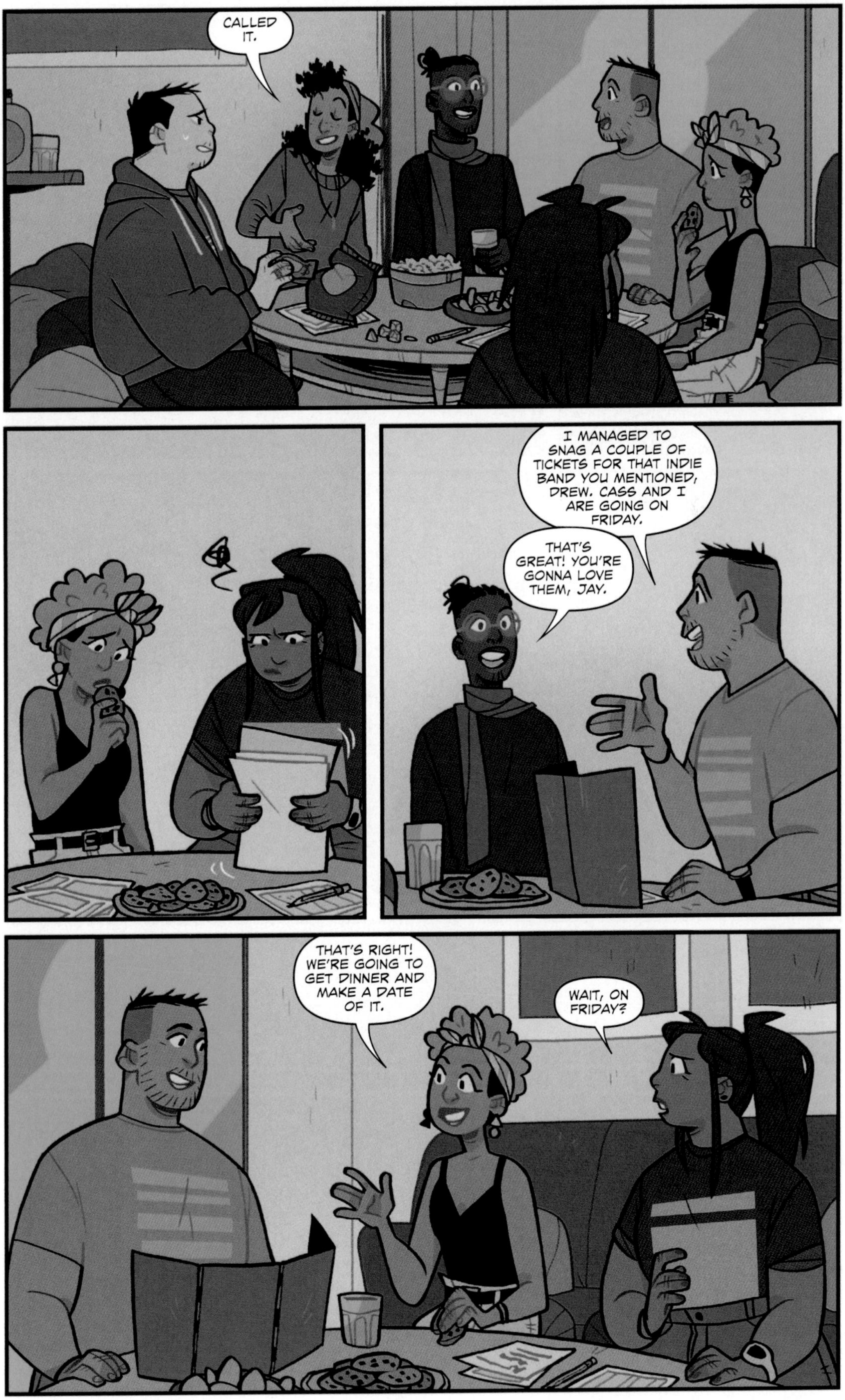
CALLED IT.
I MANAGED TO SNAG A COUPLE OF TICKETS FOR THAT INDIE BAND YOU MENTIONED, DREW. CASS AND I ARE GOING ON FRIDAY.
THAT'S GREAT! YOU'RE GONNA LOVE THEM, JAY.
THAT'S RIGHT! WE'RE GOING TO GET DINNER AND MAKE A DATE OF IT.
WAIT, ON FRIDAY?

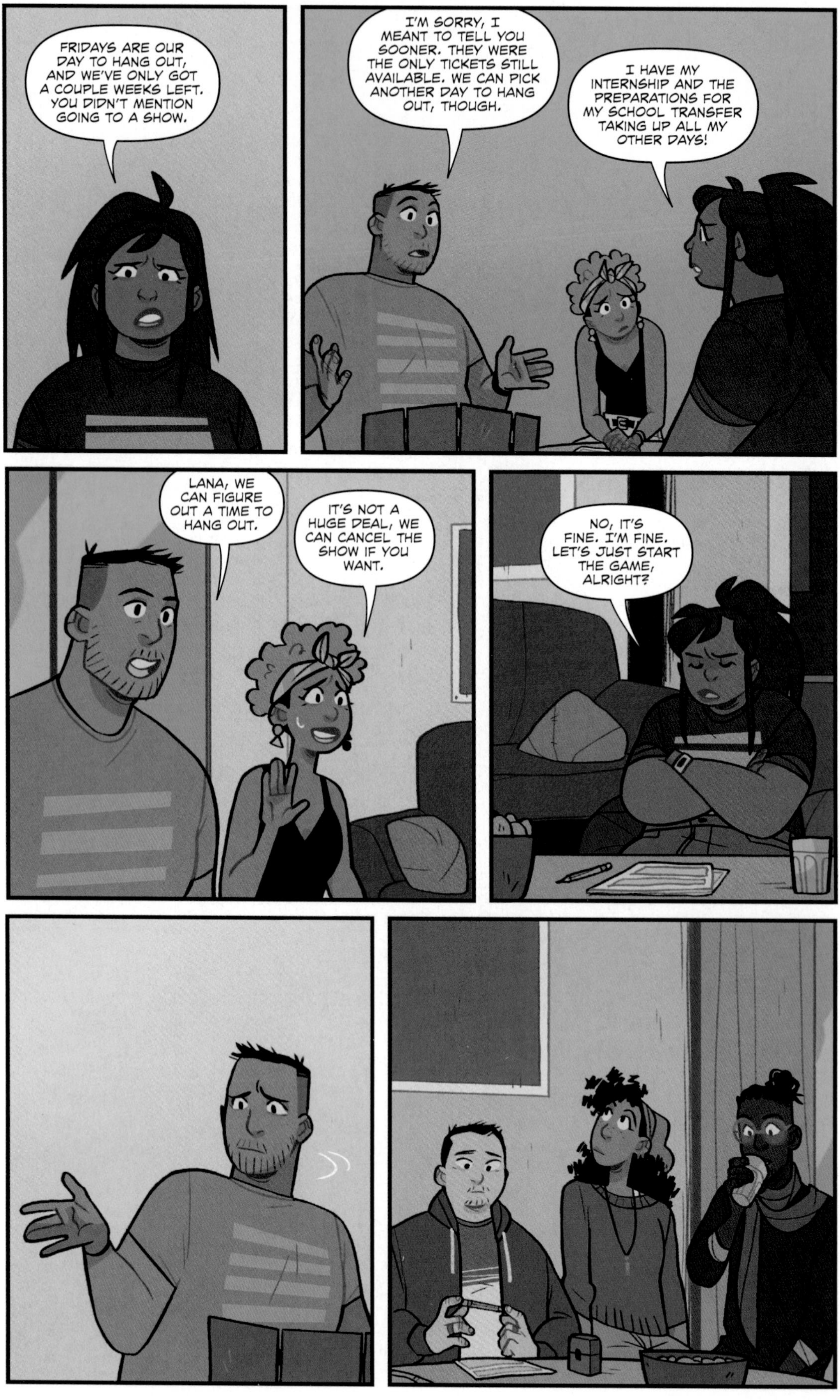
FRIDAYS ARE OUR DAY TO HANG OUT, AND WE'VE ONLY GOT A COUPLE WEEKS LEFT. YOU DIDN'T MENTION GOING TO A SHOW.
I'M SORRY, I MEANT TO TELL YOU SOONER. THEY WERE THE ONLY TICKETS STILL AVAILABLE. WE CAN PICK ANOTHER DAY TO HANG OUT, THOUGH.
I HAVE MY INTERNSHIP AND THE PREPARATIONS FOR MY SCHOOL TRANSFER TAKING UP ALL MY OTHER DAYS!
LANA, WE CAN FIGURE OUT A TIME TO HANG OUT.
IT'S NOT A HUGE DEAL, WE CAN CANCEL THE SHOW IF YOU WANT.
NO, IT'S FINE. I'M FINE. LET'S JUST START THE GAME, ALRIGHT?

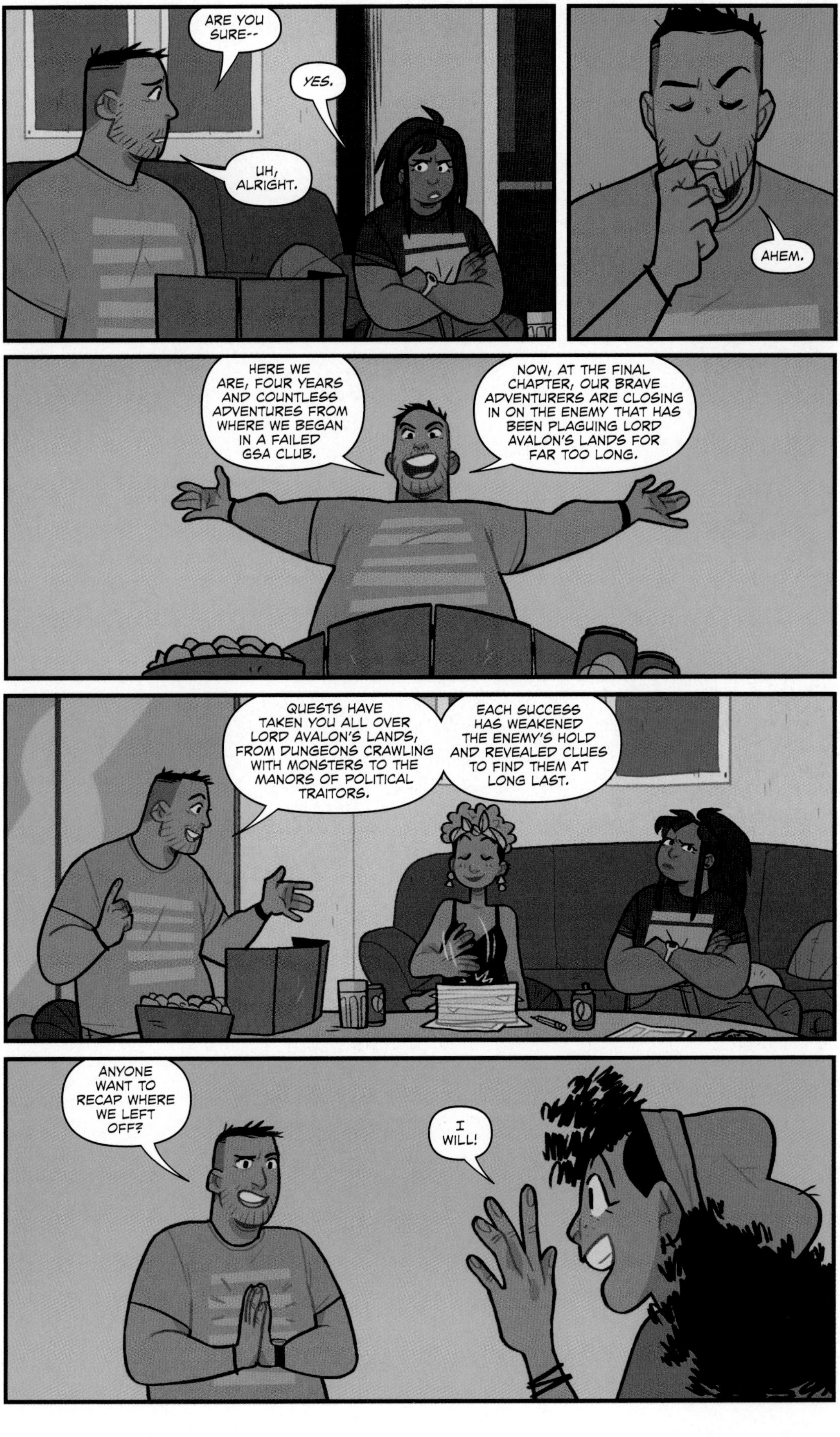
ARE YOU SURE--
YES.
UH, ALRIGHT.
AHEM.
HERE WE ARE, FOUR YEARS AND COUNTLESS ADVENTURES FROM WHERE WE BEGAN IN A FAILED GSA CLUB.
NOW, AT THE FINAL CHAPTER, OUR BRAVE ADVENTURERS ARE CLOSING IN ON THE ENEMY THAT HAS BEEN PLAGUING LORD AVALON'S LANDS FOR FAR TOO LONG.
QUESTS HAVE TAKEN YOU ALL OVER LORD AVALON'S LANDS, FROM DUNGEONS CRAWLING WITH MONSTERS TO THE MANORS OF POLITICAL TRAITORS.
EACH SUCCESS HAS WEAKENED THE ENEMY'S HOLD AND REVEALED CLUES TO FIND THEM AT LONG LAST.
ANYONE WANT TO RECAP WHERE WE LEFT OFF?
I WILL!

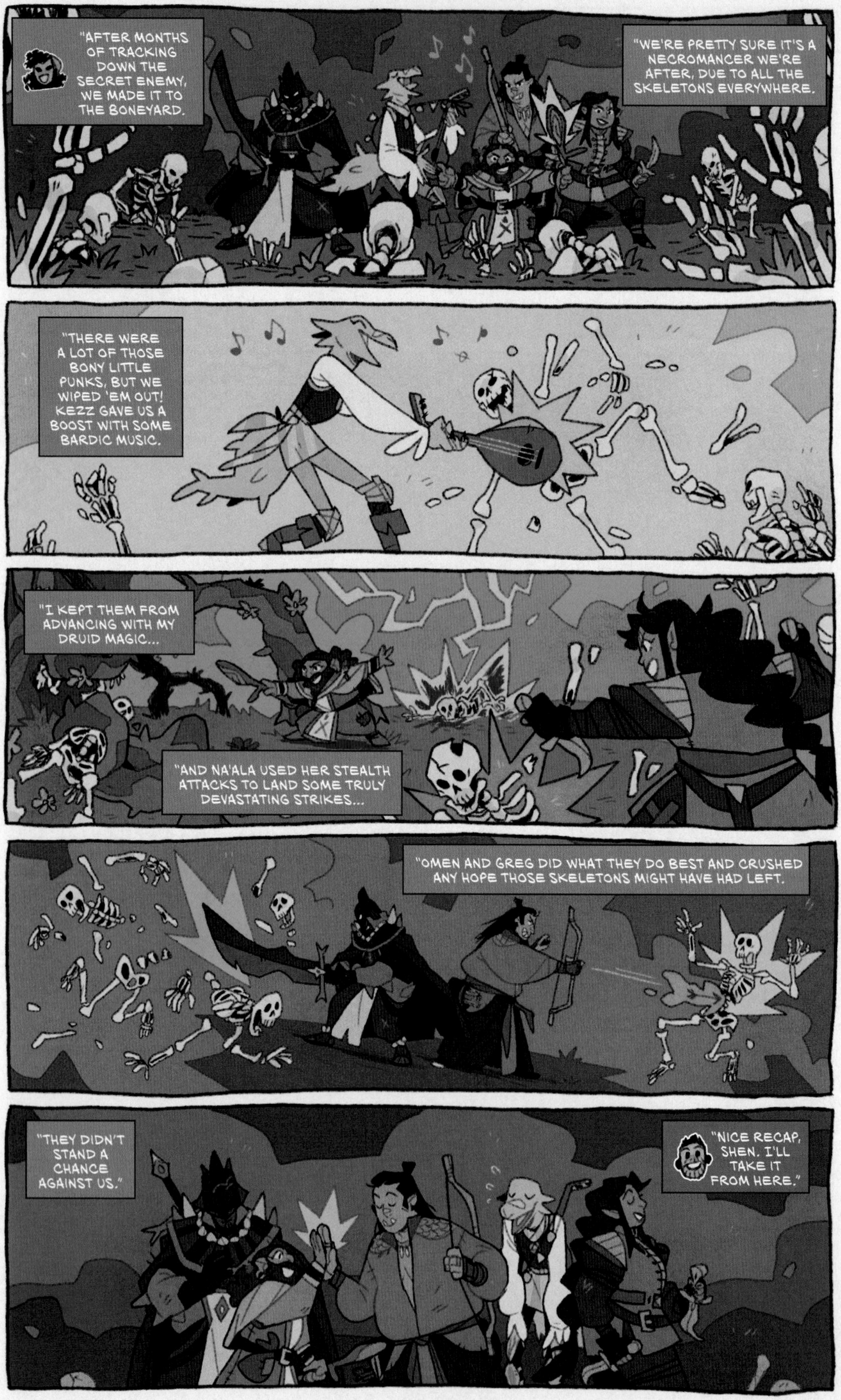

"AFTER MONTHS OF TRACKING DOWN THE SECRET ENEMY, WE MADE IT TO THE BONEYARD.
"WE'RE PRETTY SURE IT'S A NECROMANCER WE'RE AFTER, DUE TO ALL THE SKELETONS EVERYWHERE.
"THERE WERE A LOT OF THOSE BONY LITTLE PUNKS, BUT WE WIPED 'EM OUT! KEZZ GAVE US A BOOST WITH SOME BARDIC MUSIC.
"I KEPT THEM FROM ADVANCING WITH MY DRUID MAGIC...
"AND NA'ALA USED HER STEALTH ATTACKS TO LAND SOME TRULY DEVASTATING STRIKES...
"OMEN AND GREG DID WHAT THEY DO BEST AND CRUSHED ANY HOPE THOSE SKELETONS MIGHT HAVE HAD LEFT.
"THEY DIDN'T STAND A CHANCE AGAINST US."
"NICE RECAP, SHEN. I'LL TAKE IT FROM HERE."

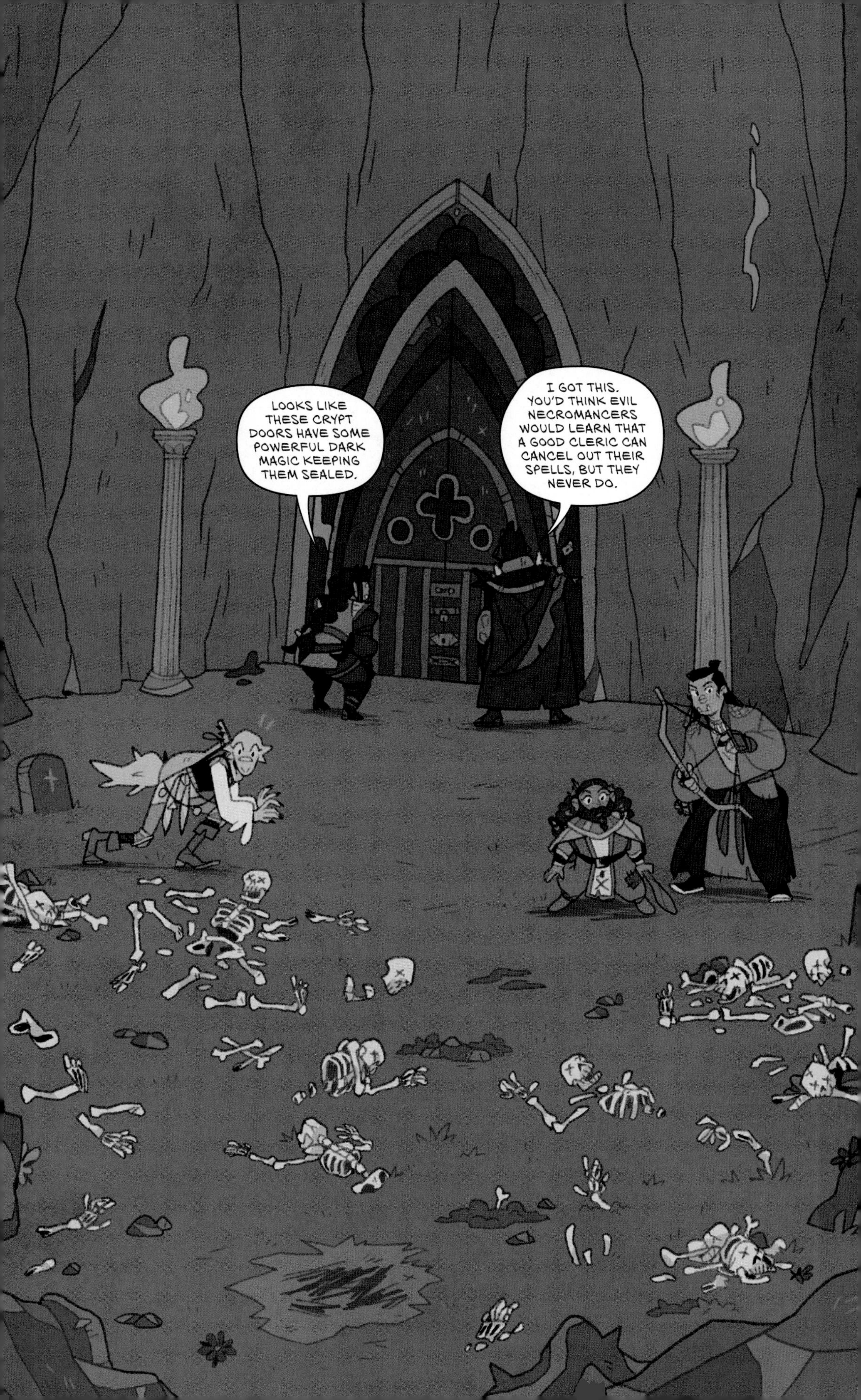
LOOKS LIKE THESE CRYPT DOORS HAVE SOME POWERFUL DARK MAGIC KEEPING THEM SEALED.
I GOT THIS. YOU'D THINK EVIL NECROMANCERS WOULD LEARN THAT A GOOD CLERIC CAN CANCEL OUT THEIR SPELLS, BUT THEY NEVER DO.

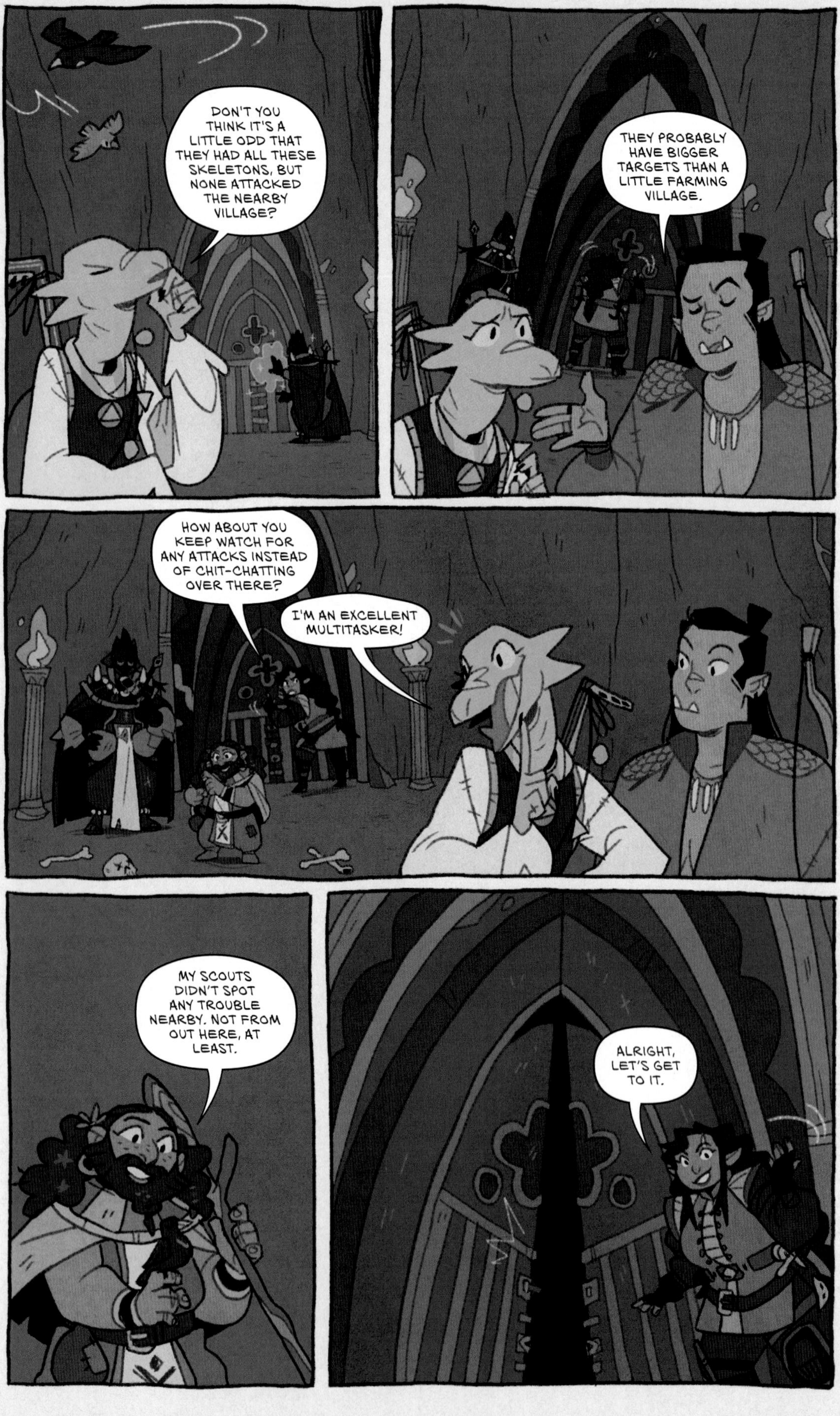
DON'T YOU THINK IT'S A LITTLE ODD THAT THEY HAD ALL THESE SKELETONS, BUT NONE ATTACKED THE NEARBY VILLAGE?
THEY PROBABLY HAVE BIGGER TARGETS THAN A LITTLE FARMING VILLAGE.
HOW ABOUT YOU KEEP WATCH FOR ANY ATTACKS INSTEAD OF CHIT-CHATTING OVER THERE?
I'M AN EXCELLENT MULTITASKER!
MY SCOUTS DIDN'T SPOT ANY TROUBLE NEARBY. NOT FROM OUT HERE, AT LEAST.
ALRIGHT, LET'S GET TO IT.

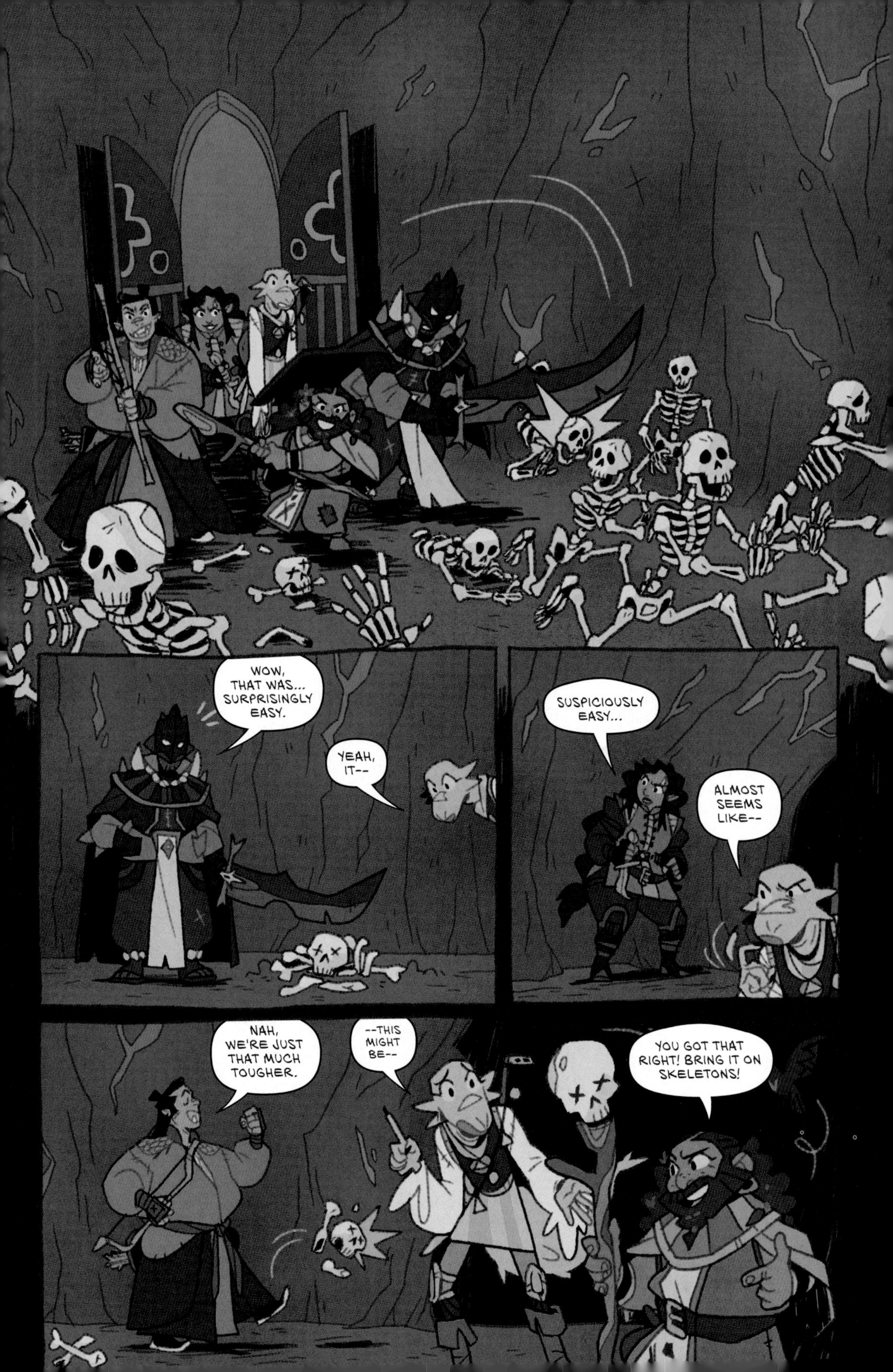
WOW, THAT WAS... SURPRISINGLY EASY.
YEAH, IT--
SUSPICIOUSLY EASY...
ALMOST SEEMS LIKE--
NAH, WE'RE JUST THAT MUCH TOUGHER.
--THIS MIGHT BE--
YOU GOT THAT RIGHT! BRING IT ON SKELETONS!

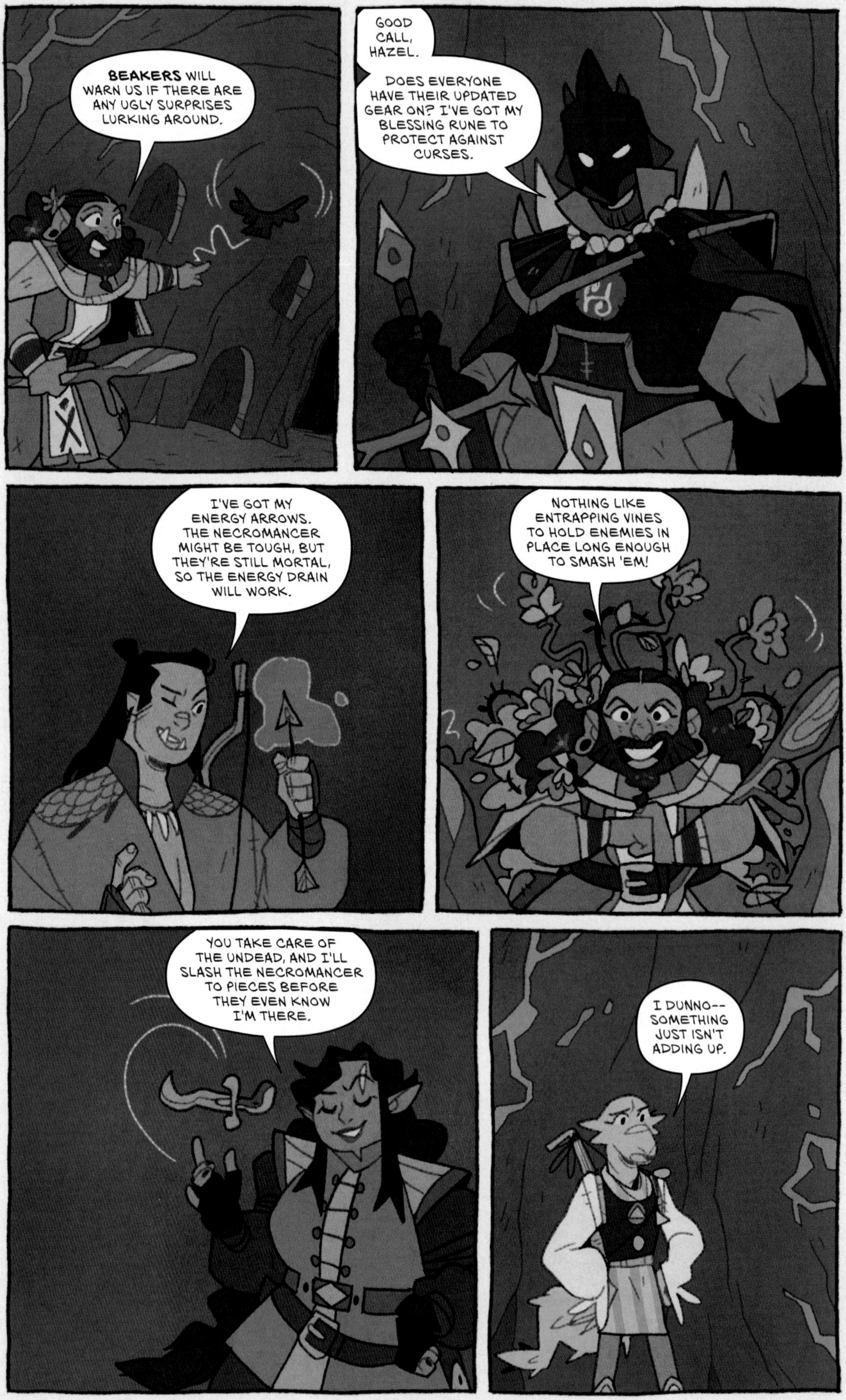
BEAKERS WILL WARN US IF THERE ARE ANY UGLY SURPRISES LURKING AROUND.
GOOD CALL, HAZEL.
DOES EVERYONE HAVE THEIR UPDATED GEAR ON? I'VE GOT MY BLESSING RUNE TO PROTECT AGAINST CURSES.
I'VE GOT MY ENERGY ARROWS. THE NECROMANCER MIGHT BE TOUGH, BUT THEY'RE STILL MORTAL, SO THE ENERGY DRAIN WILL WORK.
NOTHING LIKE ENTRAPPING VINES TO HOLD ENEMIES IN PLACE LONG ENOUGH TO SMASH 'EM!
YOU TAKE CARE OF THE UNDEAD, AND I'LL SLASH THE NECROMANCER TO PIECES BEFORE THEY EVEN KNOW I'M THERE.
I DUNNO-- SOMETHING JUST ISN'T ADDING UP.

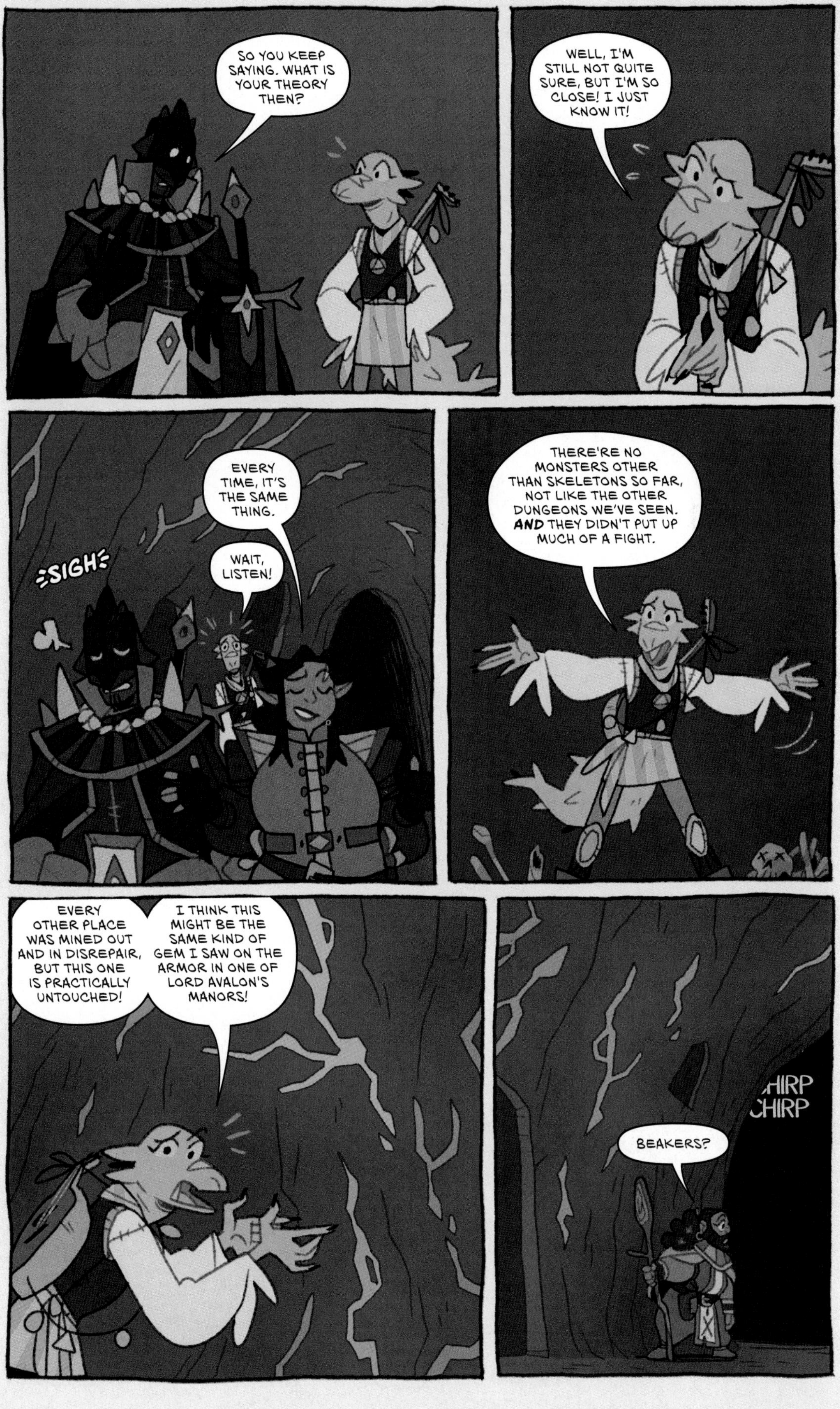
SO YOU KEEP SAYING. WHAT IS YOUR THEORY THEN?
WELL, I'M STILL NOT QUITE SURE, BUT I'M SO CLOSE! I JUST KNOW IT!
EVERY TIME, IT'S THE SAME THING.
SIGH
WAIT, LISTEN!
THERE'RE NO MONSTERS OTHER THAN SKELETONS SO FAR, NOT LIKE THE OTHER DUNGEONS WE'VE SEEN. **AND** THEY DIDN'T PUT UP MUCH OF A FIGHT.
EVERY OTHER PLACE WAS MINED OUT AND IN DISREPAIR, BUT THIS ONE IS PRACTICALLY UNTOUCHED!
I THINK THIS MIGHT BE THE SAME KIND OF GEM I SAW ON THE ARMOR IN ONE OF LORD AVALON'S MANORS!
BEAKERS?

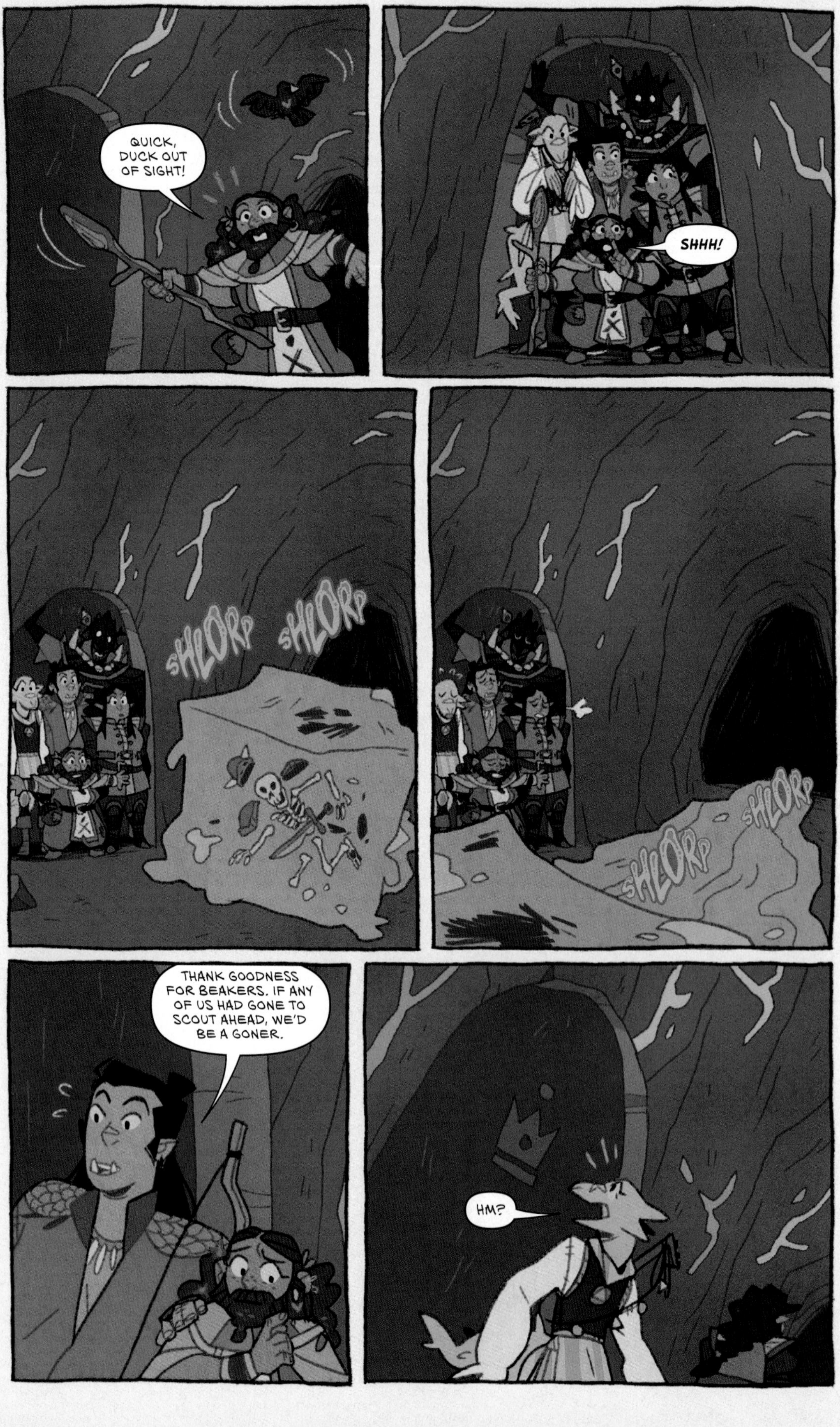
QUICK, DUCK OUT OF SIGHT!
SHHH!
sHLORP
sHLORP
sHLORP
sHLORP
THANK GOODNESS FOR BEAKERS. IF ANY OF US HAD GONE TO SCOUT AHEAD, WE'D BE A GONER.
HM?

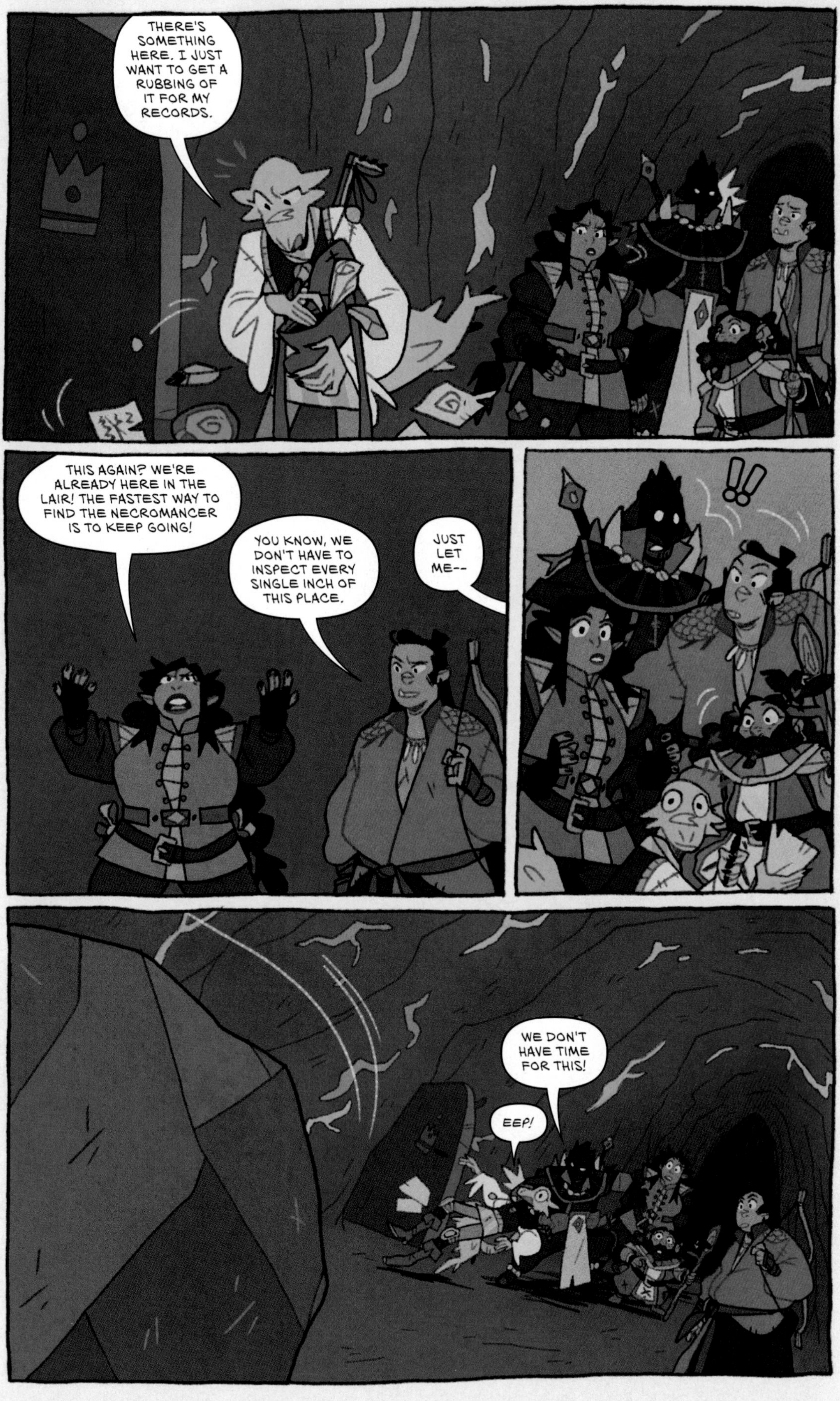
THERE'S SOMETHING HERE. I JUST WANT TO GET A RUBBING OF IT FOR MY RECORDS.
THIS AGAIN? WE'RE ALREADY HERE IN THE LAIR! THE FASTEST WAY TO FIND THE NECROMANCER IS TO KEEP GOING!
YOU KNOW, WE DON'T HAVE TO INSPECT EVERY SINGLE INCH OF THIS PLACE.
JUST LET ME--
!!
WE DON'T HAVE TIME FOR THIS!
EEP!

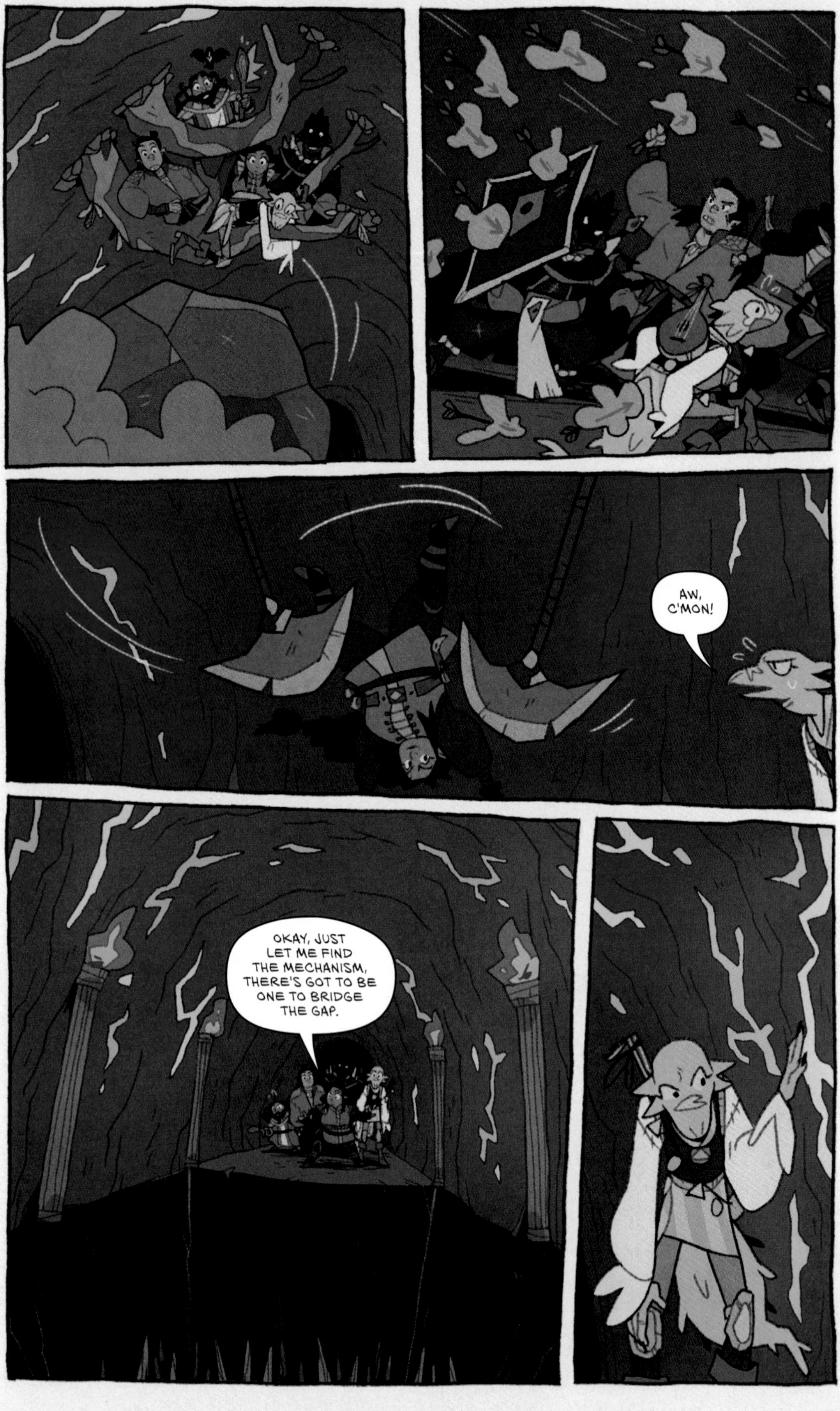
AW, C'MON!
OKAY, JUST LET ME FIND THE MECHANISM, THERE'S GOT TO BE ONE TO BRIDGE THE GAP.

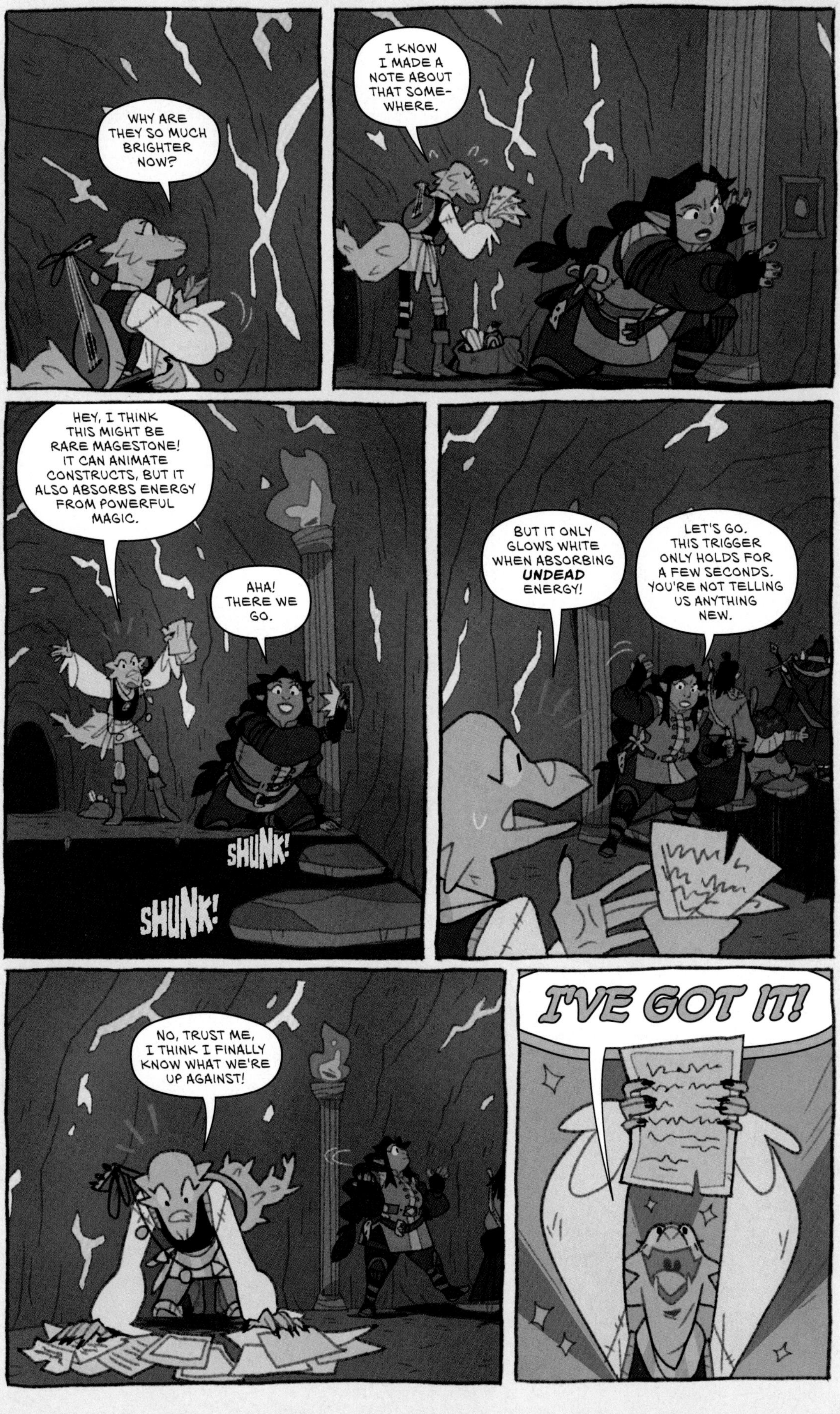
WHY ARE THEY SO MUCH BRIGHTER NOW?
I KNOW I MADE A NOTE ABOUT THAT SOME-WHERE.
HEY, I THINK THIS MIGHT BE RARE MAGESTONE! IT CAN ANIMATE CONSTRUCTS, BUT IT ALSO ABSORBS ENERGY FROM POWERFUL MAGIC.
AHA! THERE WE GO.
SHUNK!
SHUNK!
BUT IT ONLY GLOWS WHITE WHEN ABSORBING **UNDEAD** ENERGY!
LET'S GO. THIS TRIGGER ONLY HOLDS FOR A FEW SECONDS. YOU'RE NOT TELLING US ANYTHING NEW.
NO, TRUST ME, I THINK I FINALLY KNOW WHAT WE'RE UP AGAINST!
I'VE GOT IT!

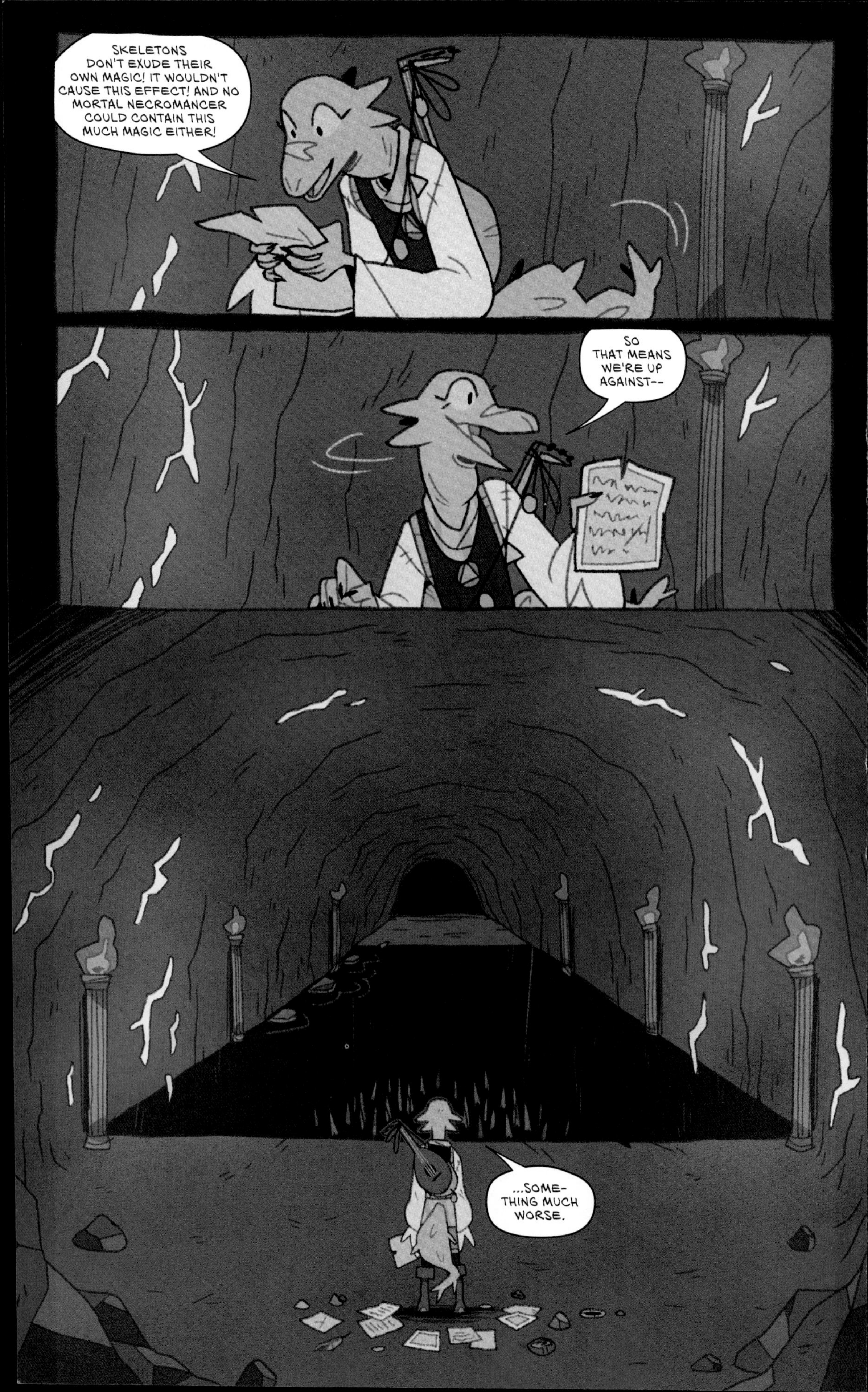
SKELETONS DON'T EXUDE THEIR OWN MAGIC! IT WOULDN'T CAUSE THIS EFFECT! AND NO MORTAL NECROMANCER COULD CONTAIN THIS MUCH MAGIC EITHER!
SO THAT MEANS WE'RE UP AGAINST--
...SOME-THING MUCH WORSE.

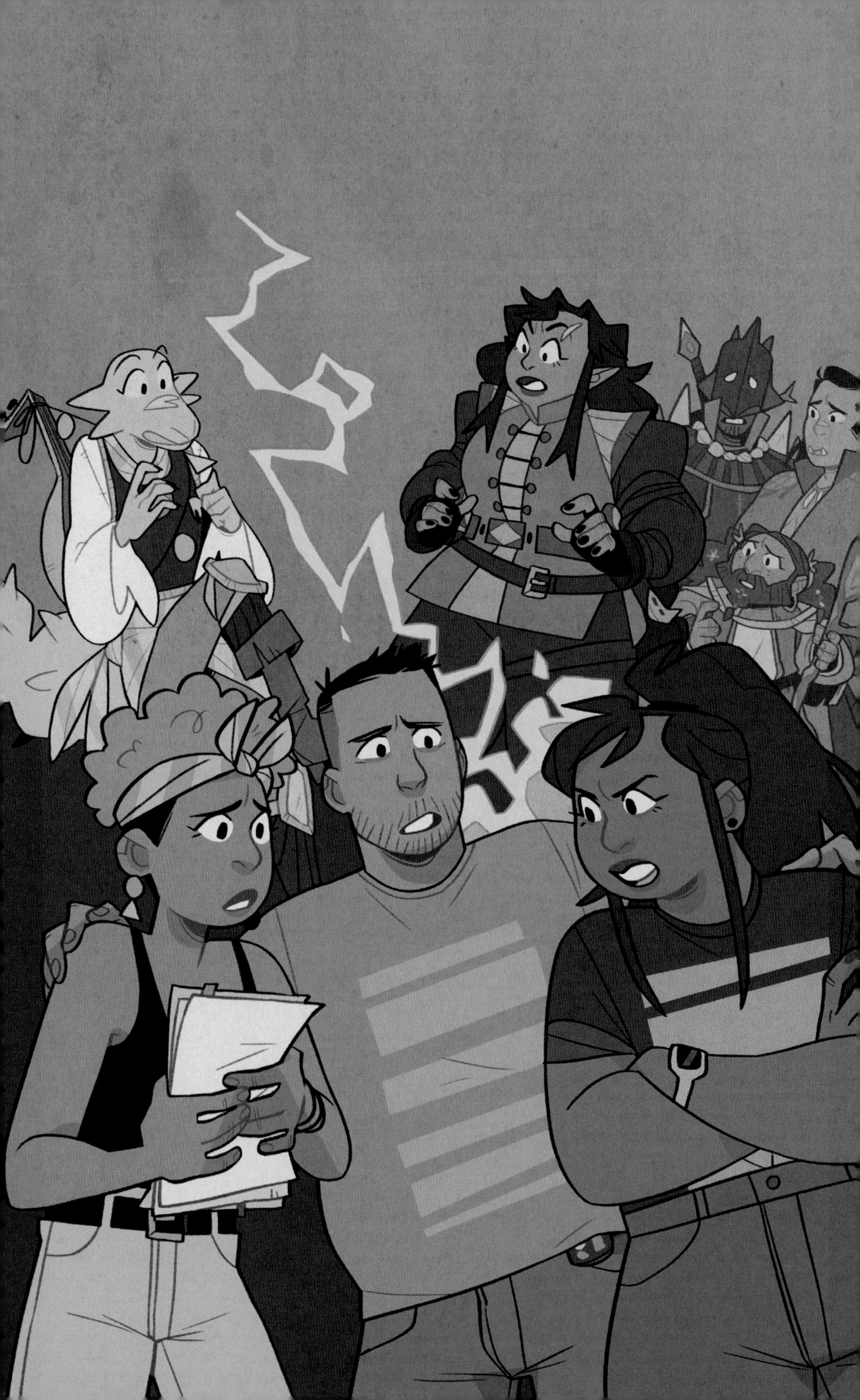

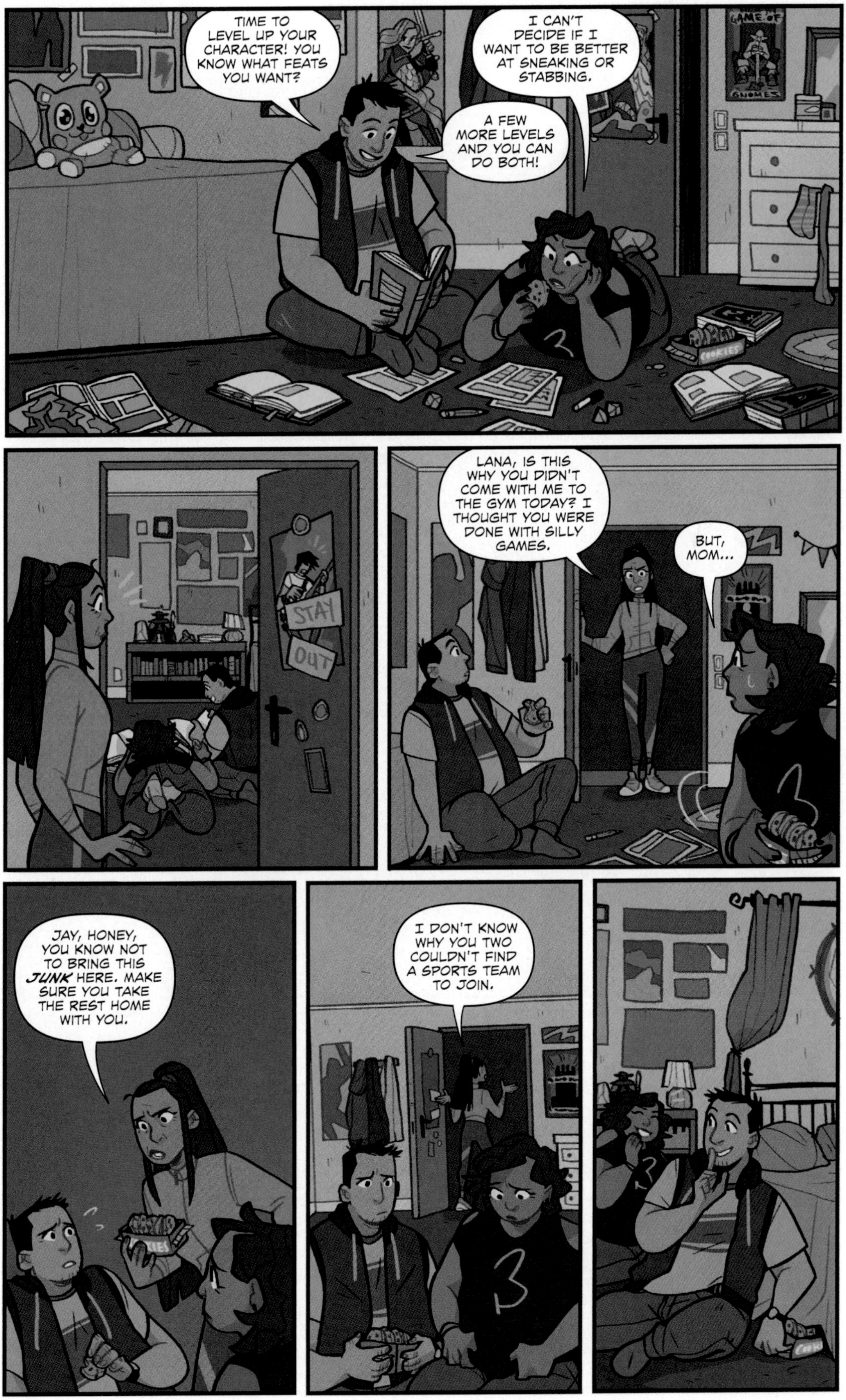
TIME TO LEVEL UP YOUR CHARACTER! YOU KNOW WHAT FEATS YOU WANT?
I CAN'T DECIDE IF I WANT TO BE BETTER AT SNEAKING OR STABBING.
A FEW MORE LEVELS AND YOU CAN DO BOTH!
GAME OF GNOMES
COOKIES
STAY OUT
LANA, IS THIS WHY YOU DIDN'T COME WITH ME TO THE GYM TODAY? I THOUGHT YOU WERE DONE WITH SILLY GAMES.
BUT, MOM...
JAY, HONEY, YOU KNOW NOT TO BRING THIS *JUNK* HERE. MAKE SURE YOU TAKE THE REST HOME WITH YOU.
I DON'T KNOW WHY YOU TWO COULDN'T FIND A SPORTS TEAM TO JOIN.

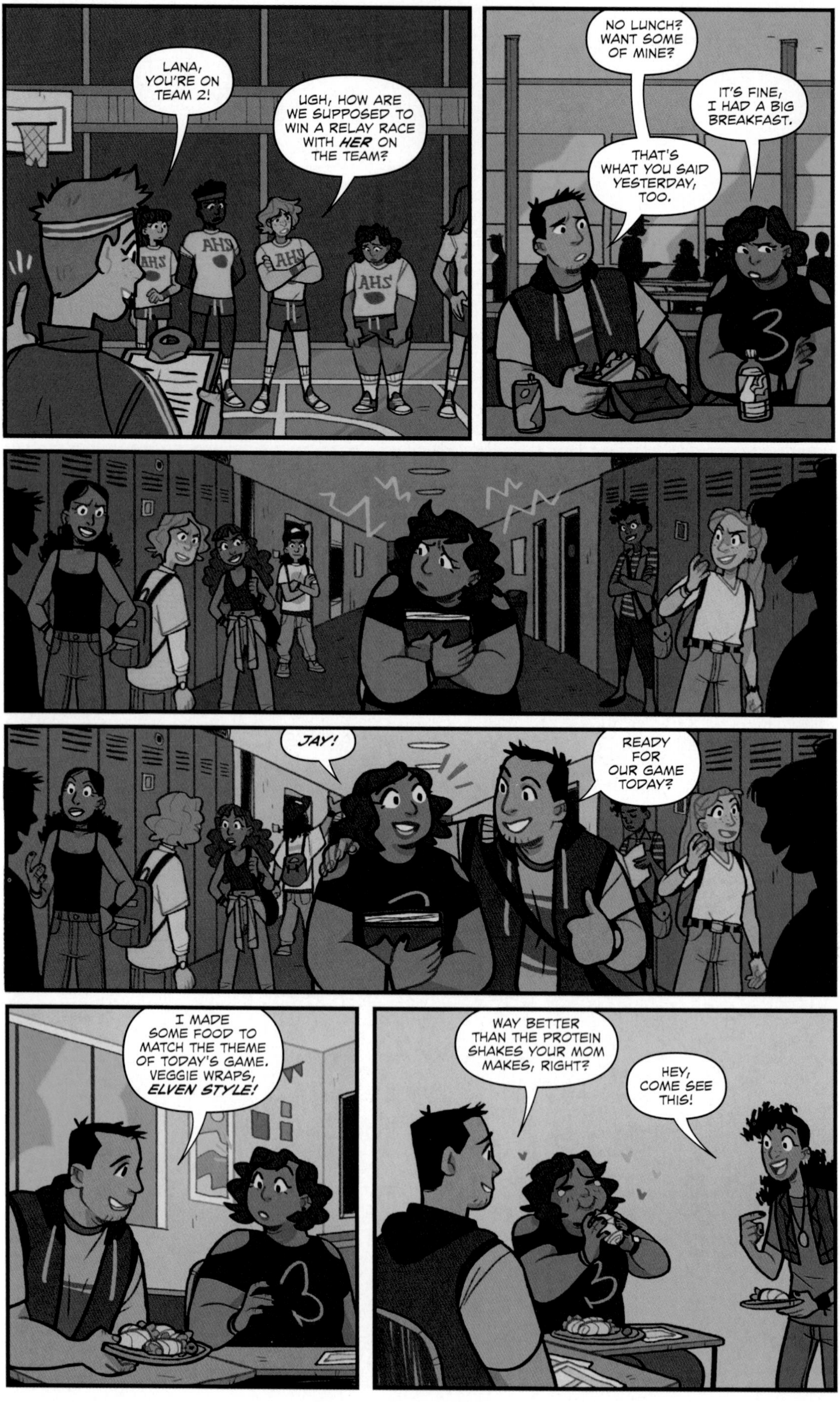
LANA, YOU'RE ON TEAM 2!
UGH, HOW ARE WE SUPPOSED TO WIN A RELAY RACE WITH *HER* ON THE TEAM?
NO LUNCH? WANT SOME OF MINE?
IT'S FINE, I HAD A BIG BREAKFAST.
THAT'S WHAT YOU SAID YESTERDAY, TOO.
JAY!
READY FOR OUR GAME TODAY?
I MADE SOME FOOD TO MATCH THE THEME OF TODAY'S GAME. VEGGIE WRAPS, *ELVEN STYLE!*
WAY BETTER THAN THE PROTEIN SHAKES YOUR MOM MAKES, RIGHT?
HEY, COME SEE THIS!

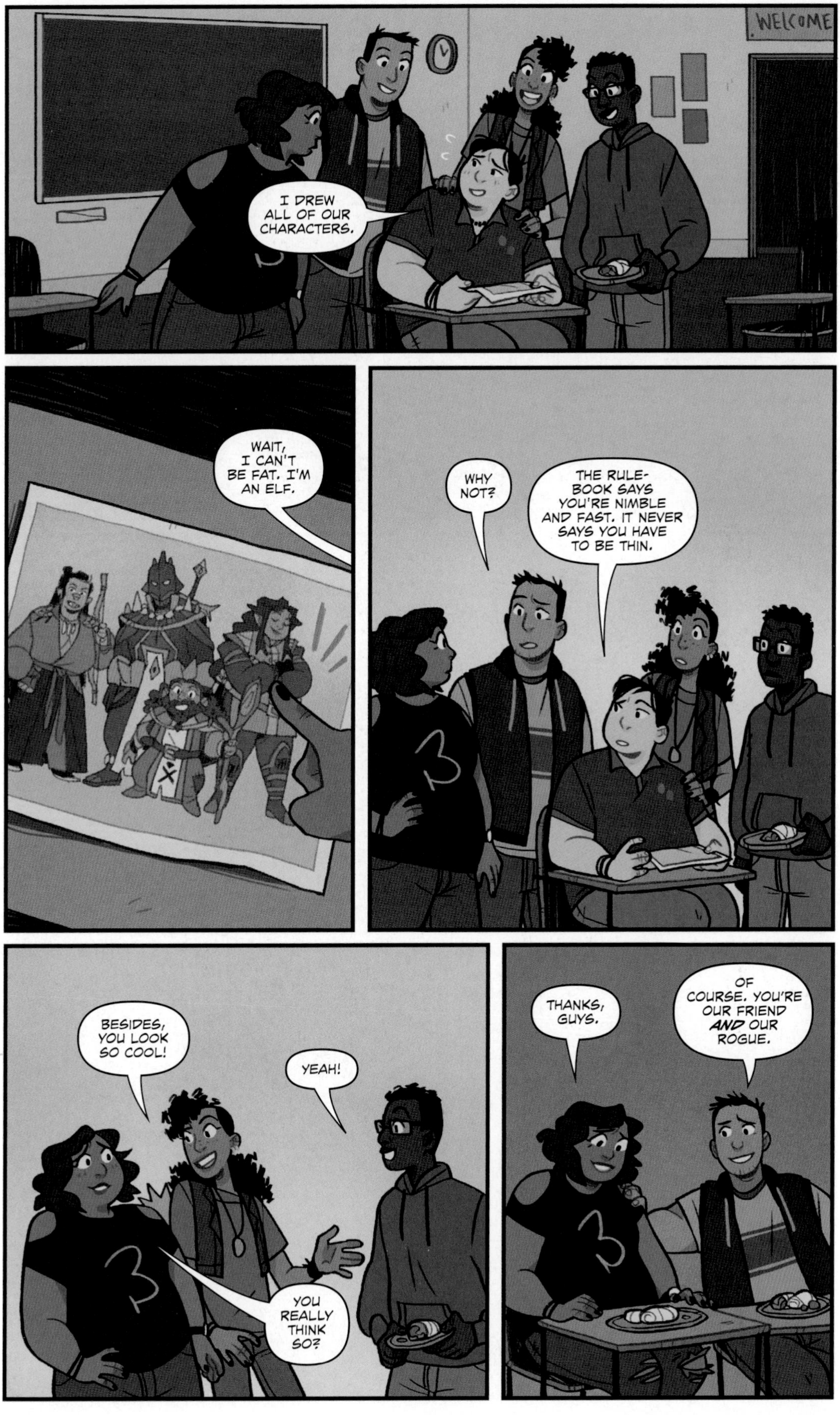
WELCOME
I DREW ALL OF OUR CHARACTERS.
WAIT, I CAN'T BE FAT. I'M AN ELF.
WHY NOT?
THE RULE-BOOK SAYS YOU'RE NIMBLE AND FAST. IT NEVER SAYS YOU HAVE TO BE THIN.
BESIDES, YOU LOOK SO COOL!
YEAH!
YOU REALLY THINK SO?
THANKS, GUYS.
OF COURSE. YOU'RE OUR FRIEND ***AND*** OUR ROGUE.

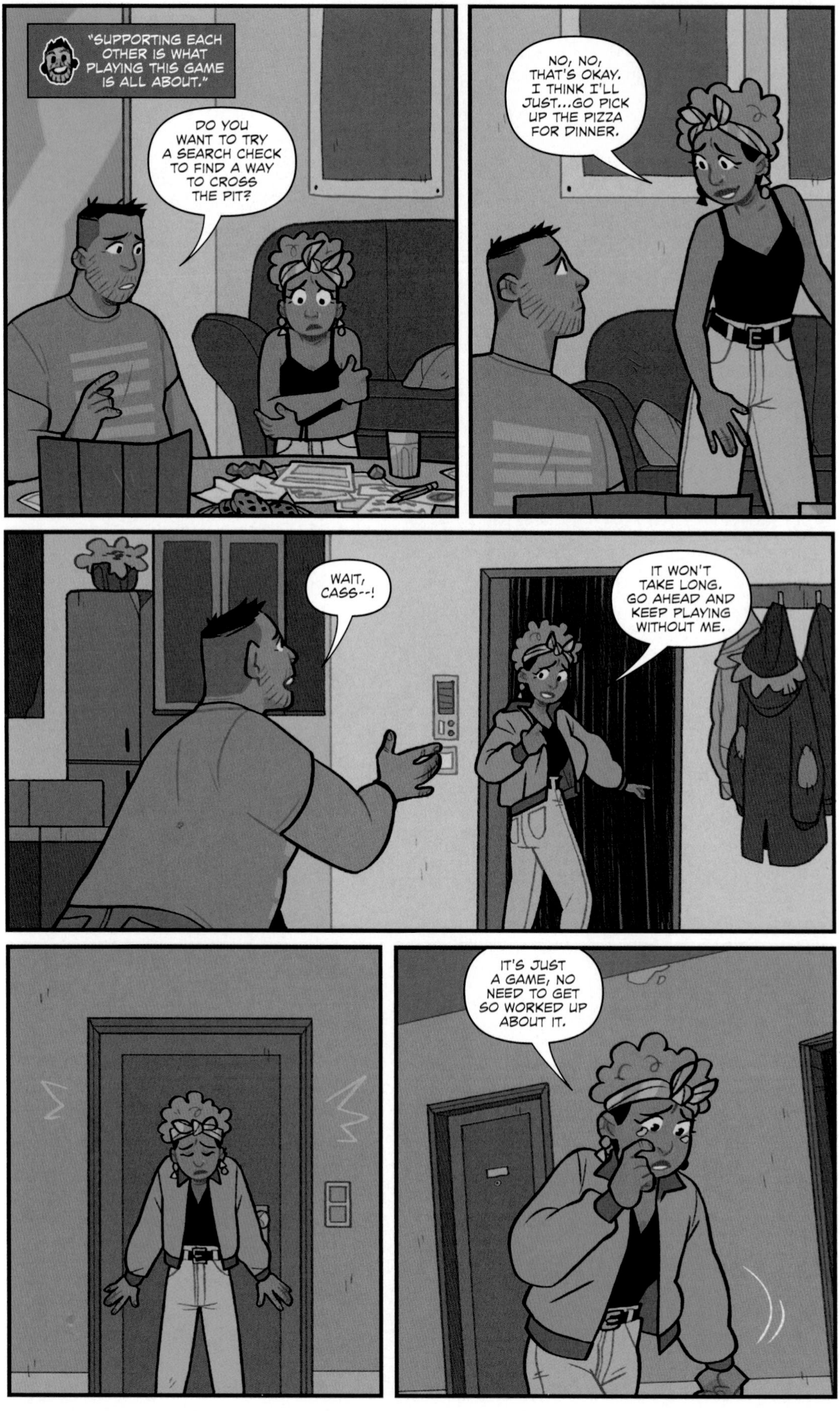
"SUPPORTING EACH OTHER IS WHAT PLAYING THIS GAME IS ALL ABOUT."
DO YOU WANT TO TRY A SEARCH CHECK TO FIND A WAY TO CROSS THE PIT?
NO, NO, THAT'S OKAY. I THINK I'LL JUST...GO PICK UP THE PIZZA FOR DINNER.
WAIT, CASS--!
IT WON'T TAKE LONG. GO AHEAD AND KEEP PLAYING WITHOUT ME.
IT'S JUST A GAME, NO NEED TO GET SO WORKED UP ABOUT IT.

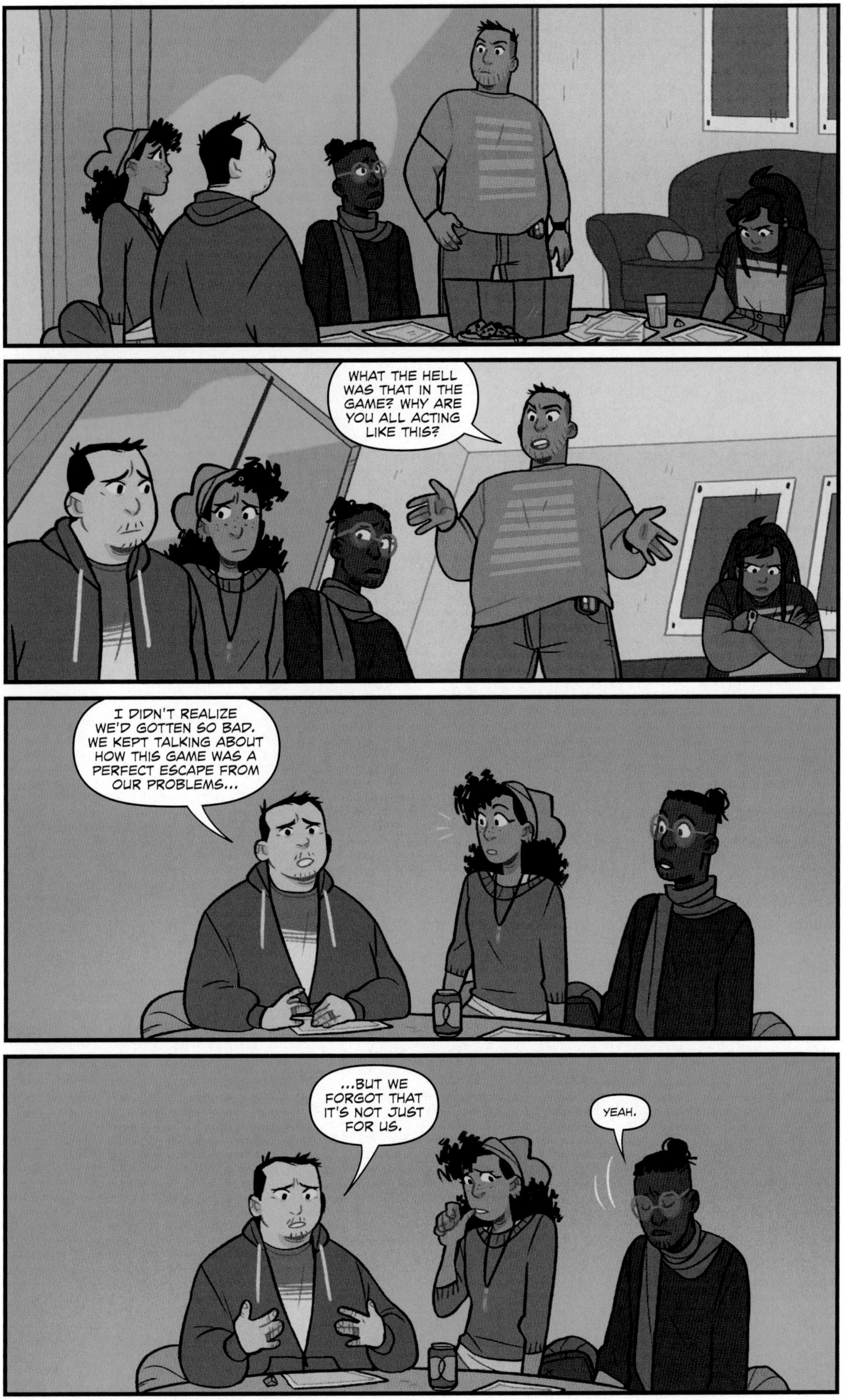
WHAT THE HELL WAS THAT IN THE GAME? WHY ARE YOU ALL ACTING LIKE THIS?
I DIDN'T REALIZE WE'D GOTTEN SO BAD. WE KEPT TALKING ABOUT HOW THIS GAME WAS A PERFECT ESCAPE FROM OUR PROBLEMS...
...BUT WE FORGOT THAT IT'S NOT JUST FOR US.
YEAH.

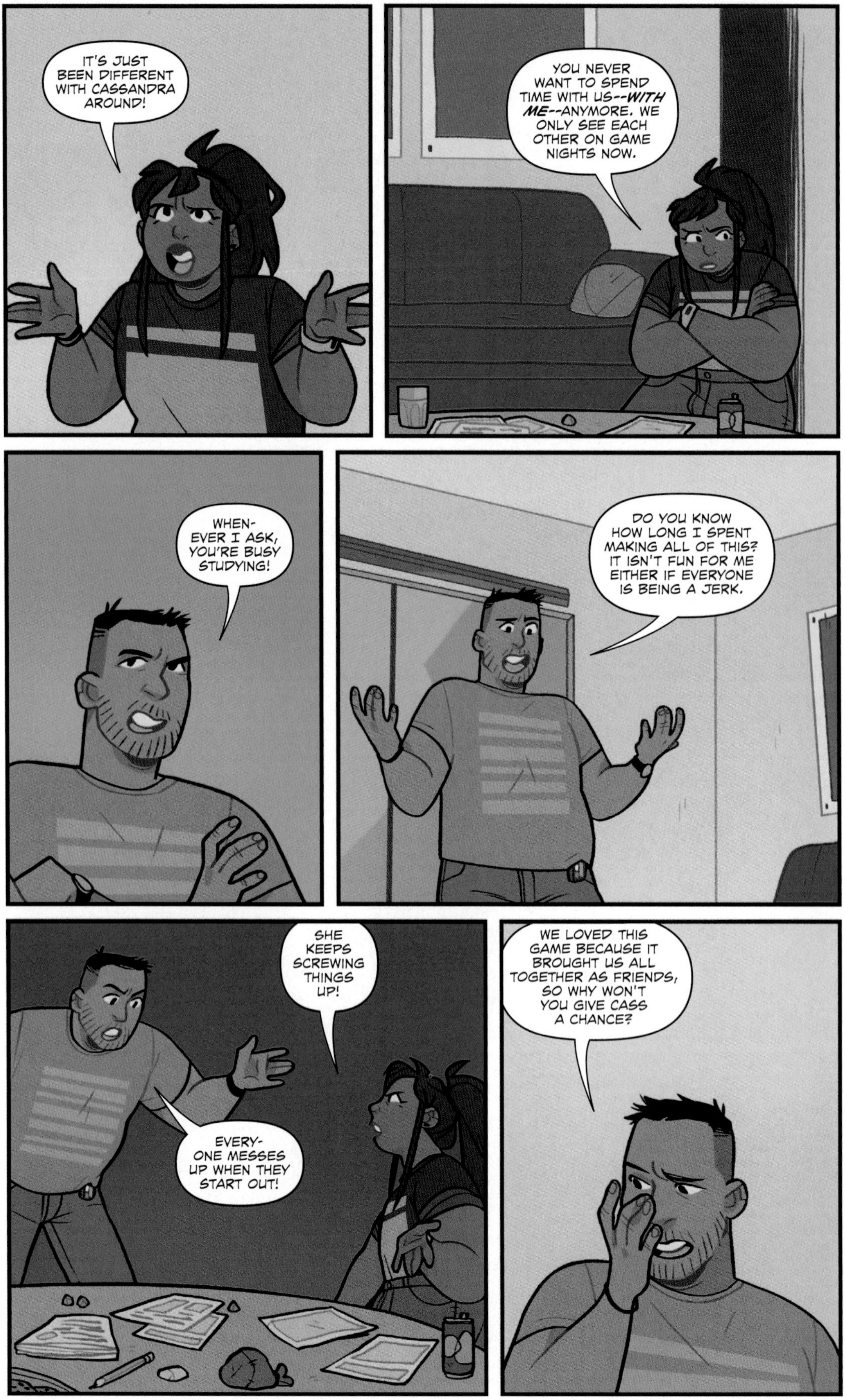
IT'S JUST BEEN DIFFERENT WITH CASSANDRA AROUND!
YOU NEVER WANT TO SPEND TIME WITH US--*WITH ME*--ANYMORE. WE ONLY SEE EACH OTHER ON GAME NIGHTS NOW.
WHEN-EVER I ASK, YOU'RE BUSY STUDYING!
DO YOU KNOW HOW LONG I SPENT MAKING ALL OF THIS? IT ISN'T FUN FOR ME EITHER IF EVERYONE IS BEING A JERK.
SHE KEEPS SCREWING THINGS UP!
EVERY-ONE MESSES UP WHEN THEY START OUT!
WE LOVED THIS GAME BECAUSE IT BROUGHT US ALL TOGETHER AS FRIENDS, SO WHY WON'T YOU GIVE CASS A CHANCE?

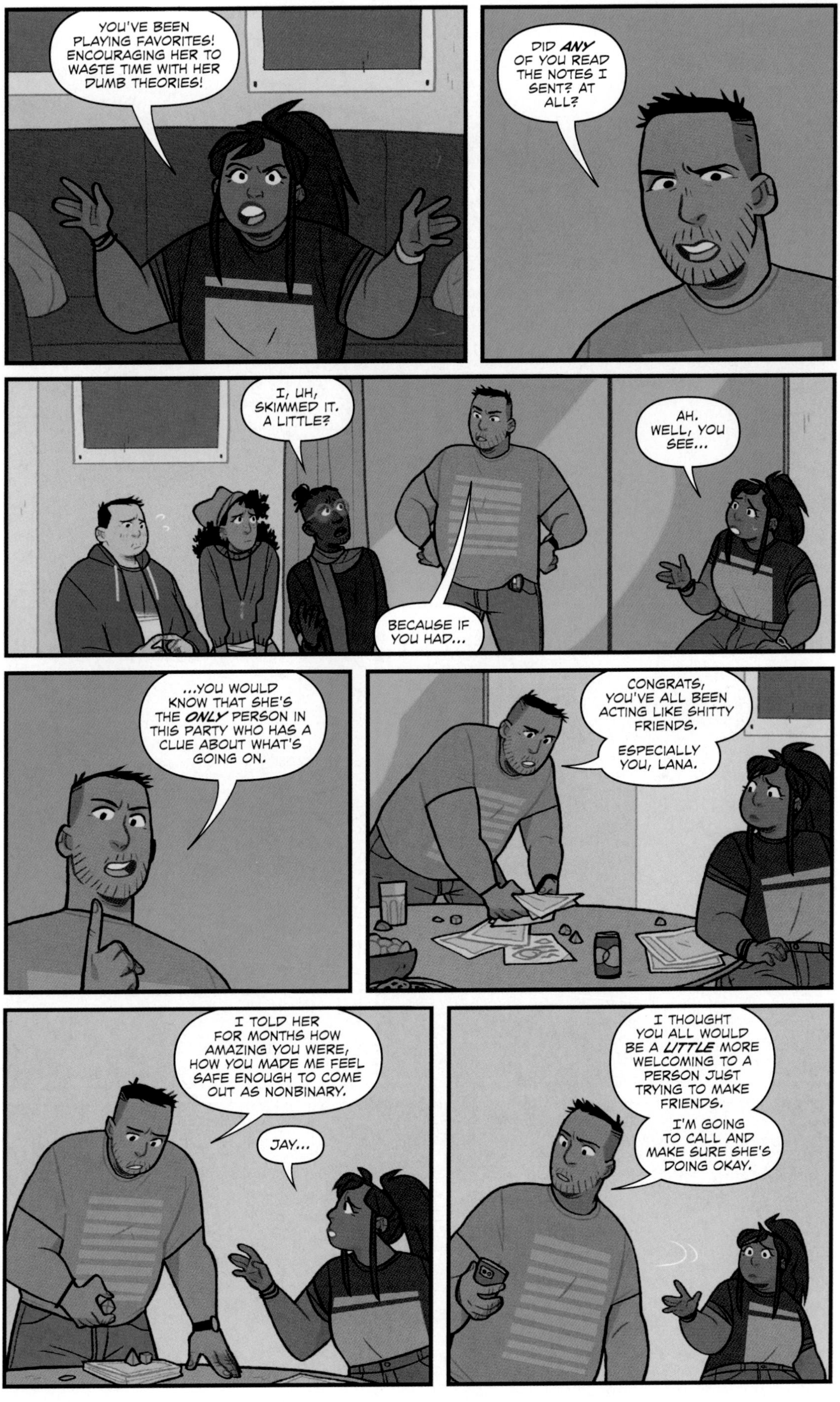
YOU'VE BEEN PLAYING FAVORITES! ENCOURAGING HER TO WASTE TIME WITH HER DUMB THEORIES!
DID ANY OF YOU READ THE NOTES I SENT? AT ALL?
I, UH, SKIMMED IT. A LITTLE?
BECAUSE IF YOU HAD...
AH. WELL, YOU SEE...
...YOU WOULD KNOW THAT SHE'S THE ONLY PERSON IN THIS PARTY WHO HAS A CLUE ABOUT WHAT'S GOING ON.
CONGRATS, YOU'VE ALL BEEN ACTING LIKE SHITTY FRIENDS.
ESPECIALLY YOU, LANA.
I TOLD HER FOR MONTHS HOW AMAZING YOU WERE, HOW YOU MADE ME FEEL SAFE ENOUGH TO COME OUT AS NONBINARY.
JAY...
I THOUGHT YOU ALL WOULD BE A LITTLE MORE WELCOMING TO A PERSON JUST TRYING TO MAKE FRIENDS.
I'M GOING TO CALL AND MAKE SURE SHE'S DOING OKAY.

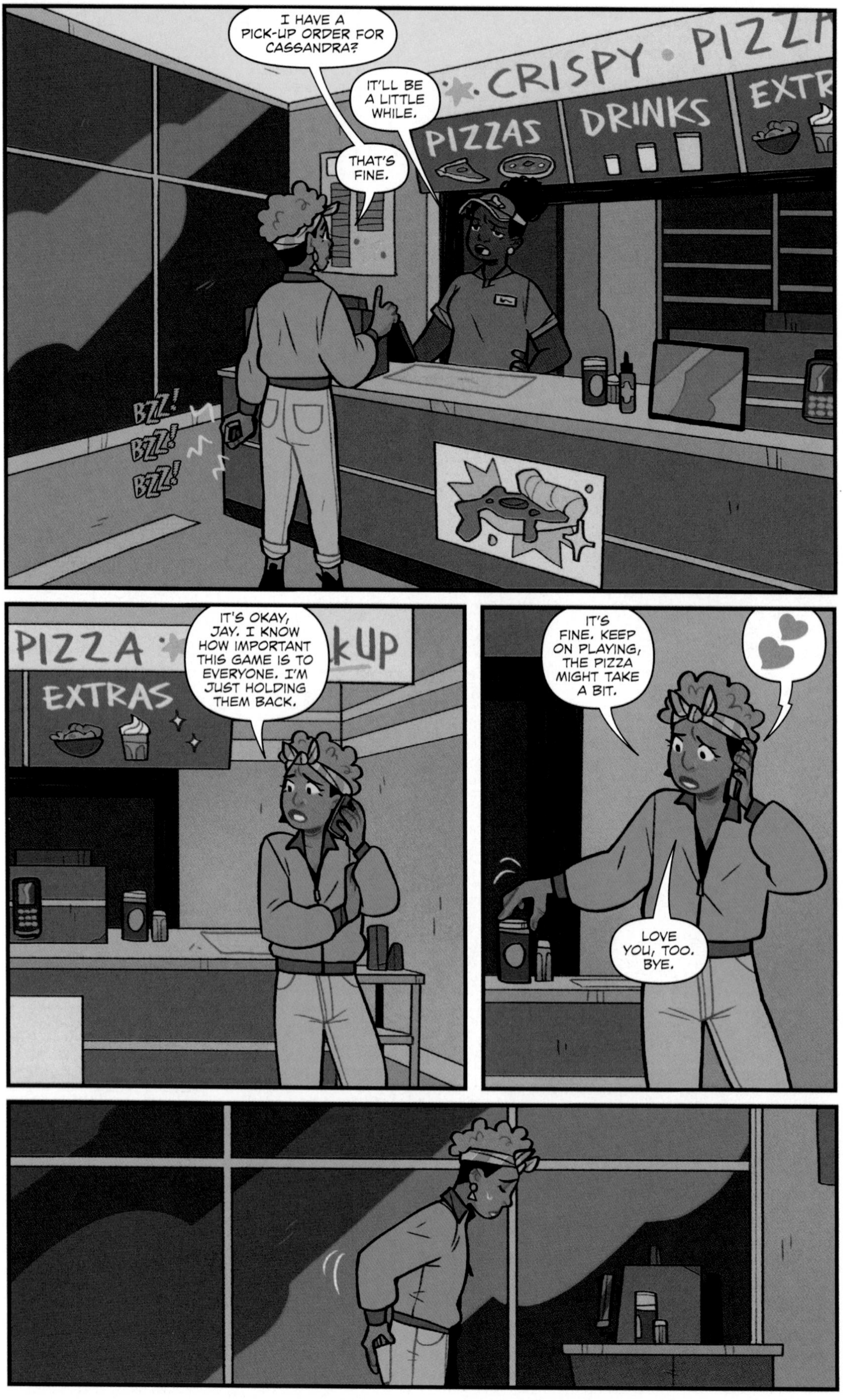
CRISPY • PIZZA
PIZZAS
DRINKS
EXTR
I HAVE A PICK-UP ORDER FOR CASSANDRA?
IT'LL BE A LITTLE WHILE.
THAT'S FINE.
BZZ!
BZZ!
BZZ!
PIZZA
kUP
EXTRAS
IT'S OKAY, JAY. I KNOW HOW IMPORTANT THIS GAME IS TO EVERYONE. I'M JUST HOLDING THEM BACK.
IT'S FINE. KEEP ON PLAYING, THE PIZZA MIGHT TAKE A BIT.
LOVE YOU, TOO. BYE.

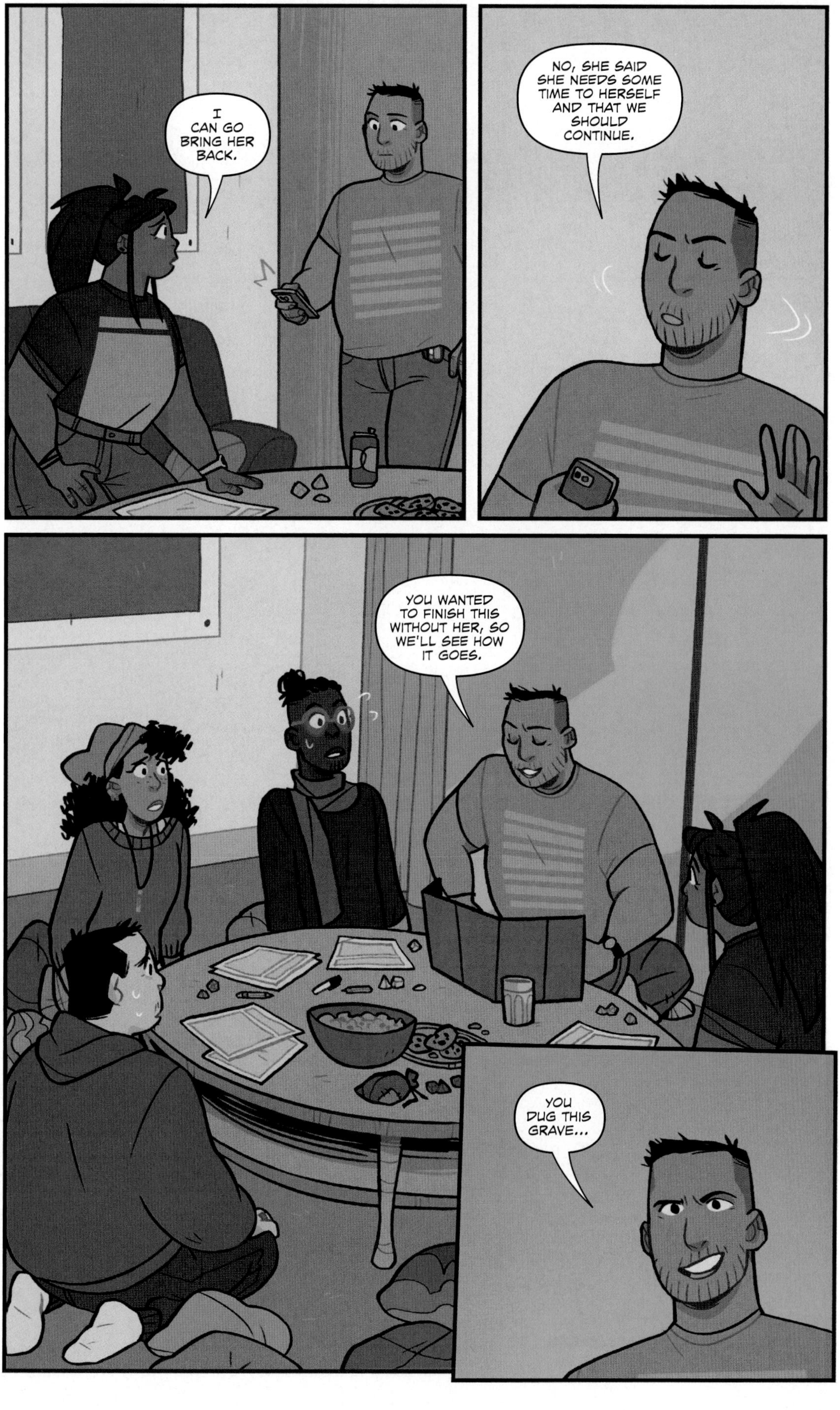
I CAN GO BRING HER BACK.
NO, SHE SAID SHE NEEDS SOME TIME TO HERSELF AND THAT WE SHOULD CONTINUE.
YOU WANTED TO FINISH THIS WITHOUT HER, SO WE'LL SEE HOW IT GOES.
YOU DUG THIS GRAVE...

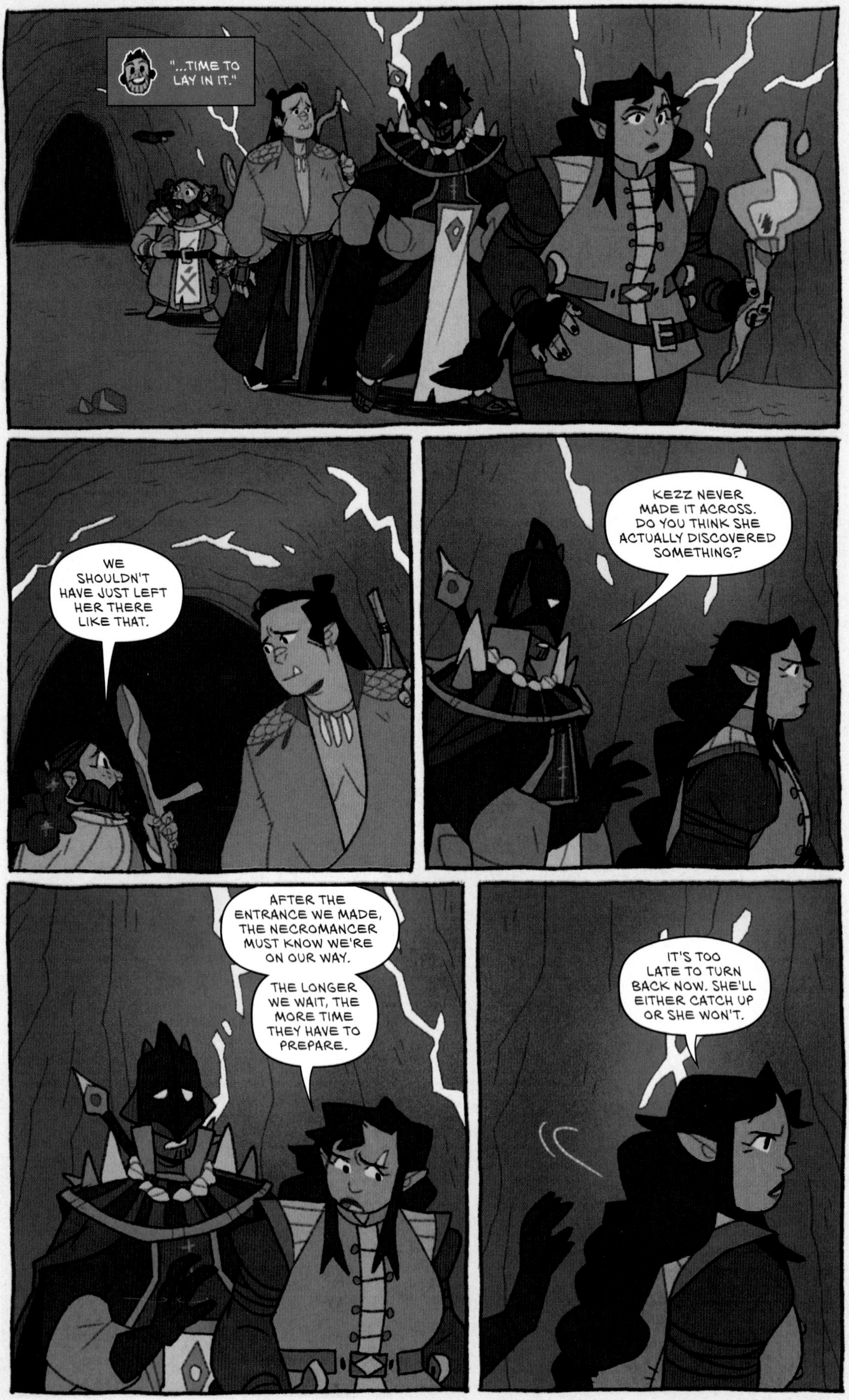
"...TIME TO LAY IN IT."
WE SHOULDN'T HAVE JUST LEFT HER THERE LIKE THAT.
KEZZ NEVER MADE IT ACROSS. DO YOU THINK SHE ACTUALLY DISCOVERED SOMETHING?
AFTER THE ENTRANCE WE MADE, THE NECROMANCER MUST KNOW WE'RE ON OUR WAY.
THE LONGER WE WAIT, THE MORE TIME THEY HAVE TO PREPARE.
IT'S TOO LATE TO TURN BACK NOW. SHE'LL EITHER CATCH UP OR SHE WON'T.

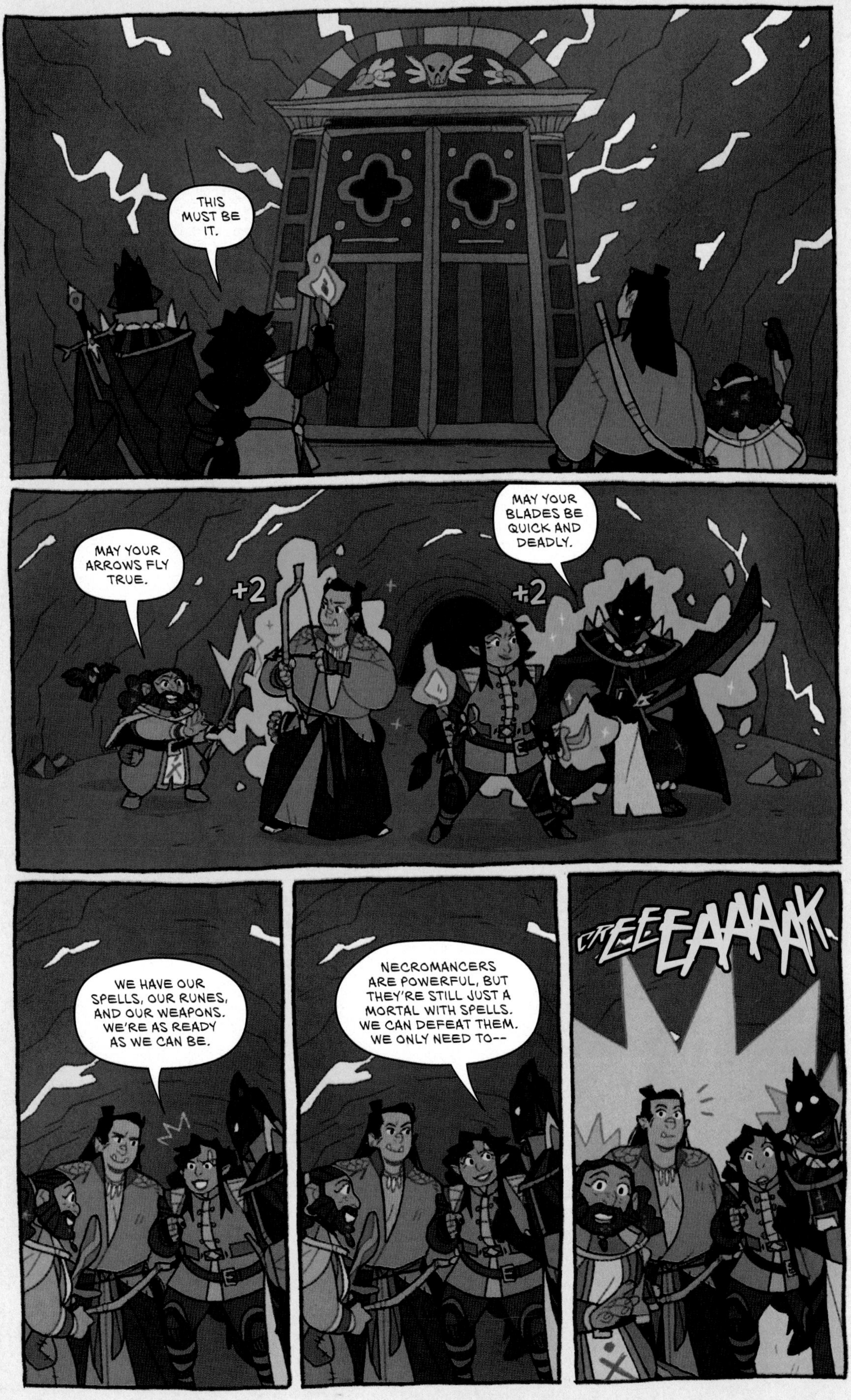
THIS MUST BE IT.
MAY YOUR ARROWS FLY TRUE.
+2
MAY YOUR BLADES BE QUICK AND DEADLY.
+2
WE HAVE OUR SPELLS, OUR RUNES, AND OUR WEAPONS. WE'RE AS READY AS WE CAN BE.
NECROMANCERS ARE POWERFUL, BUT THEY'RE STILL JUST A MORTAL WITH SPELLS. WE CAN DEFEAT THEM. WE ONLY NEED TO--
CREEEAAAAK

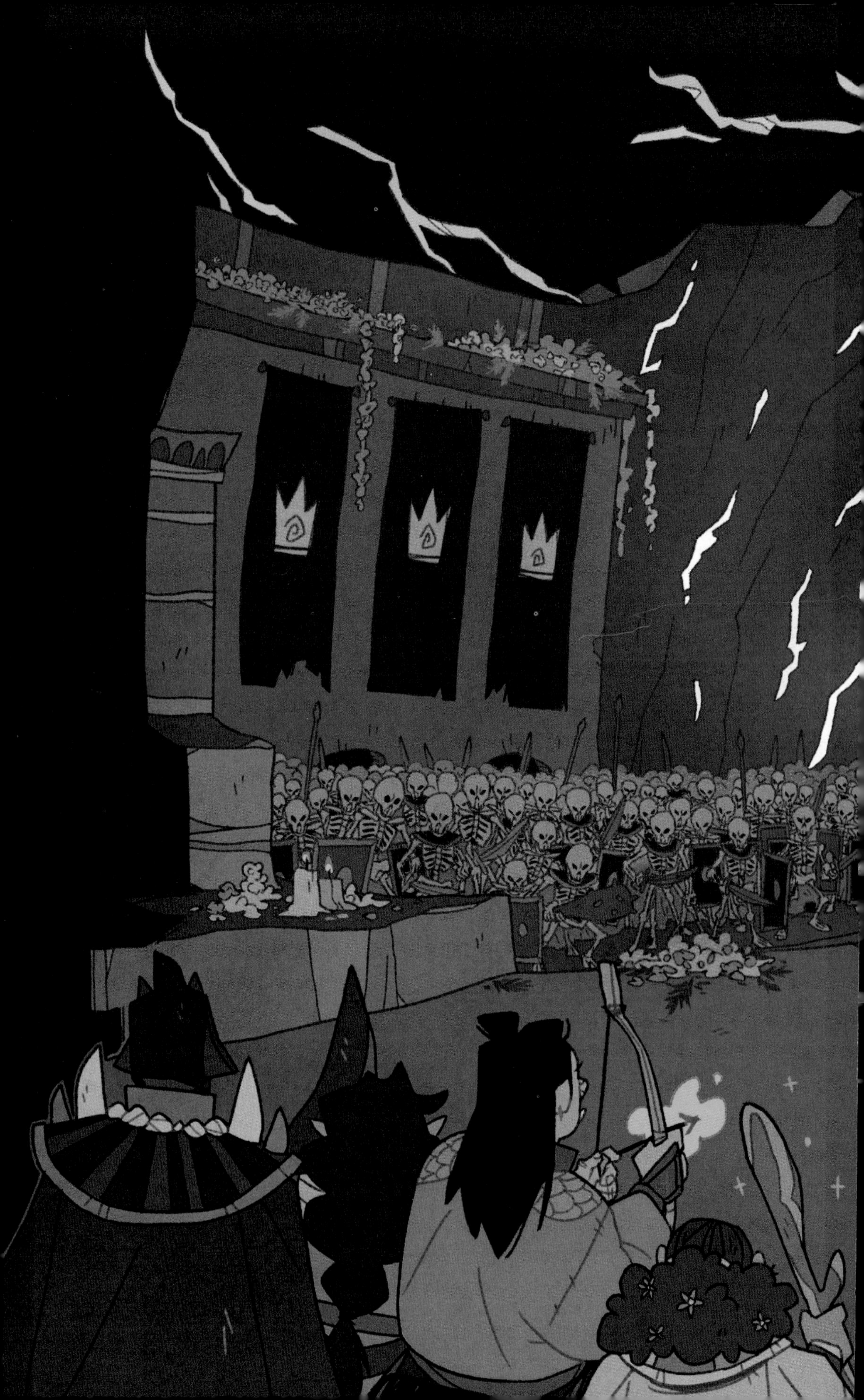

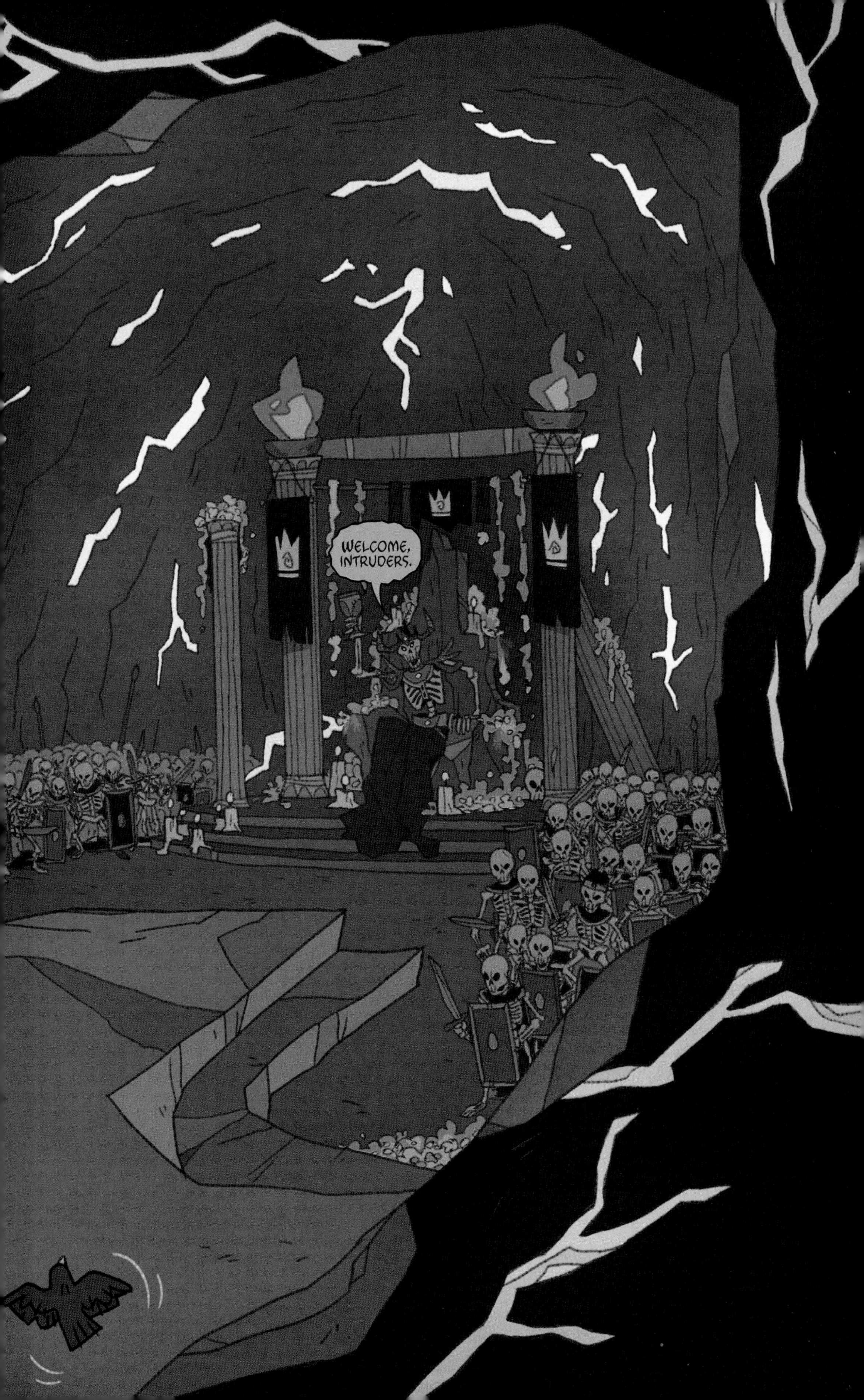
WELCOME, INTRUDERS.

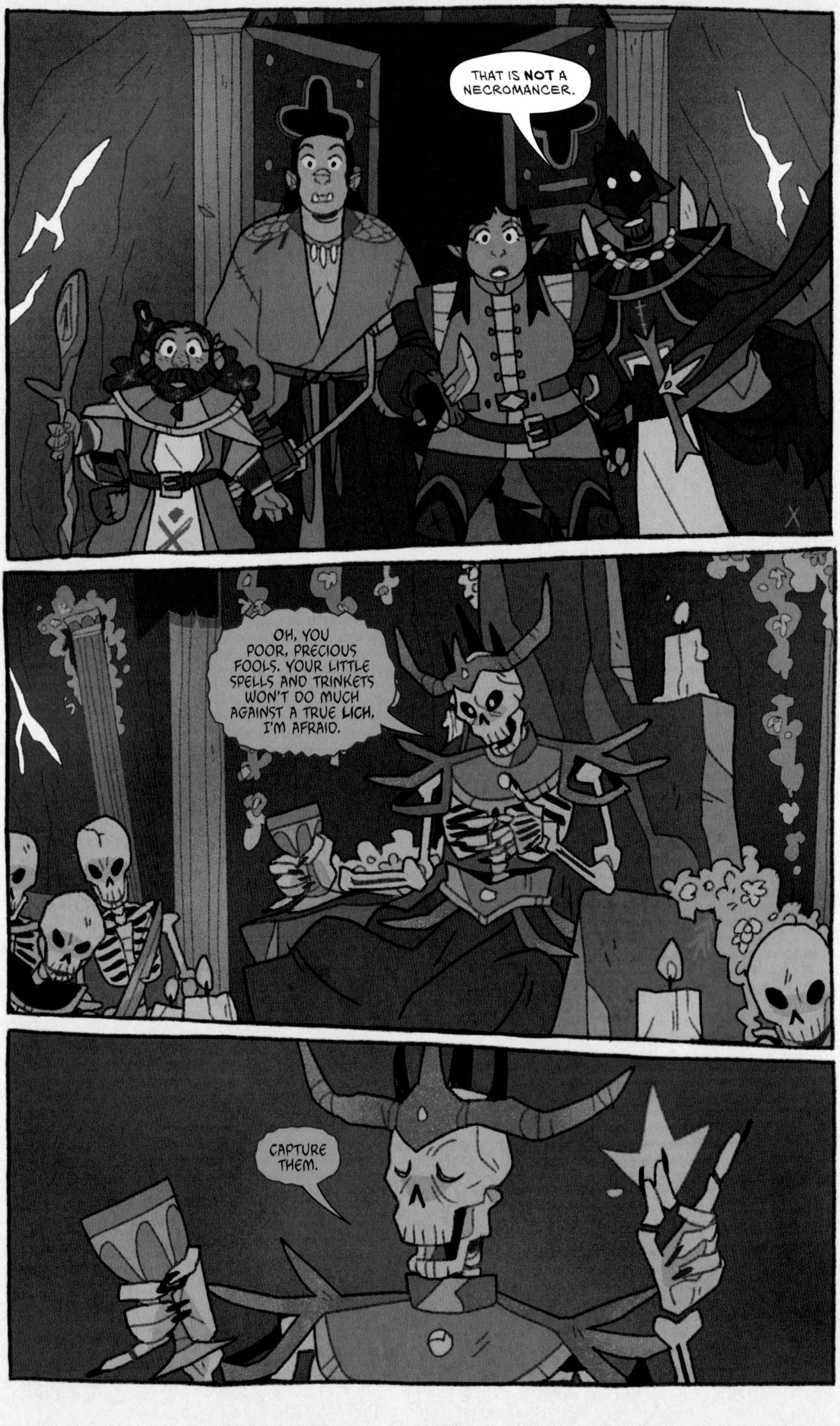
THAT IS NOT A NECROMANCER.
OH, YOU POOR, PRECIOUS FOOLS. YOUR LITTLE SPELLS AND TRINKETS WON'T DO MUCH AGAINST A TRUE LICH, I'M AFRAID.
CAPTURE THEM.

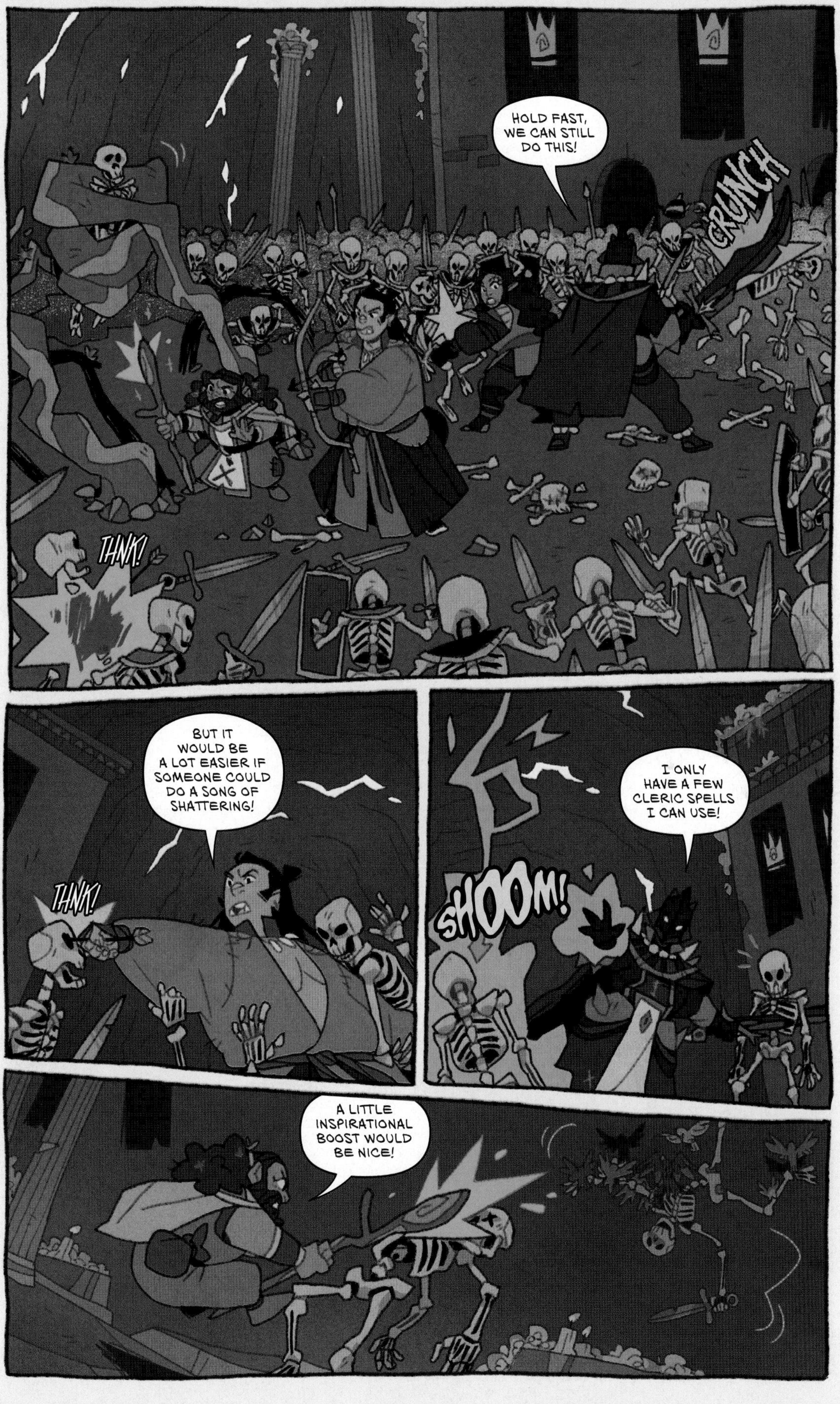
HOLD FAST, WE CAN STILL DO THIS!
CRUNCH
THNK!
BUT IT WOULD BE A LOT EASIER IF SOMEONE COULD DO A SONG OF SHATTERING!
THNK!
I ONLY HAVE A FEW CLERIC SPELLS I CAN USE!
SHOOM!
A LITTLE INSPIRATIONAL BOOST WOULD BE NICE!

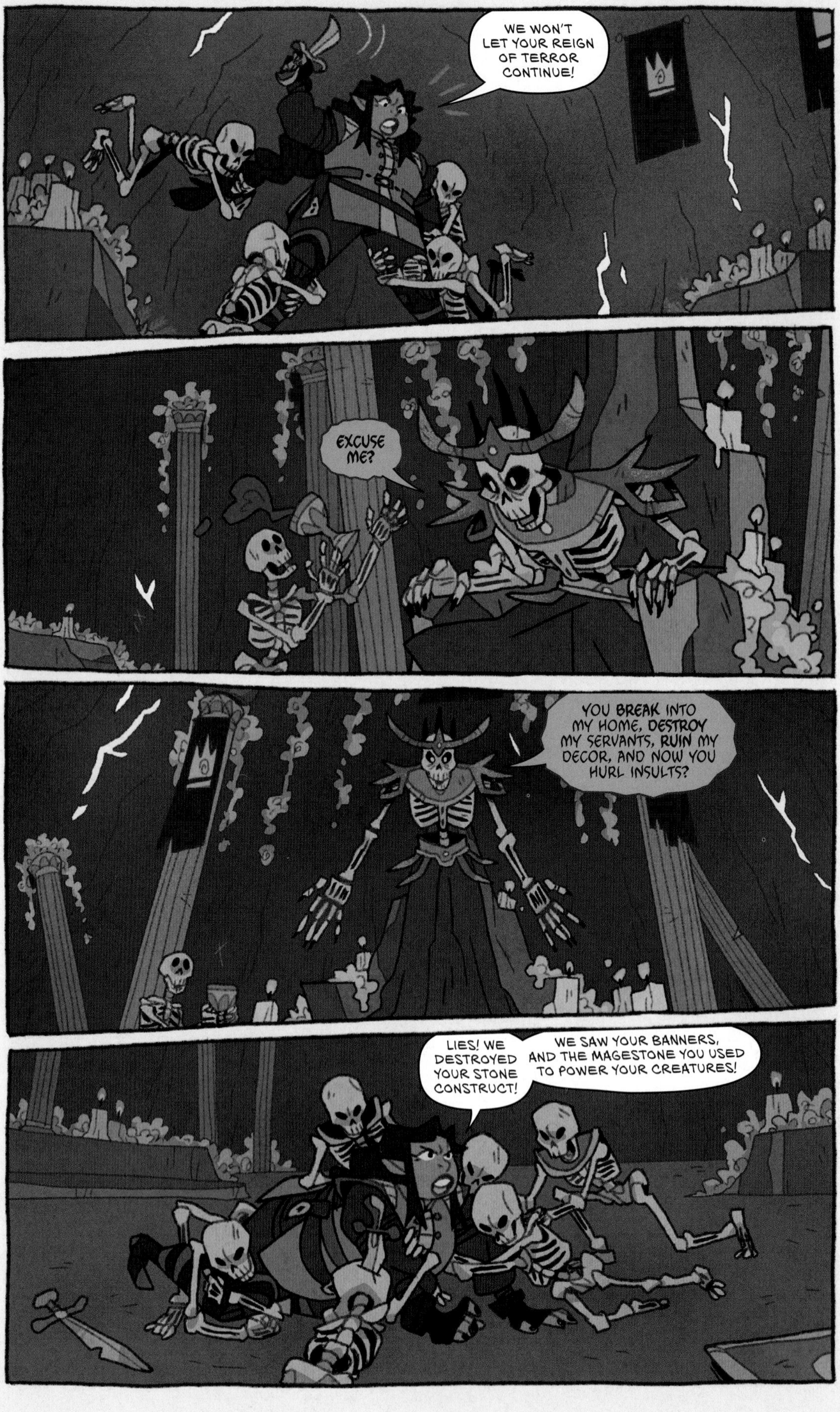
WE WON'T LET YOUR REIGN OF TERROR CONTINUE!
EXCUSE ME?
YOU BREAK INTO MY HOME, DESTROY MY SERVANTS, RUIN MY DECOR, AND NOW YOU HURL INSULTS?
LIES! WE DESTROYED YOUR STONE CONSTRUCT!
WE SAW YOUR BANNERS, AND THE MAGESTONE YOU USED TO POWER YOUR CREATURES!

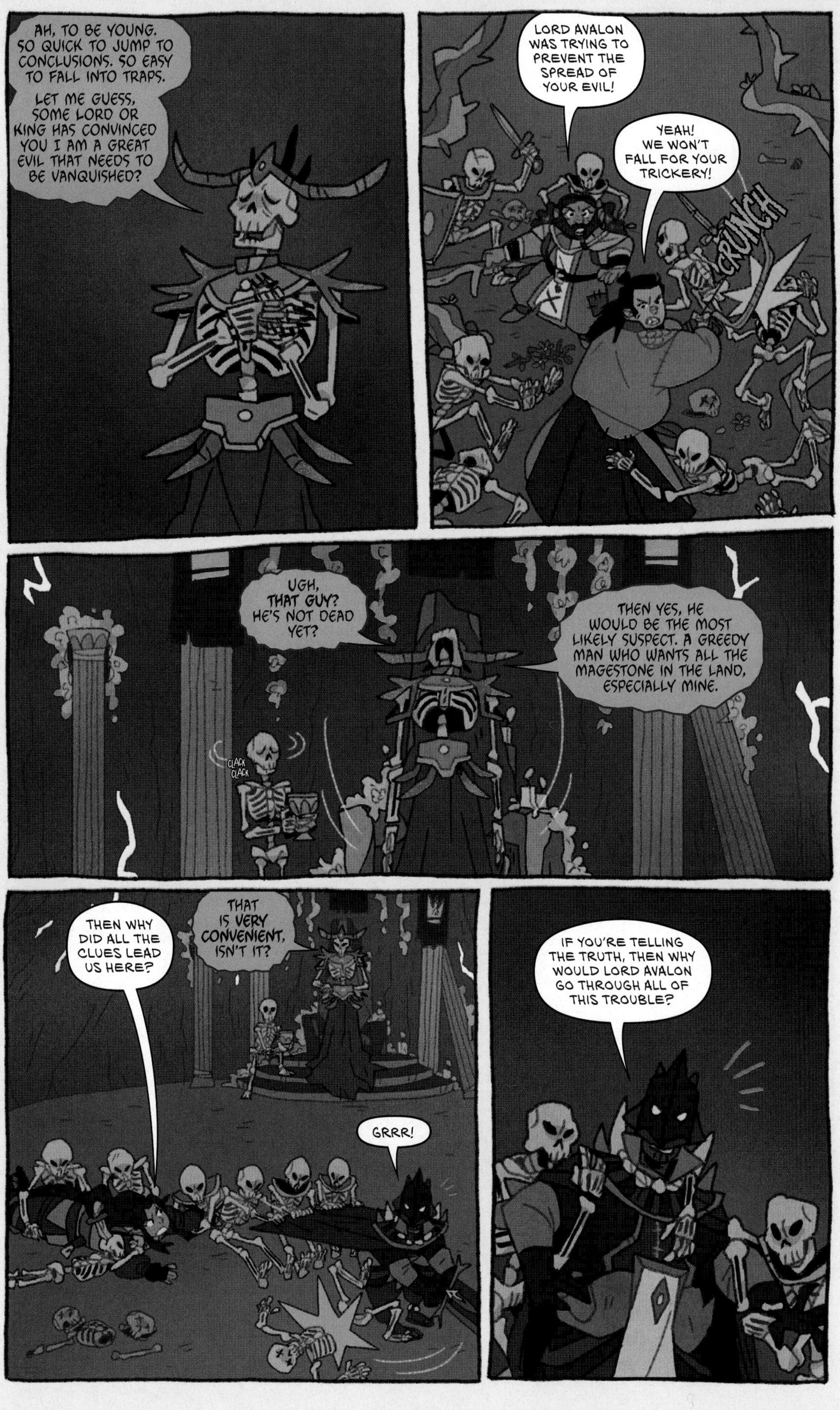
AH, TO BE YOUNG. SO QUICK TO JUMP TO CONCLUSIONS. SO EASY TO FALL INTO TRAPS.
LET ME GUESS, SOME LORD OR KING HAS CONVINCED YOU I AM A GREAT EVIL THAT NEEDS TO BE VANQUISHED?
LORD AVALON WAS TRYING TO PREVENT THE SPREAD OF YOUR EVIL!
YEAH! WE WON'T FALL FOR YOUR TRICKERY!
CRUNCH
UGH, THAT GUY? HE'S NOT DEAD YET?
THEN YES, HE WOULD BE THE MOST LIKELY SUSPECT. A GREEDY MAN WHO WANTS ALL THE MAGESTONE IN THE LAND, ESPECIALLY MINE.
CLACK CLACK
THEN WHY DID ALL THE CLUES LEAD US HERE?
THAT IS VERY CONVENIENT, ISN'T IT?
GRRR!
IF YOU'RE TELLING THE TRUTH, THEN WHY WOULD LORD AVALON GO THROUGH ALL OF THIS TROUBLE?

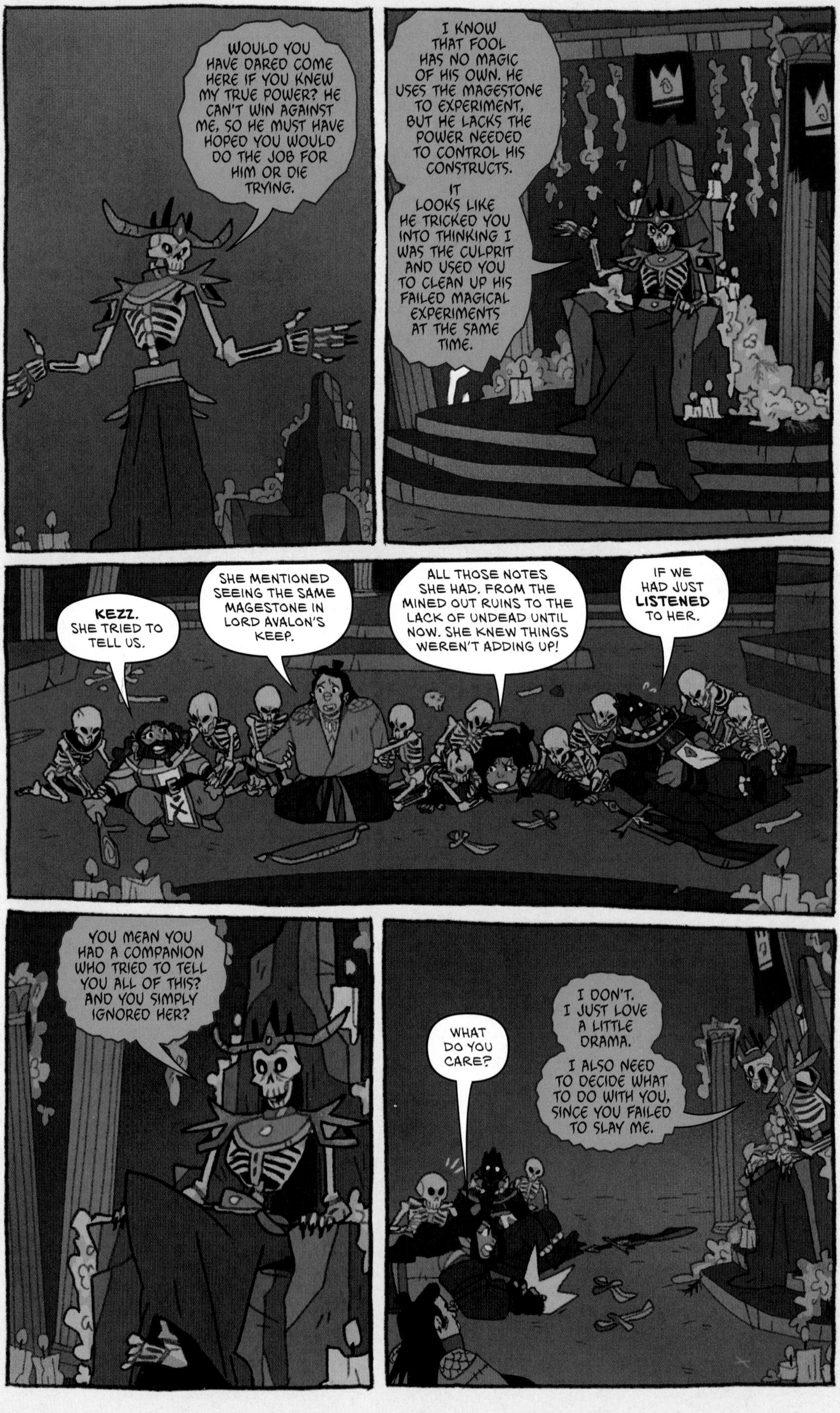
WOULD YOU HAVE DARED COME HERE IF YOU KNEW MY TRUE POWER? HE CAN'T WIN AGAINST ME, SO HE MUST HAVE HOPED YOU WOULD DO THE JOB FOR HIM OR DIE TRYING.
I KNOW THAT FOOL HAS NO MAGIC OF HIS OWN. HE USES THE MAGESTONE TO EXPERIMENT, BUT HE LACKS THE POWER NEEDED TO CONTROL HIS CONSTRUCTS.
IT LOOKS LIKE HE TRICKED YOU INTO THINKING I WAS THE CULPRIT AND USED YOU TO CLEAN UP HIS FAILED MAGICAL EXPERIMENTS AT THE SAME TIME.
KEZZ. SHE TRIED TO TELL US.
SHE MENTIONED SEEING THE SAME MAGESTONE IN LORD AVALON'S KEEP.
ALL THOSE NOTES SHE HAD. FROM THE MINED OUT RUINS TO THE LACK OF UNDEAD UNTIL NOW. SHE KNEW THINGS WEREN'T ADDING UP!
IF WE HAD JUST LISTENED TO HER.
YOU MEAN YOU HAD A COMPANION WHO TRIED TO TELL YOU ALL OF THIS? AND YOU SIMPLY IGNORED HER?
WHAT DO YOU CARE?
I DON'T. I JUST LOVE A LITTLE DRAMA.
I ALSO NEED TO DECIDE WHAT TO DO WITH YOU, SINCE YOU FAILED TO SLAY ME.

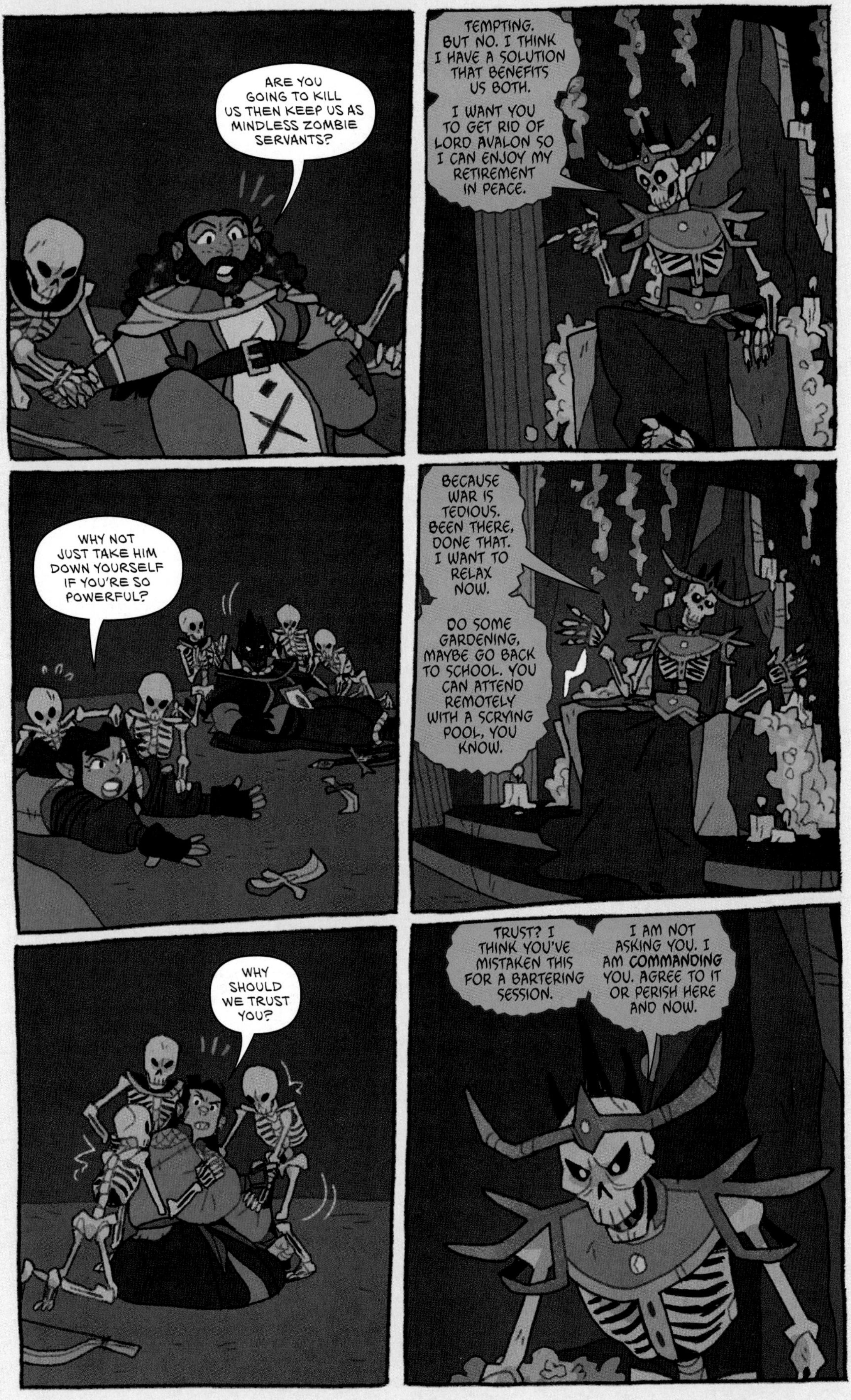
ARE YOU GOING TO KILL US THEN KEEP US AS MINDLESS ZOMBIE SERVANTS?
TEMPTING. BUT NO. I THINK I HAVE A SOLUTION THAT BENEFITS US BOTH.
I WANT YOU TO GET RID OF LORD AVALON SO I CAN ENJOY MY RETIREMENT IN PEACE.
WHY NOT JUST TAKE HIM DOWN YOURSELF IF YOU'RE SO POWERFUL?
BECAUSE WAR IS TEDIOUS. BEEN THERE, DONE THAT. I WANT TO RELAX NOW.
DO SOME GARDENING, MAYBE GO BACK TO SCHOOL. YOU CAN ATTEND REMOTELY WITH A SCRYING POOL, YOU KNOW.
WHY SHOULD WE TRUST YOU?
TRUST? I THINK YOU'VE MISTAKEN THIS FOR A BARTERING SESSION.
I AM NOT ASKING YOU. I AM COMMANDING YOU. AGREE TO IT OR PERISH HERE AND NOW.

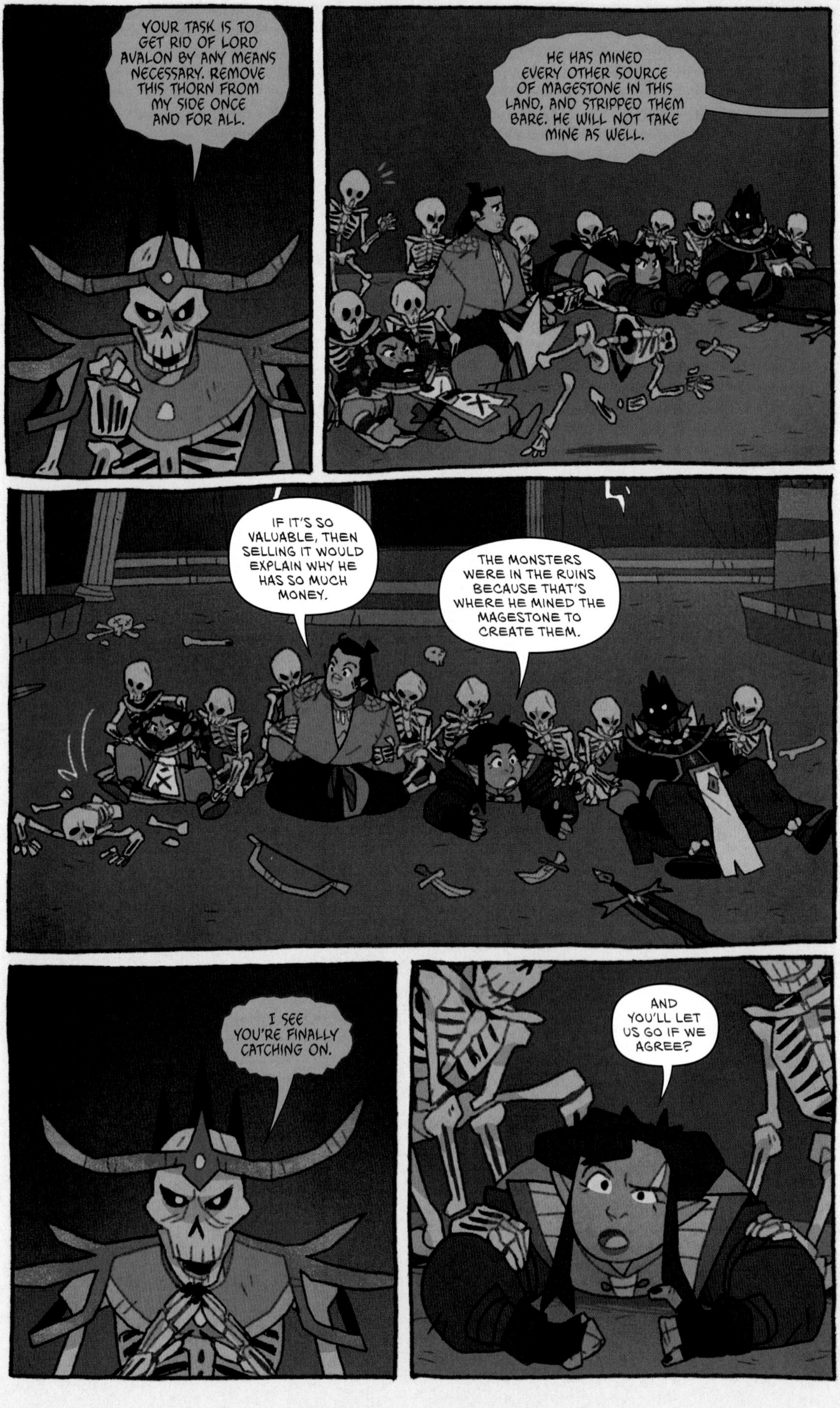
YOUR TASK IS TO GET RID OF LORD AVALON BY ANY MEANS NECESSARY. REMOVE THIS THORN FROM MY SIDE ONCE AND FOR ALL.
HE HAS MINED EVERY OTHER SOURCE OF MAGESTONE IN THIS LAND, AND STRIPPED THEM BARE. HE WILL NOT TAKE MINE AS WELL.
IF IT'S SO VALUABLE, THEN SELLING IT WOULD EXPLAIN WHY HE HAS SO MUCH MONEY.
THE MONSTERS WERE IN THE RUINS BECAUSE THAT'S WHERE HE MINED THE MAGESTONE TO CREATE THEM.
I SEE YOU'RE FINALLY CATCHING ON.
AND YOU'LL LET US GO IF WE AGREE?

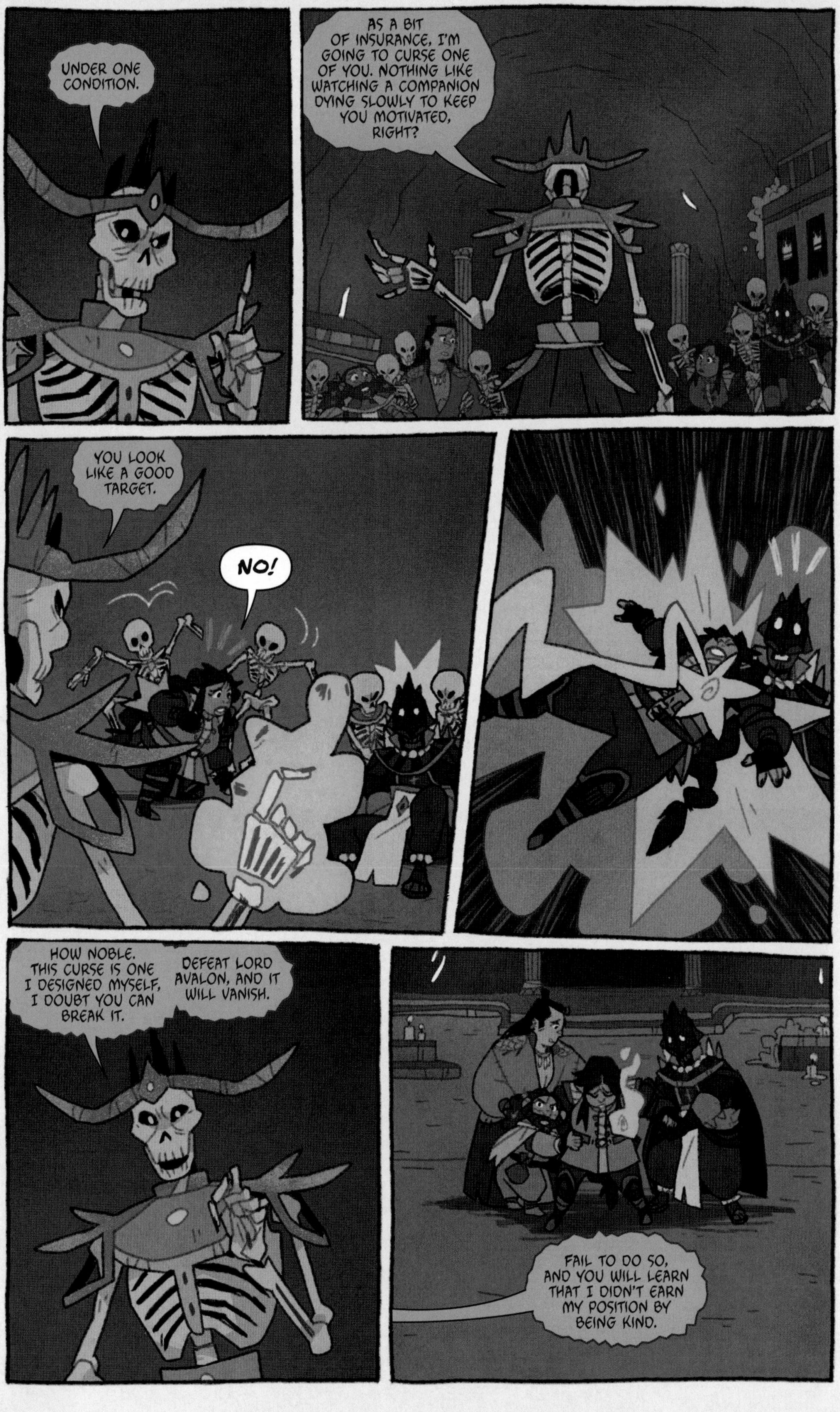

UNDER ONE CONDITION.
AS A BIT OF INSURANCE, I'M GOING TO CURSE ONE OF YOU. NOTHING LIKE WATCHING A COMPANION DYING SLOWLY TO KEEP YOU MOTIVATED, RIGHT?
YOU LOOK LIKE A GOOD TARGET.
NO!
HOW NOBLE. THIS CURSE IS ONE I DESIGNED MYSELF, I DOUBT YOU CAN BREAK IT.
DEFEAT LORD AVALON, AND IT WILL VANISH.
FAIL TO DO SO, AND YOU WILL LEARN THAT I DIDN'T EARN MY POSITION BY BEING KIND.

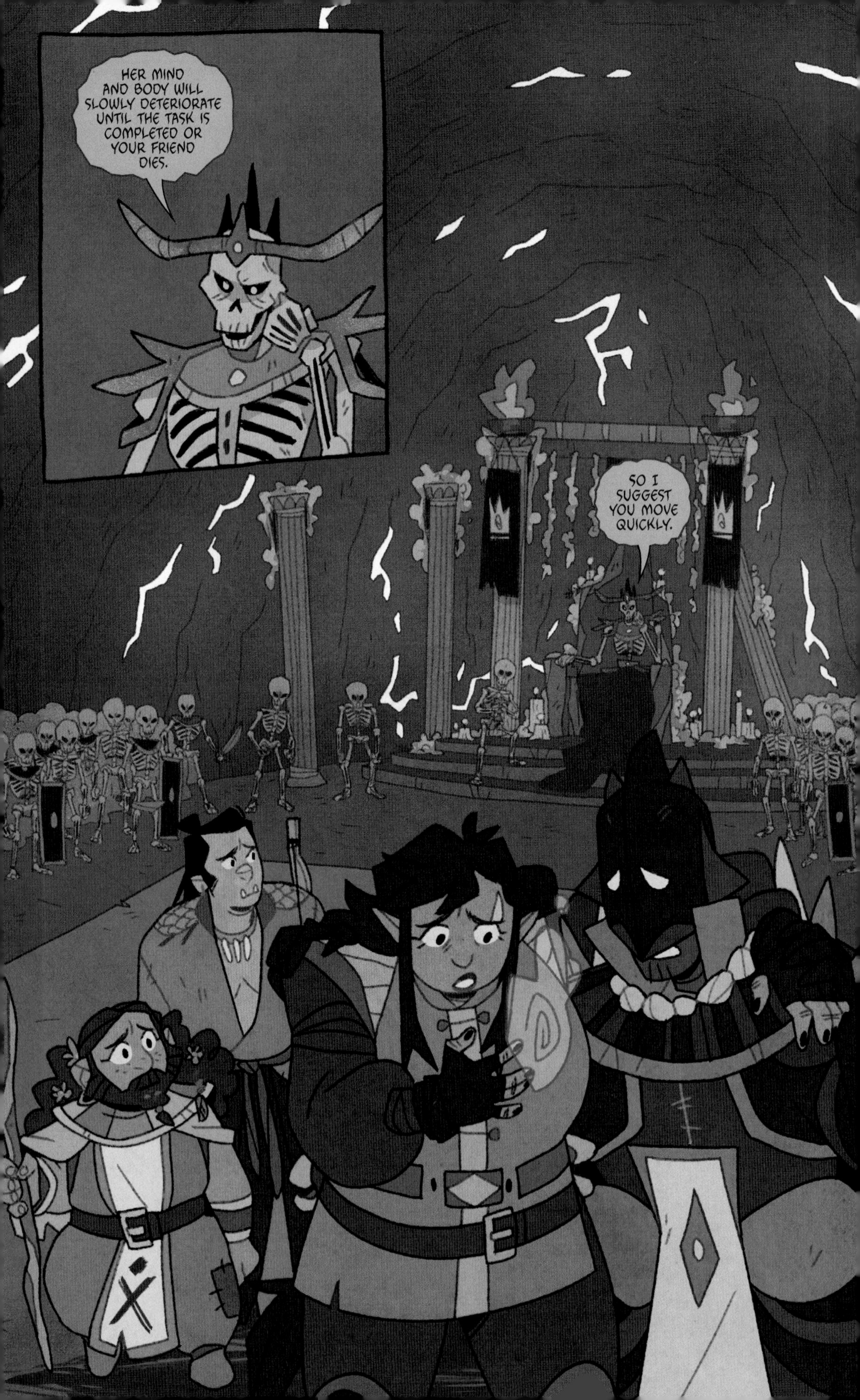
HER MIND AND BODY WILL SLOWLY DETERIORATE UNTIL THE TASK IS COMPLETED OR YOUR FRIEND DIES.
SO I SUGGEST YOU MOVE QUICKLY.

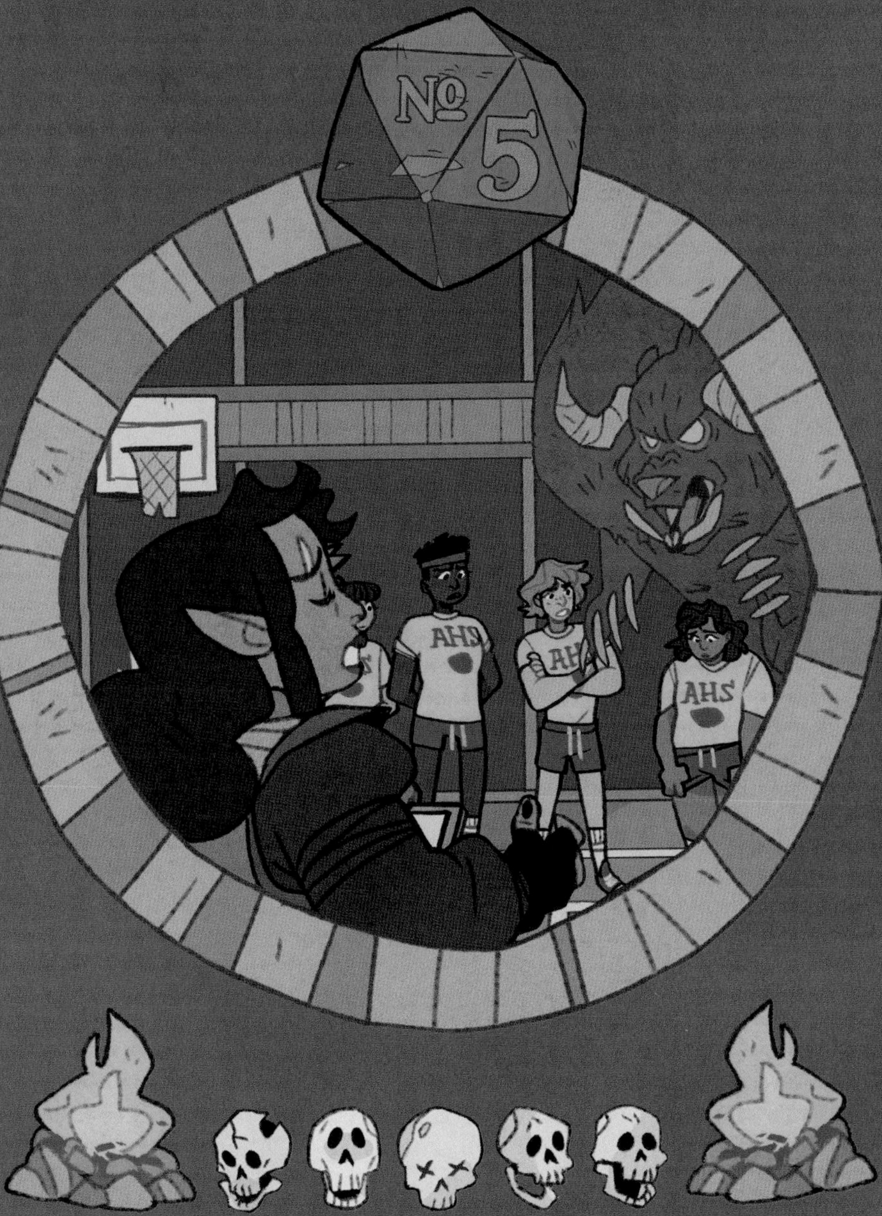
№ 5
AHS
AHS
AHS

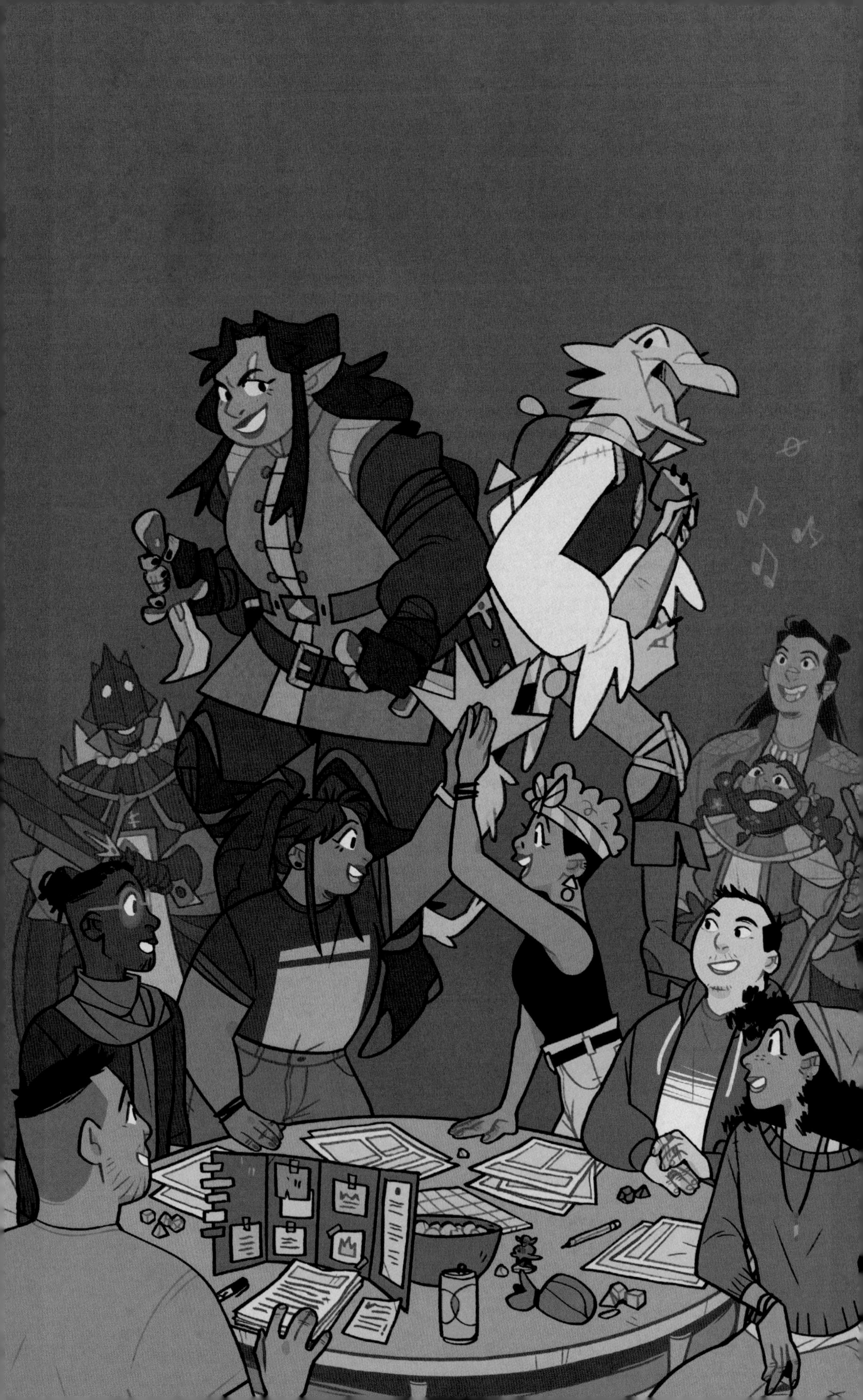

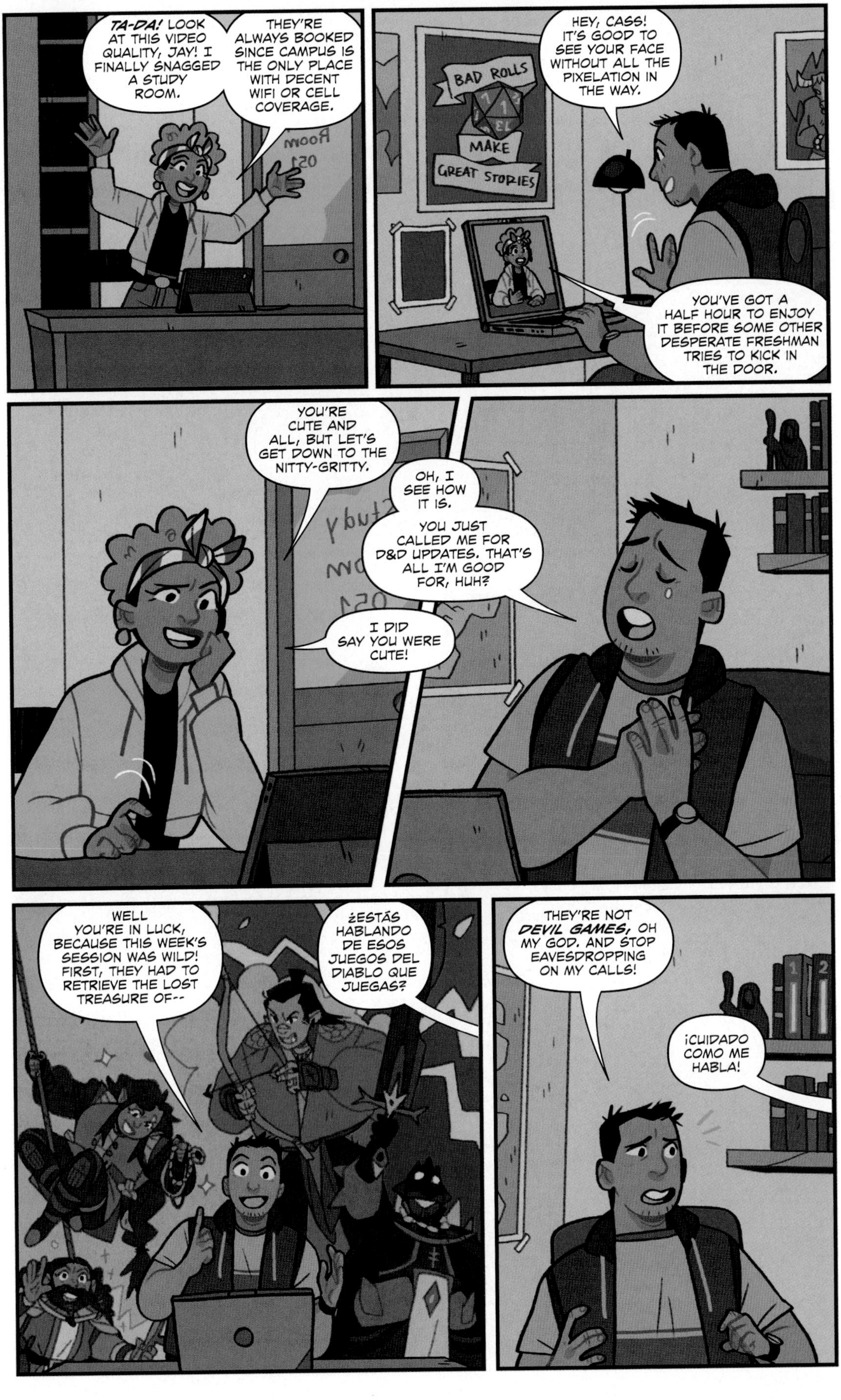
TA-DA! LOOK AT THIS VIDEO QUALITY, JAY! I FINALLY SNAGGED A STUDY ROOM.
THEY'RE ALWAYS BOOKED SINCE CAMPUS IS THE ONLY PLACE WITH DECENT WIFI OR CELL COVERAGE.
Room 051
BAD ROLLS MAKE GREAT STORIES
HEY, CASS! IT'S GOOD TO SEE YOUR FACE WITHOUT ALL THE PIXELATION IN THE WAY.
YOU'VE GOT A HALF HOUR TO ENJOY IT BEFORE SOME OTHER DESPERATE FRESHMAN TRIES TO KICK IN THE DOOR.
YOU'RE CUTE AND ALL, BUT LET'S GET DOWN TO THE NITTY-GRITTY.
OH, I SEE HOW IT IS.
YOU JUST CALLED ME FOR D&D UPDATES. THAT'S ALL I'M GOOD FOR, HUH?
I DID SAY YOU WERE CUTE!
WELL YOU'RE IN LUCK, BECAUSE THIS WEEK'S SESSION WAS WILD! FIRST, THEY HAD TO RETRIEVE THE LOST TREASURE OF--
¿ESTÁS HABLANDO DE ESOS JUEGOS DEL DIABLO QUE JUEGAS?
THEY'RE NOT DEVIL GAMES, OH MY GOD. AND STOP EAVESDROPPING ON MY CALLS!
¡CUIDADO COMO ME HABLA!

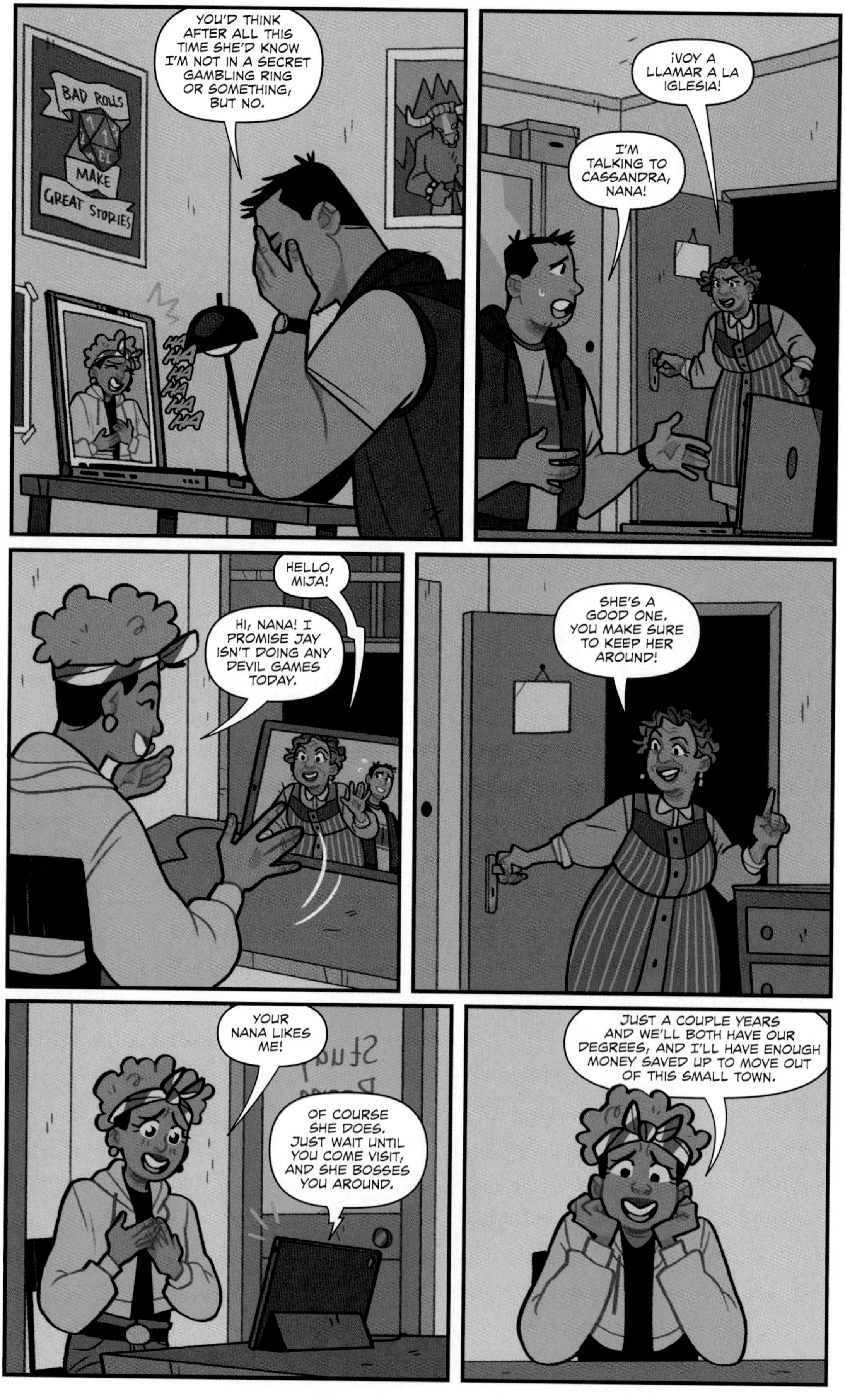
BAD ROLLS
MAKE
GREAT STORIES
YOU'D THINK AFTER ALL THIS TIME SHE'D KNOW I'M NOT IN A SECRET GAMBLING RING OR SOMETHING, BUT NO.
HA HA HA HA HA HA
¡VOY A LLAMAR A LA IGLESIA!
I'M TALKING TO CASSANDRA, NANA!
HELLO, MIJA!
HI, NANA! I PROMISE JAY ISN'T DOING ANY DEVIL GAMES TODAY.
SHE'S A GOOD ONE. YOU MAKE SURE TO KEEP HER AROUND!
YOUR NANA LIKES ME!
OF COURSE SHE DOES. JUST WAIT UNTIL YOU COME VISIT, AND SHE BOSSES YOU AROUND.
JUST A COUPLE YEARS AND WE'LL BOTH HAVE OUR DEGREES, AND I'LL HAVE ENOUGH MONEY SAVED UP TO MOVE OUT OF THIS SMALL TOWN.

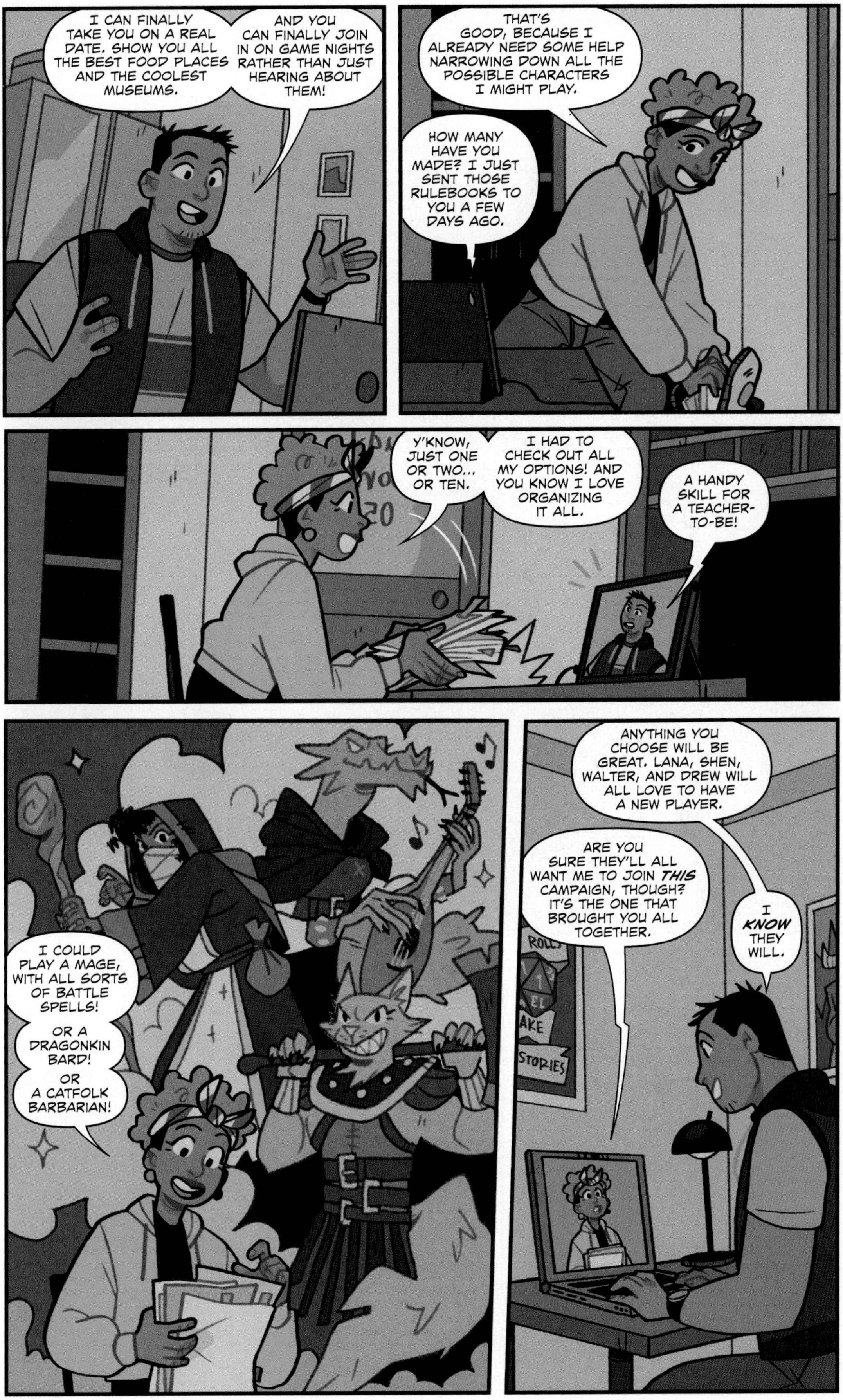
I CAN FINALLY TAKE YOU ON A REAL DATE. SHOW YOU ALL THE BEST FOOD PLACES AND THE COOLEST MUSEUMS.
AND YOU CAN FINALLY JOIN IN ON GAME NIGHTS RATHER THAN JUST HEARING ABOUT THEM!
THAT'S GOOD, BECAUSE I ALREADY NEED SOME HELP NARROWING DOWN ALL THE POSSIBLE CHARACTERS I MIGHT PLAY.
HOW MANY HAVE YOU MADE? I JUST SENT THOSE RULEBOOKS TO YOU A FEW DAYS AGO.
Y'KNOW, JUST ONE OR TWO... OR TEN.
I HAD TO CHECK OUT ALL MY OPTIONS! AND YOU KNOW I LOVE ORGANIZING IT ALL.
A HANDY SKILL FOR A TEACHER-TO-BE!
I COULD PLAY A MAGE, WITH ALL SORTS OF BATTLE SPELLS!
OR A DRAGONKIN BARD!
OR A CATFOLK BARBARIAN!
ANYTHING YOU CHOOSE WILL BE GREAT. LANA, SHEN, WALTER, AND DREW WILL ALL LOVE TO HAVE A NEW PLAYER.
ARE YOU SURE THEY'LL ALL WANT ME TO JOIN *THIS* CAMPAIGN, THOUGH? IT'S THE ONE THAT BROUGHT YOU ALL TOGETHER.
I *KNOW* THEY WILL.

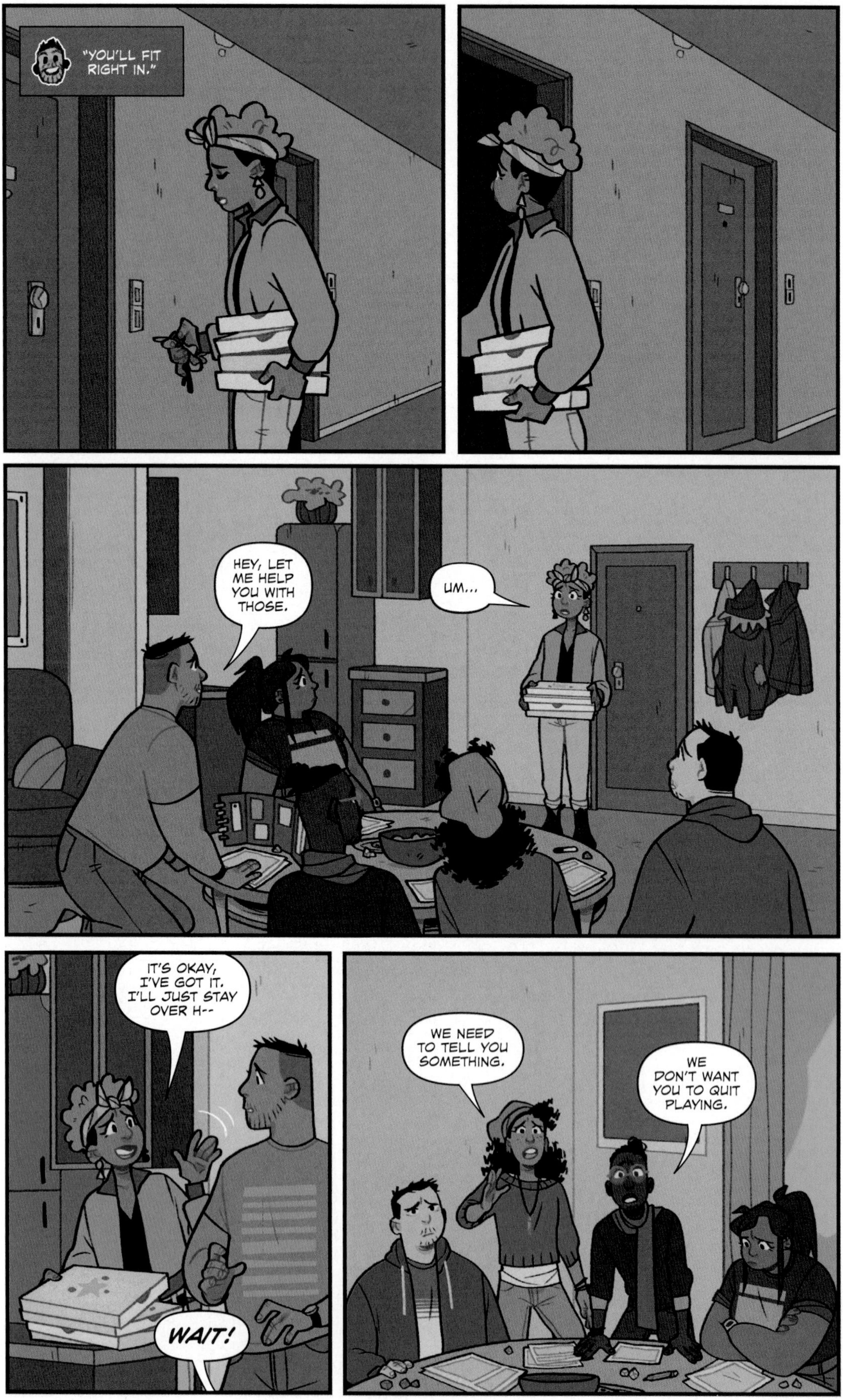
"YOU'LL FIT RIGHT IN."
HEY, LET ME HELP YOU WITH THOSE.
UM...
IT'S OKAY, I'VE GOT IT. I'LL JUST STAY OVER H--
WAIT!
WE NEED TO TELL YOU SOMETHING.
WE DON'T WANT YOU TO QUIT PLAYING.

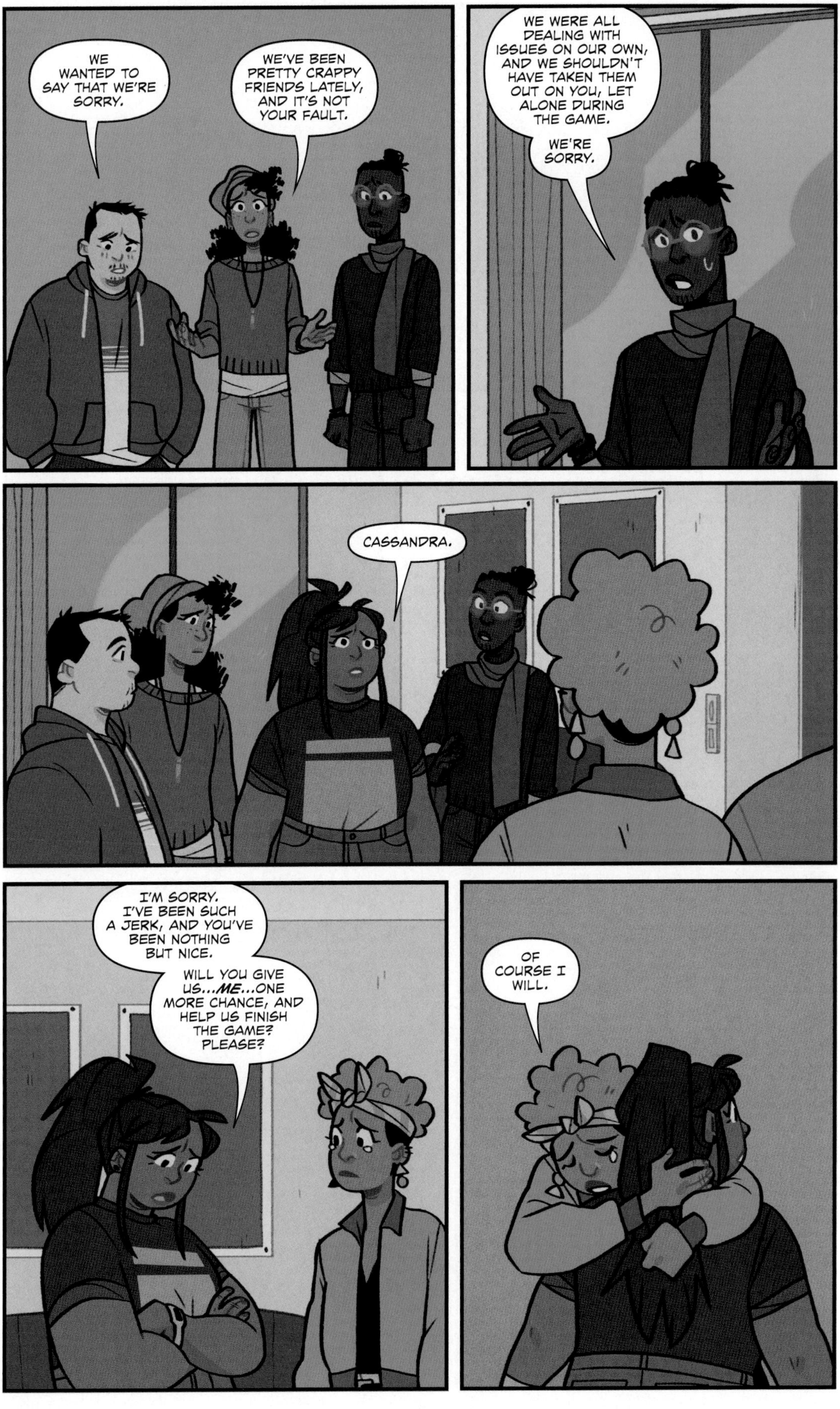
WE WANTED TO SAY THAT WE'RE SORRY.
WE'VE BEEN PRETTY CRAPPY FRIENDS LATELY, AND IT'S NOT YOUR FAULT.
WE WERE ALL DEALING WITH ISSUES ON OUR OWN, AND WE SHOULDN'T HAVE TAKEN THEM OUT ON YOU, LET ALONE DURING THE GAME.
WE'RE SORRY.
CASSANDRA.
I'M SORRY. I'VE BEEN SUCH A JERK, AND YOU'VE BEEN NOTHING BUT NICE.
WILL YOU GIVE US...*ME*...ONE MORE CHANCE, AND HELP US FINISH THE GAME? PLEASE?
OF COURSE I WILL.

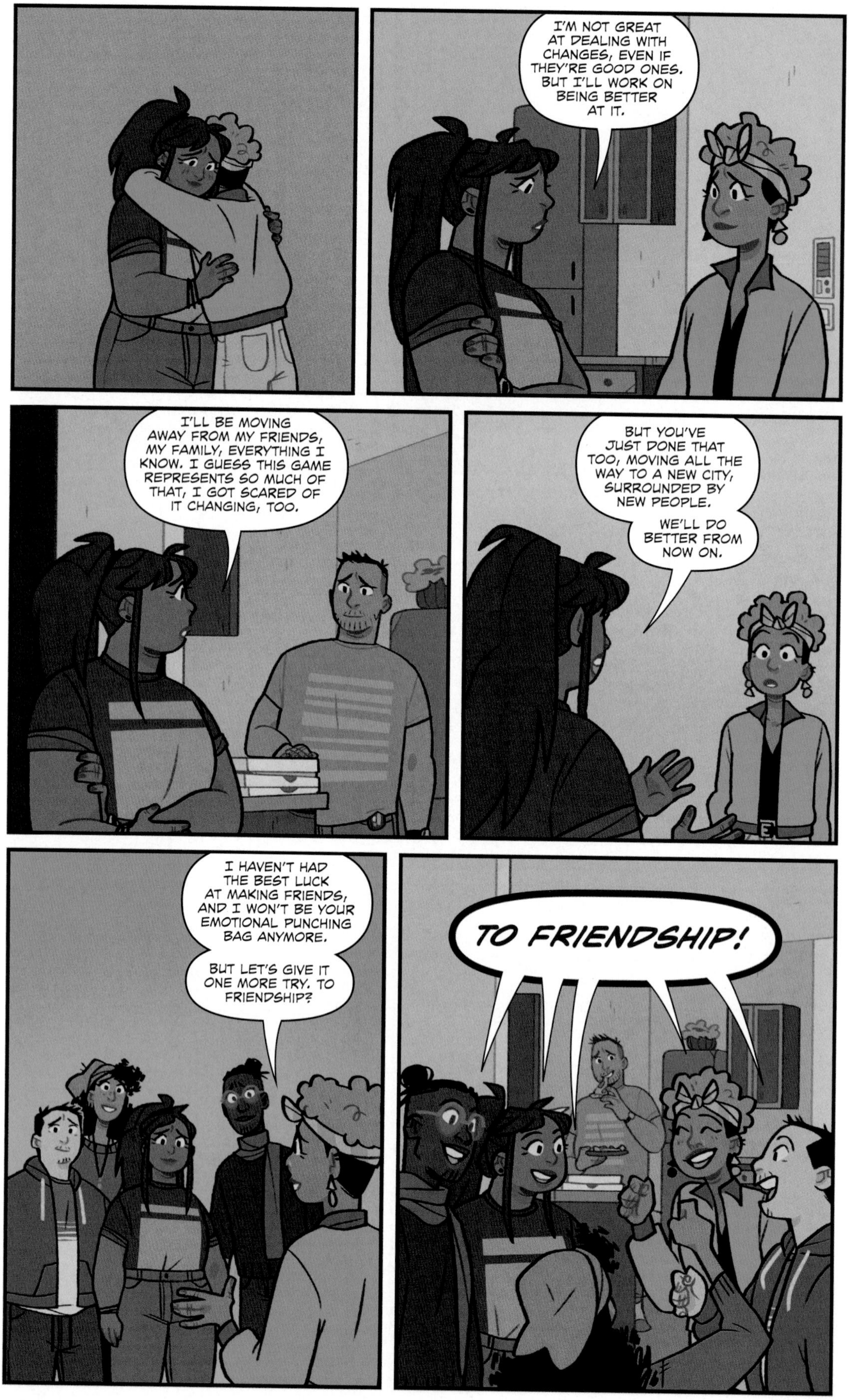
I'M NOT GREAT AT DEALING WITH CHANGES, EVEN IF THEY'RE GOOD ONES. BUT I'LL WORK ON BEING BETTER AT IT.
I'LL BE MOVING AWAY FROM MY FRIENDS, MY FAMILY, EVERYTHING I KNOW. I GUESS THIS GAME REPRESENTS SO MUCH OF THAT, I GOT SCARED OF IT CHANGING, TOO.
BUT YOU'VE JUST DONE THAT TOO, MOVING ALL THE WAY TO A NEW CITY, SURROUNDED BY NEW PEOPLE.
WE'LL DO BETTER FROM NOW ON.
I HAVEN'T HAD THE BEST LUCK AT MAKING FRIENDS, AND I WON'T BE YOUR EMOTIONAL PUNCHING BAG ANYMORE.
BUT LET'S GIVE IT ONE MORE TRY. TO FRIENDSHIP?
TO FRIENDSHIP!

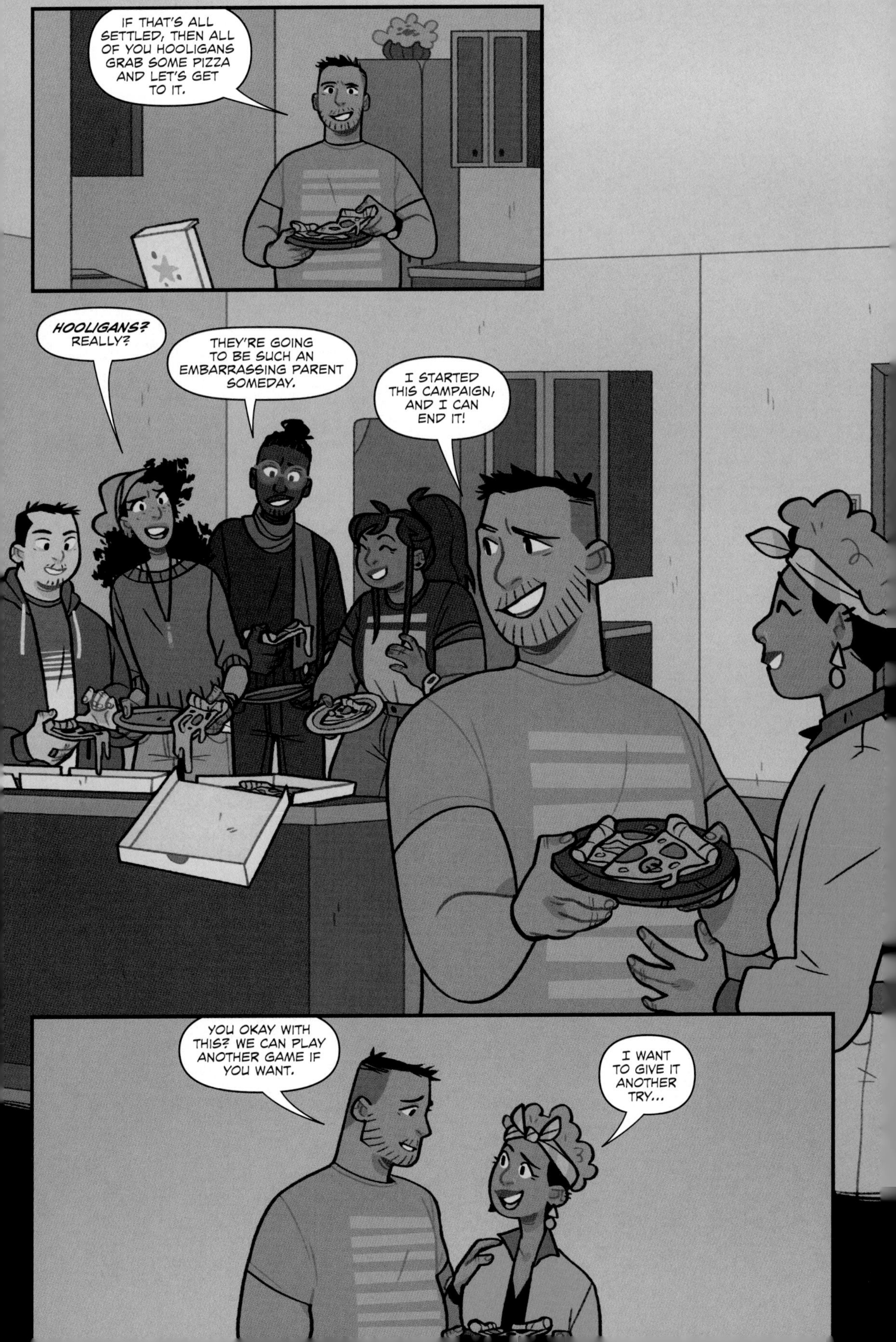
IF THAT'S ALL SETTLED, THEN ALL OF YOU HOOLIGANS GRAB SOME PIZZA AND LET'S GET TO IT.
HOOLIGANS? REALLY?
THEY'RE GOING TO BE SUCH AN EMBARRASSING PARENT SOMEDAY.
I STARTED THIS CAMPAIGN, AND I CAN END IT!
YOU OKAY WITH THIS? WE CAN PLAY ANOTHER GAME IF YOU WANT.
I WANT TO GIVE IT ANOTHER TRY...

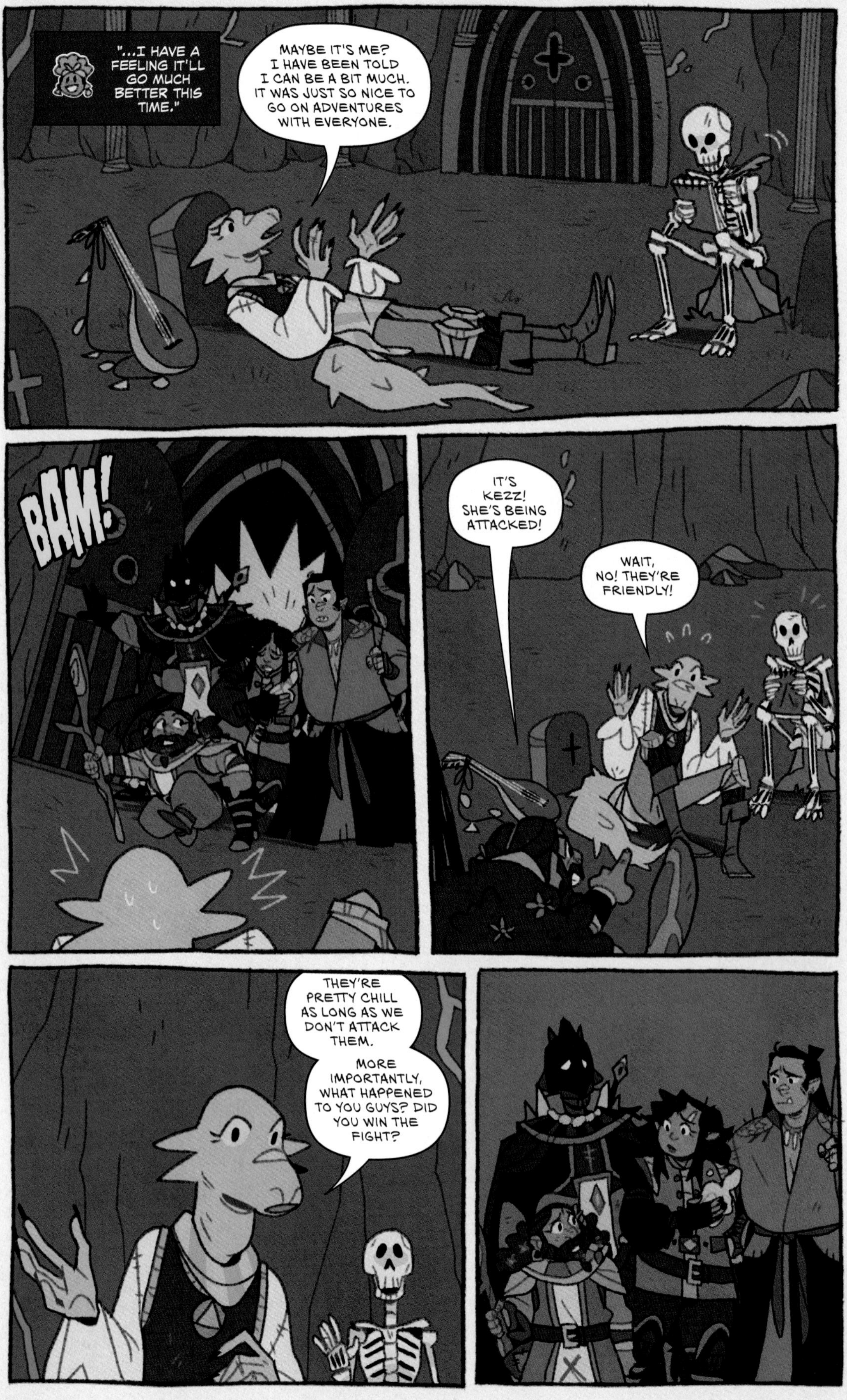
"...I HAVE A FEELING IT'LL GO MUCH BETTER THIS TIME."
MAYBE IT'S ME? I HAVE BEEN TOLD I CAN BE A BIT MUCH. IT WAS JUST SO NICE TO GO ON ADVENTURES WITH EVERYONE.
BAM!
IT'S KEZZ! SHE'S BEING ATTACKED!
WAIT, NO! THEY'RE FRIENDLY!
THEY'RE PRETTY CHILL AS LONG AS WE DON'T ATTACK THEM.
MORE IMPORTANTLY, WHAT HAPPENED TO YOU GUYS? DID YOU WIN THE FIGHT?

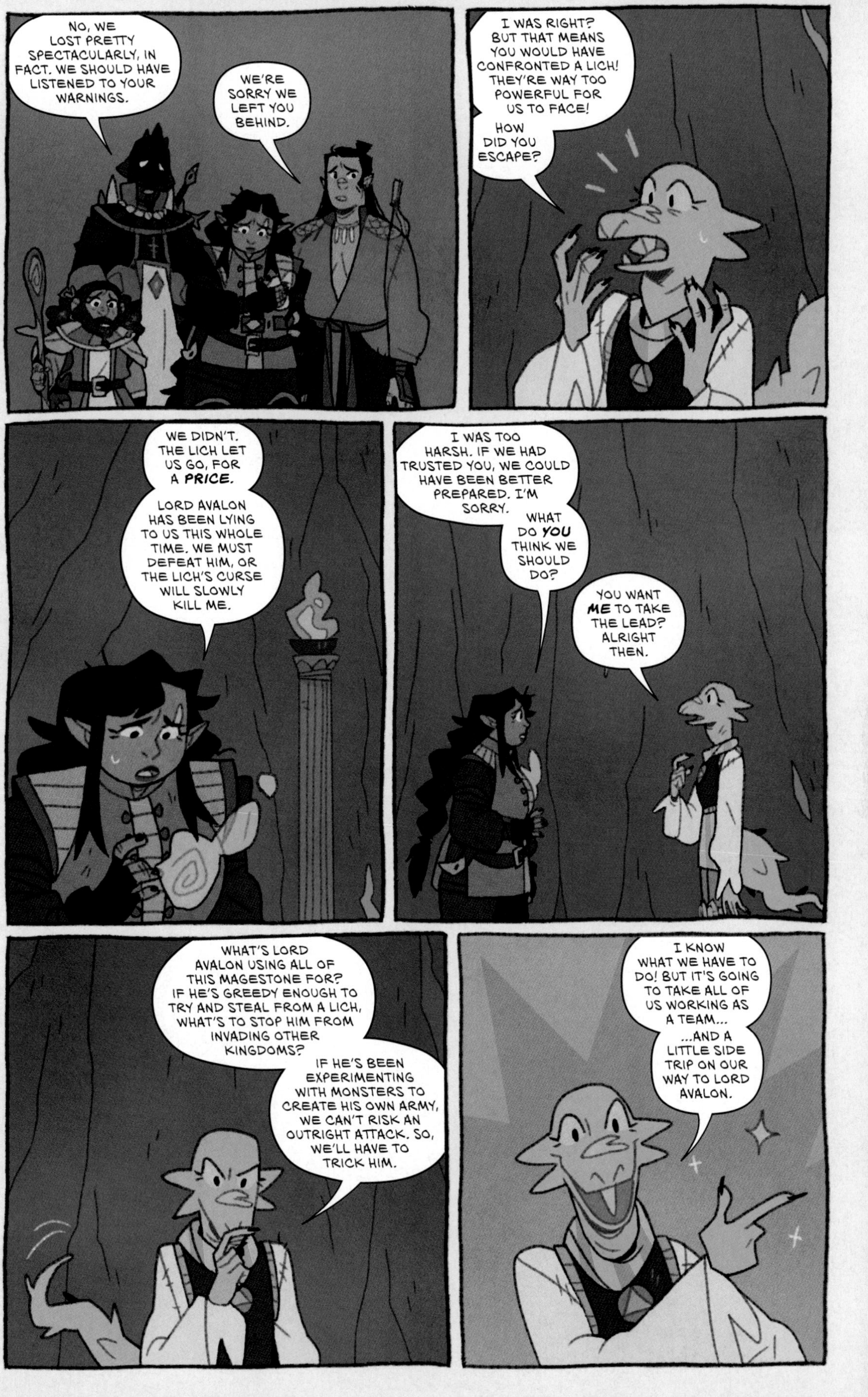
NO, WE LOST PRETTY SPECTACULARLY, IN FACT. WE SHOULD HAVE LISTENED TO YOUR WARNINGS.
WE'RE SORRY WE LEFT YOU BEHIND.
I WAS RIGHT? BUT THAT MEANS YOU WOULD HAVE CONFRONTED A LICH! THEY'RE WAY TOO POWERFUL FOR US TO FACE!
HOW DID YOU ESCAPE?
WE DIDN'T. THE LICH LET US GO, FOR A **PRICE.**
LORD AVALON HAS BEEN LYING TO US THIS WHOLE TIME. WE MUST DEFEAT HIM, OR THE LICH'S CURSE WILL SLOWLY KILL ME.
I WAS TOO HARSH. IF WE HAD TRUSTED YOU, WE COULD HAVE BEEN BETTER PREPARED. I'M SORRY.
WHAT DO ***YOU*** THINK WE SHOULD DO?
YOU WANT ***ME*** TO TAKE THE LEAD? ALRIGHT THEN.
WHAT'S LORD AVALON USING ALL OF THIS MAGESTONE FOR? IF HE'S GREEDY ENOUGH TO TRY AND STEAL FROM A LICH, WHAT'S TO STOP HIM FROM INVADING OTHER KINGDOMS?
IF HE'S BEEN EXPERIMENTING WITH MONSTERS TO CREATE HIS OWN ARMY, WE CAN'T RISK AN OUTRIGHT ATTACK. SO, WE'LL HAVE TO TRICK HIM.
I KNOW WHAT WE HAVE TO DO! BUT IT'S GOING TO TAKE ALL OF US WORKING AS A TEAM...
...AND A LITTLE SIDE TRIP ON OUR WAY TO LORD AVALON.

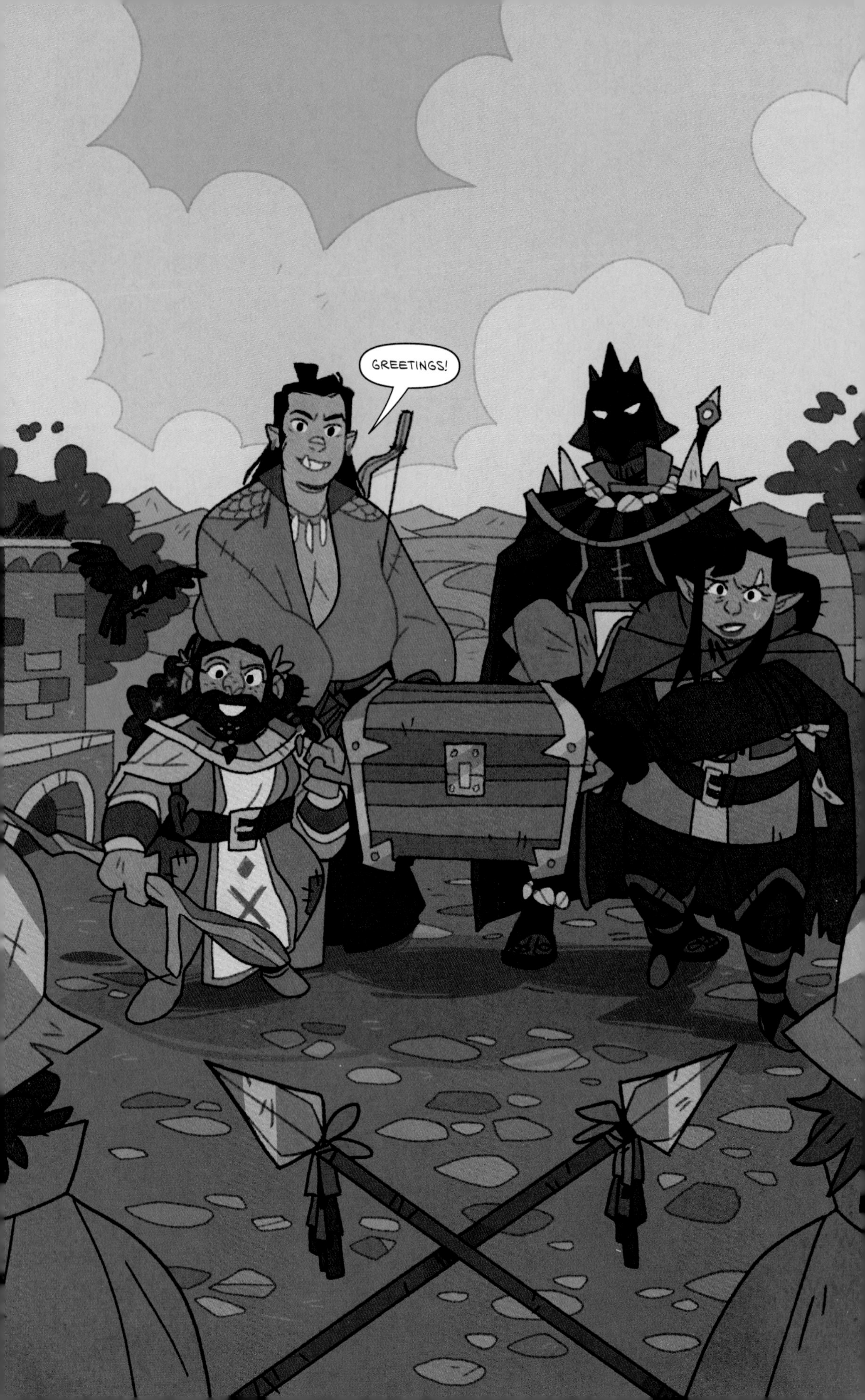
GREETINGS!

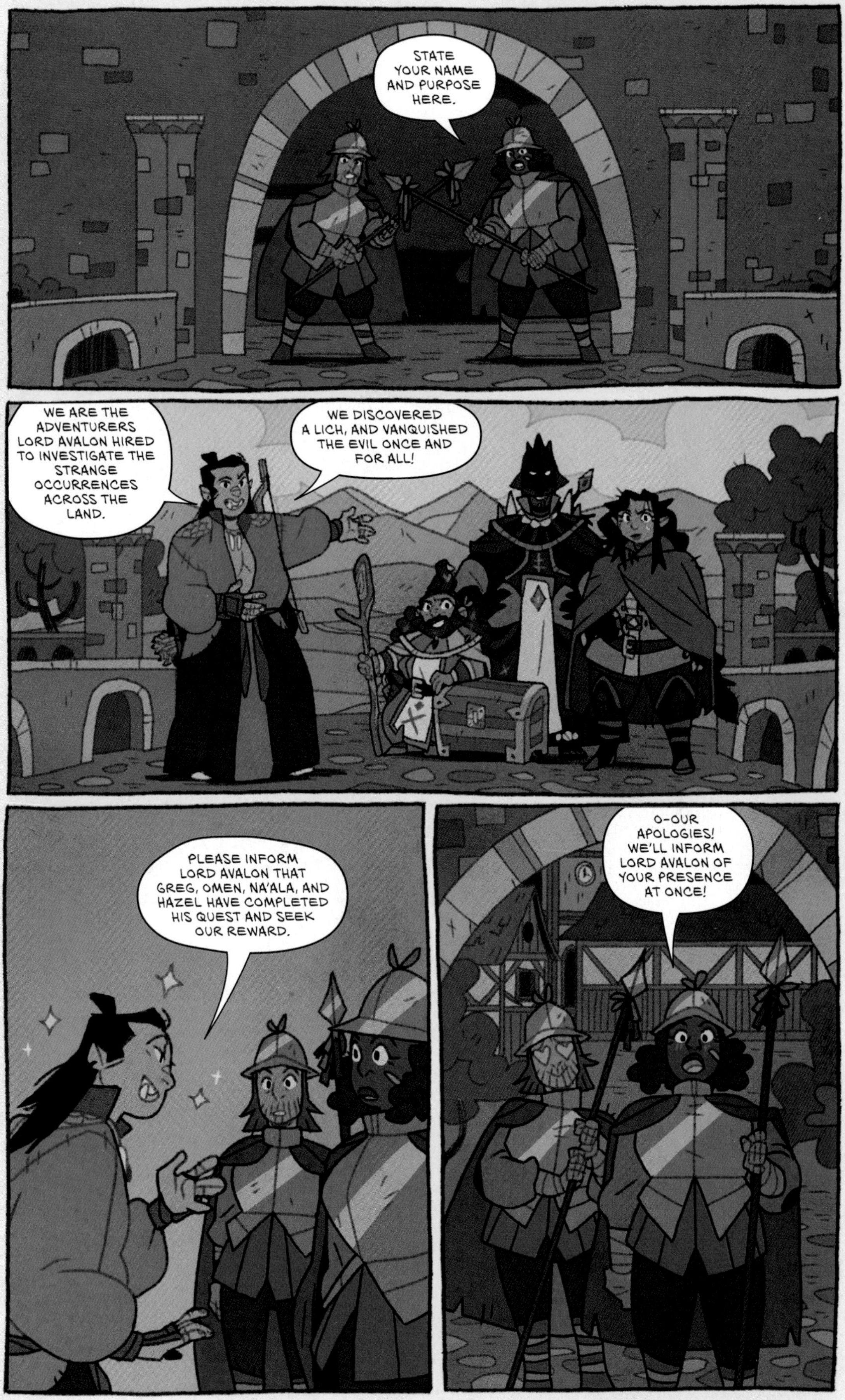
STATE YOUR NAME AND PURPOSE HERE.
WE ARE THE ADVENTURERS LORD AVALON HIRED TO INVESTIGATE THE STRANGE OCCURRENCES ACROSS THE LAND.
WE DISCOVERED A LICH, AND VANQUISHED THE EVIL ONCE AND FOR ALL!
PLEASE INFORM LORD AVALON THAT GREG, OMEN, NA'ALA, AND HAZEL HAVE COMPLETED HIS QUEST AND SEEK OUR REWARD.
O-OUR APOLOGIES! WE'LL INFORM LORD AVALON OF YOUR PRESENCE AT ONCE!

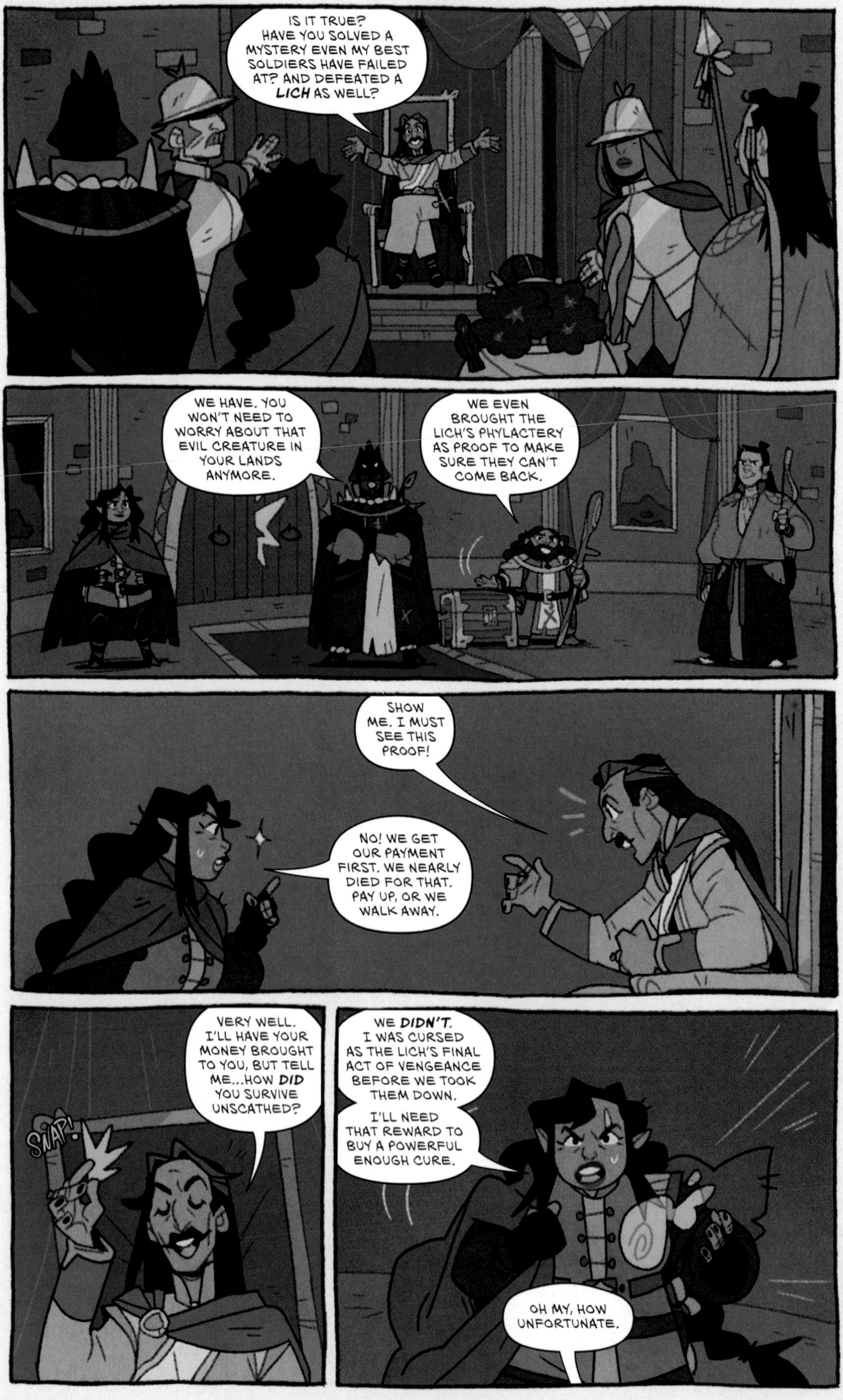
IS IT TRUE? HAVE YOU SOLVED A MYSTERY EVEN MY BEST SOLDIERS HAVE FAILED AT? AND DEFEATED A LICH AS WELL?
WE HAVE. YOU WON'T NEED TO WORRY ABOUT THAT EVIL CREATURE IN YOUR LANDS ANYMORE.
WE EVEN BROUGHT THE LICH'S PHYLACTERY AS PROOF TO MAKE SURE THEY CAN'T COME BACK.
SHOW ME. I MUST SEE THIS PROOF!
NO! WE GET OUR PAYMENT FIRST. WE NEARLY DIED FOR THAT. PAY UP, OR WE WALK AWAY.
VERY WELL. I'LL HAVE YOUR MONEY BROUGHT TO YOU, BUT TELL ME...HOW DID YOU SURVIVE UNSCATHED?
SNAP!
WE DIDN'T. I WAS CURSED AS THE LICH'S FINAL ACT OF VENGEANCE BEFORE WE TOOK THEM DOWN.
I'LL NEED THAT REWARD TO BUY A POWERFUL ENOUGH CURE.
OH MY, HOW UNFORTUNATE.

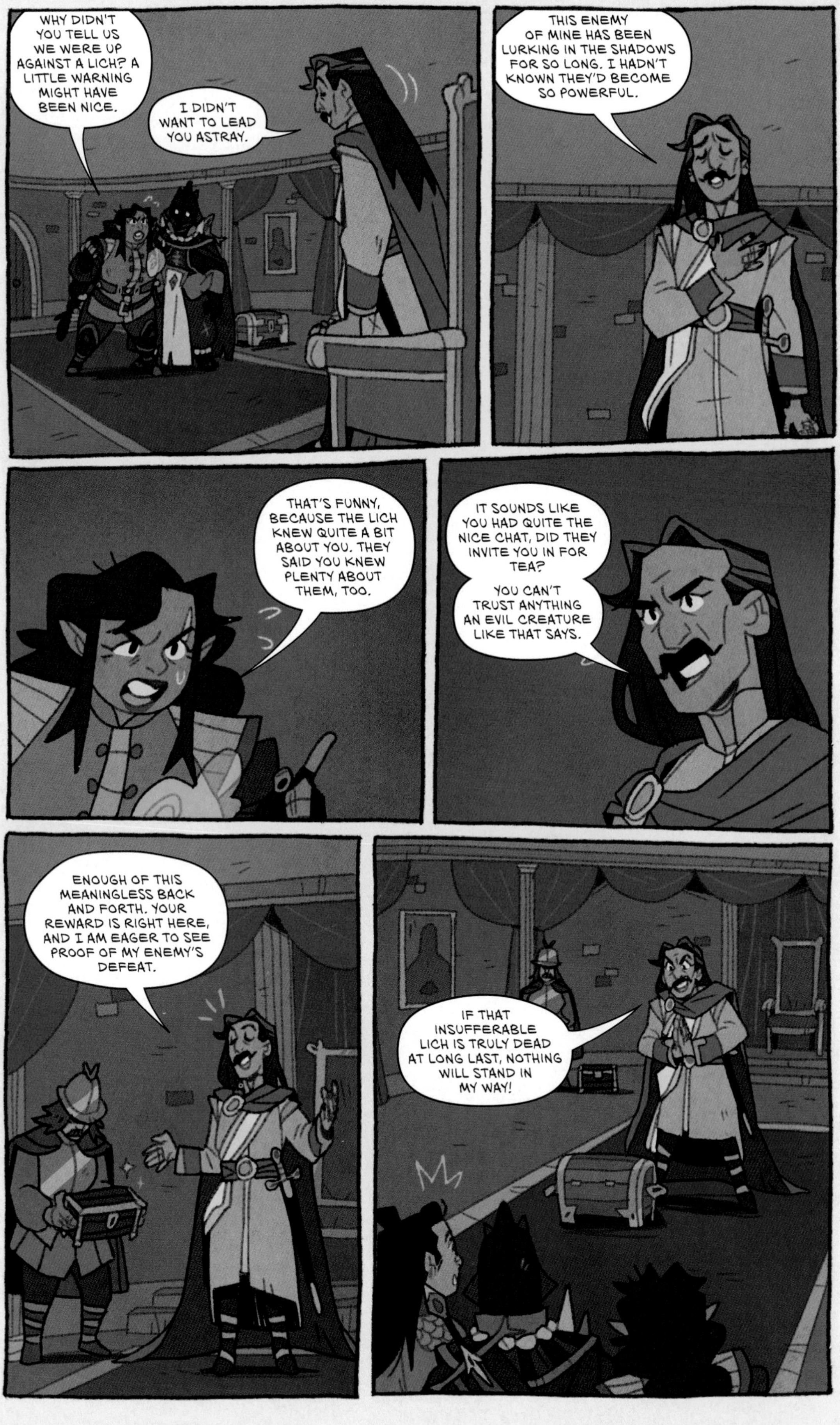
WHY DIDN'T YOU TELL US WE WERE UP AGAINST A LICH? A LITTLE WARNING MIGHT HAVE BEEN NICE.
I DIDN'T WANT TO LEAD YOU ASTRAY.
THIS ENEMY OF MINE HAS BEEN LURKING IN THE SHADOWS FOR SO LONG. I HADN'T KNOWN THEY'D BECOME SO POWERFUL.
THAT'S FUNNY, BECAUSE THE LICH KNEW QUITE A BIT ABOUT YOU. THEY SAID YOU KNEW PLENTY ABOUT THEM, TOO.
IT SOUNDS LIKE YOU HAD QUITE THE NICE CHAT, DID THEY INVITE YOU IN FOR TEA?
YOU CAN'T TRUST ANYTHING AN EVIL CREATURE LIKE THAT SAYS.
ENOUGH OF THIS MEANINGLESS BACK AND FORTH. YOUR REWARD IS RIGHT HERE, AND I AM EAGER TO SEE PROOF OF MY ENEMY'S DEFEAT.
IF THAT INSUFFERABLE LICH IS TRULY DEAD AT LONG LAST, NOTHING WILL STAND IN MY WAY!

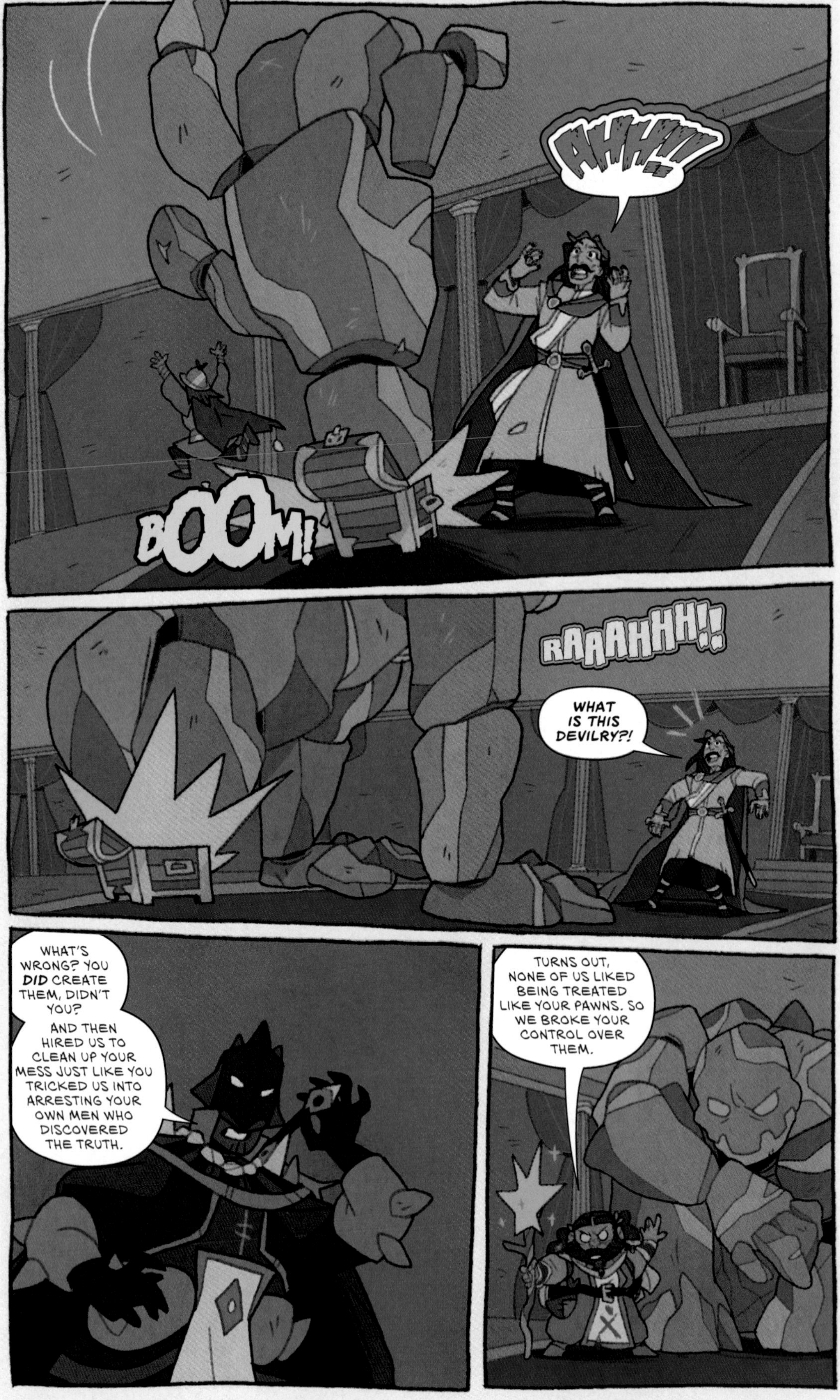
AHH?!!
BOOM!
RAAAHHH!!
WHAT IS THIS DEVILRY?!
WHAT'S WRONG? YOU DID CREATE THEM, DIDN'T YOU?
AND THEN HIRED US TO CLEAN UP YOUR MESS JUST LIKE YOU TRICKED US INTO ARRESTING YOUR OWN MEN WHO DISCOVERED THE TRUTH.
TURNS OUT, NONE OF US LIKED BEING TREATED LIKE YOUR PAWNS. SO WE BROKE YOUR CONTROL OVER THEM.

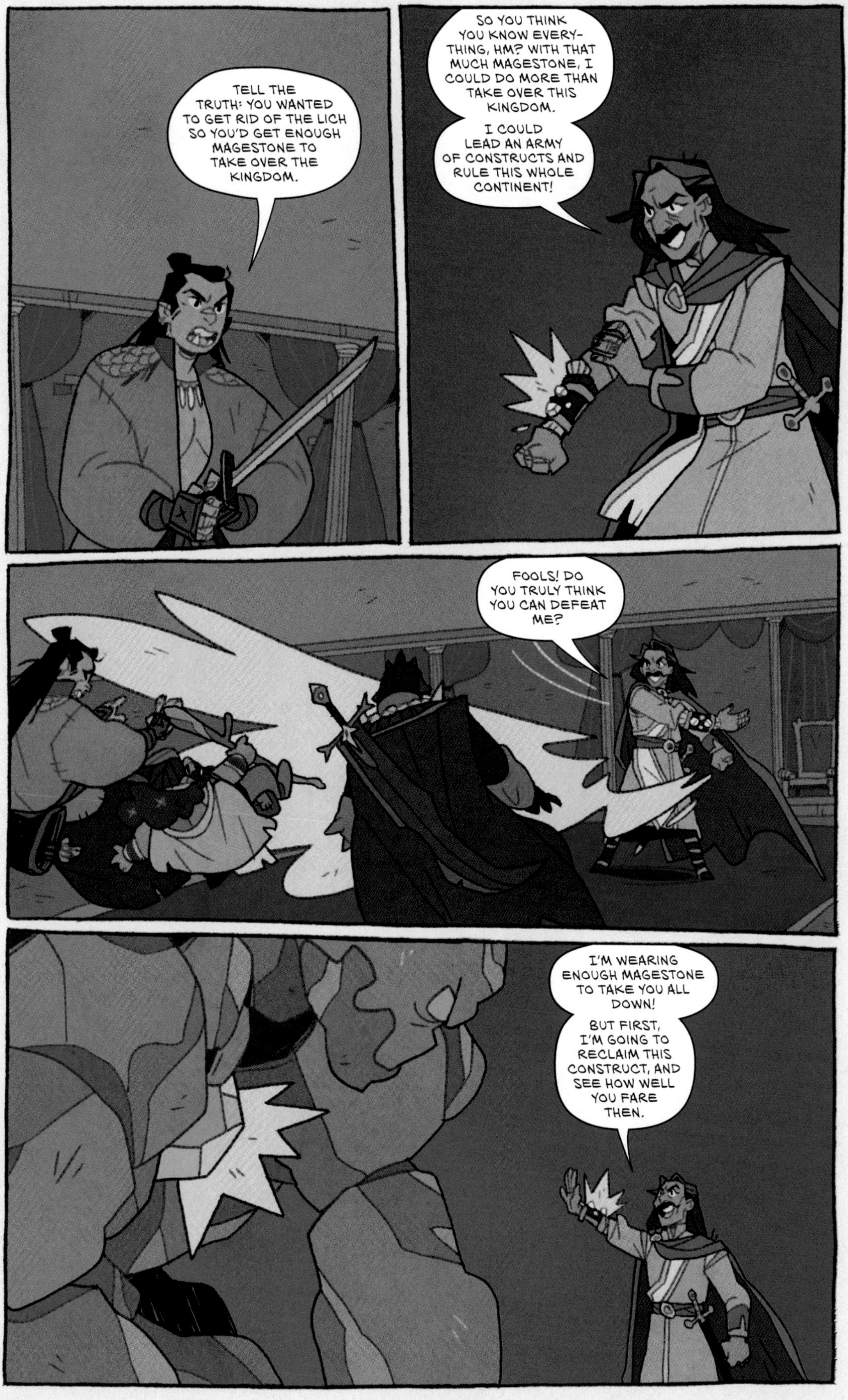
TELL THE TRUTH: YOU WANTED TO GET RID OF THE LICH SO YOU'D GET ENOUGH MAGESTONE TO TAKE OVER THE KINGDOM.
SO YOU THINK YOU KNOW EVERY-THING, HM? WITH THAT MUCH MAGESTONE, I COULD DO MORE THAN TAKE OVER THIS KINGDOM.
I COULD LEAD AN ARMY OF CONSTRUCTS AND RULE THIS WHOLE CONTINENT!
FOOLS! DO YOU TRULY THINK YOU CAN DEFEAT ME?
I'M WEARING ENOUGH MAGESTONE TO TAKE YOU ALL DOWN!
BUT FIRST, I'M GOING TO RECLAIM THIS CONSTRUCT, AND SEE HOW WELL YOU FARE THEN.

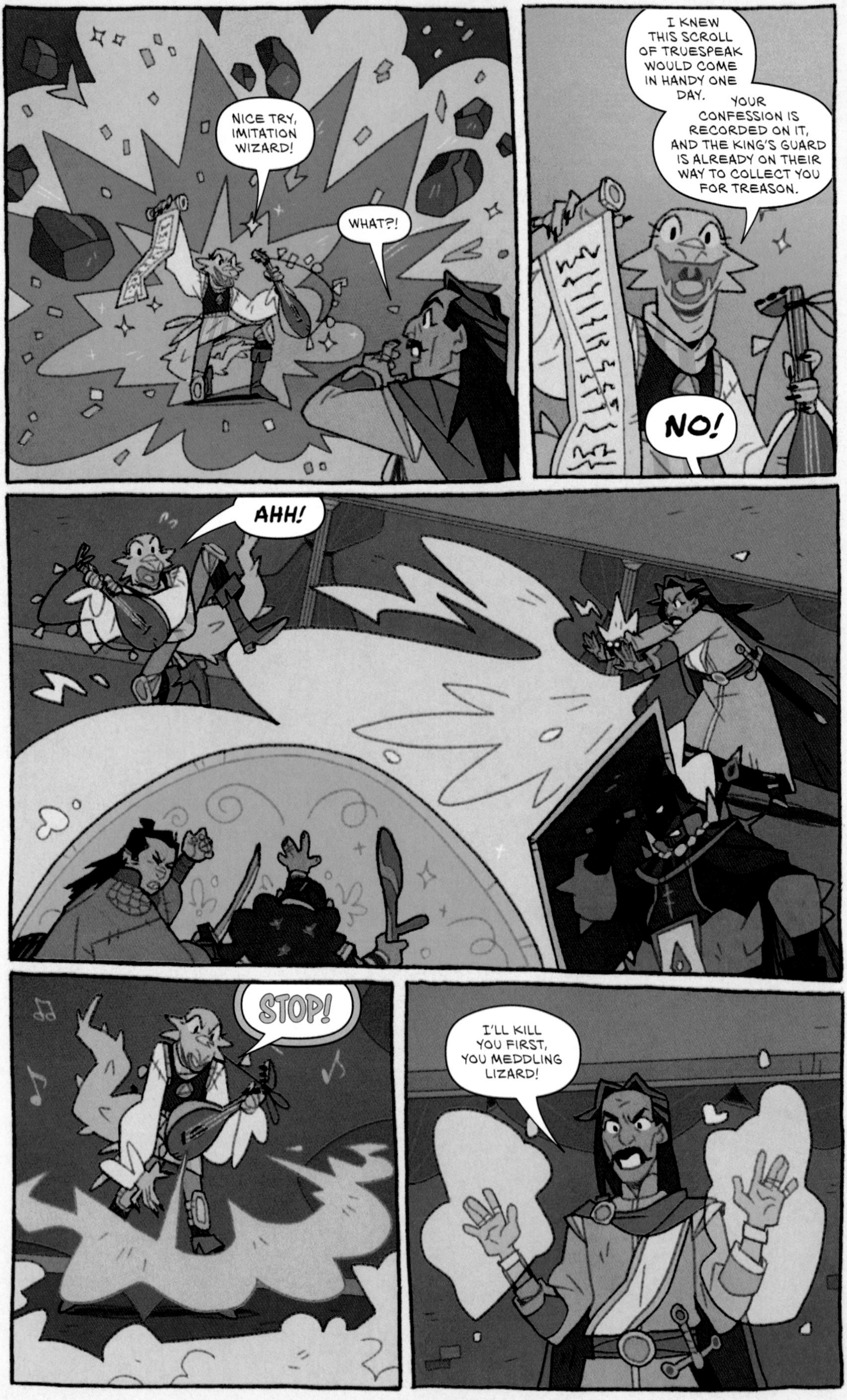
NICE TRY, IMITATION WIZARD!
WHAT?!
I KNEW THIS SCROLL OF TRUESPEAK WOULD COME IN HANDY ONE DAY.
YOUR CONFESSION IS RECORDED ON IT, AND THE KING'S GUARD IS ALREADY ON THEIR WAY TO COLLECT YOU FOR TREASON.
NO!
AHH!
STOP!
I'LL KILL YOU FIRST, YOU MEDDLING LIZARD!

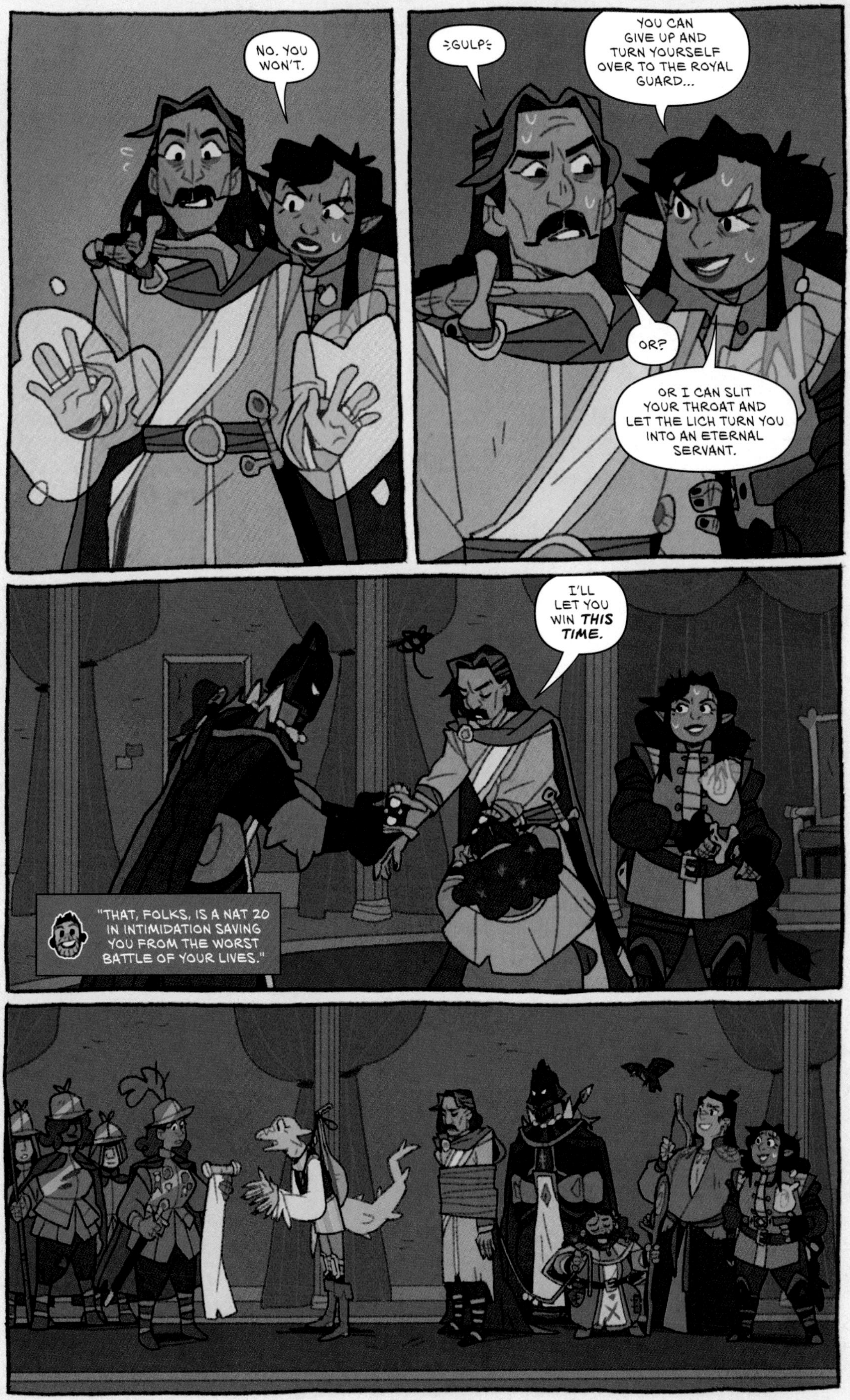
NO. YOU WON'T.
=GULP=
YOU CAN GIVE UP AND TURN YOURSELF OVER TO THE ROYAL GUARD...
OR?
OR I CAN SLIT YOUR THROAT AND LET THE LICH TURN YOU INTO AN ETERNAL SERVANT.
I'LL LET YOU WIN *THIS TIME.*
"THAT, FOLKS, IS A NAT 20 IN INTIMIDATION SAVING YOU FROM THE WORST BATTLE OF YOUR LIVES."

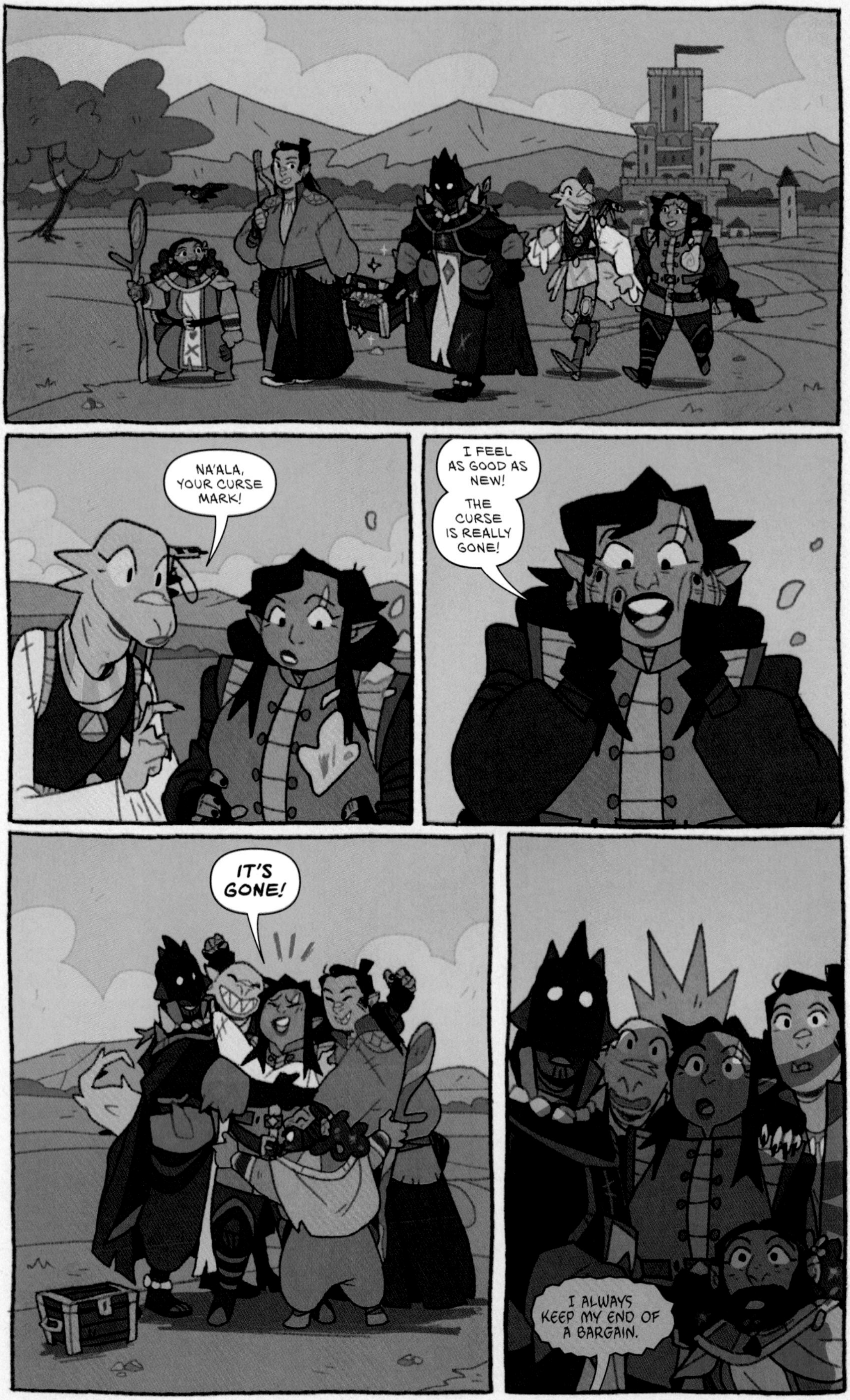
NA'ALA, YOUR CURSE MARK!
I FEEL AS GOOD AS NEW!
THE CURSE IS REALLY GONE!
IT'S GONE!
I ALWAYS KEEP MY END OF A BARGAIN.

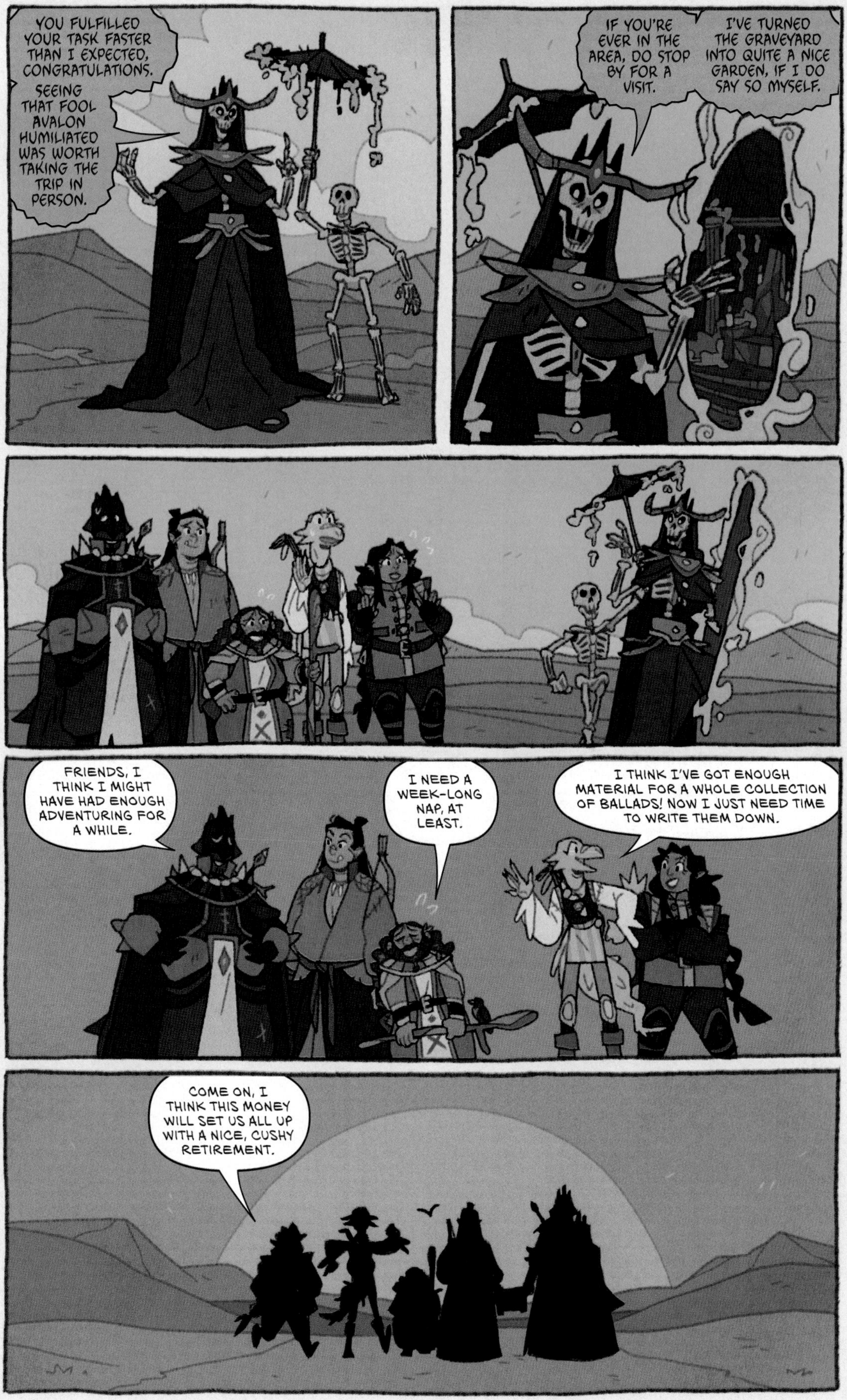
YOU FULFILLED YOUR TASK FASTER THAN I EXPECTED, CONGRATULATIONS.
SEEING THAT FOOL AVALON HUMILIATED WAS WORTH TAKING THE TRIP IN PERSON.
IF YOU'RE EVER IN THE AREA, DO STOP BY FOR A VISIT.
I'VE TURNED THE GRAVEYARD INTO QUITE A NICE GARDEN, IF I DO SAY SO MYSELF.
FRIENDS, I THINK I MIGHT HAVE HAD ENOUGH ADVENTURING FOR A WHILE.
I NEED A WEEK-LONG NAP, AT LEAST.
I THINK I'VE GOT ENOUGH MATERIAL FOR A WHOLE COLLECTION OF BALLADS! NOW I JUST NEED TIME TO WRITE THEM DOWN.
COME ON, I THINK THIS MONEY WILL SET US ALL UP WITH A NICE, CUSHY RETIREMENT.

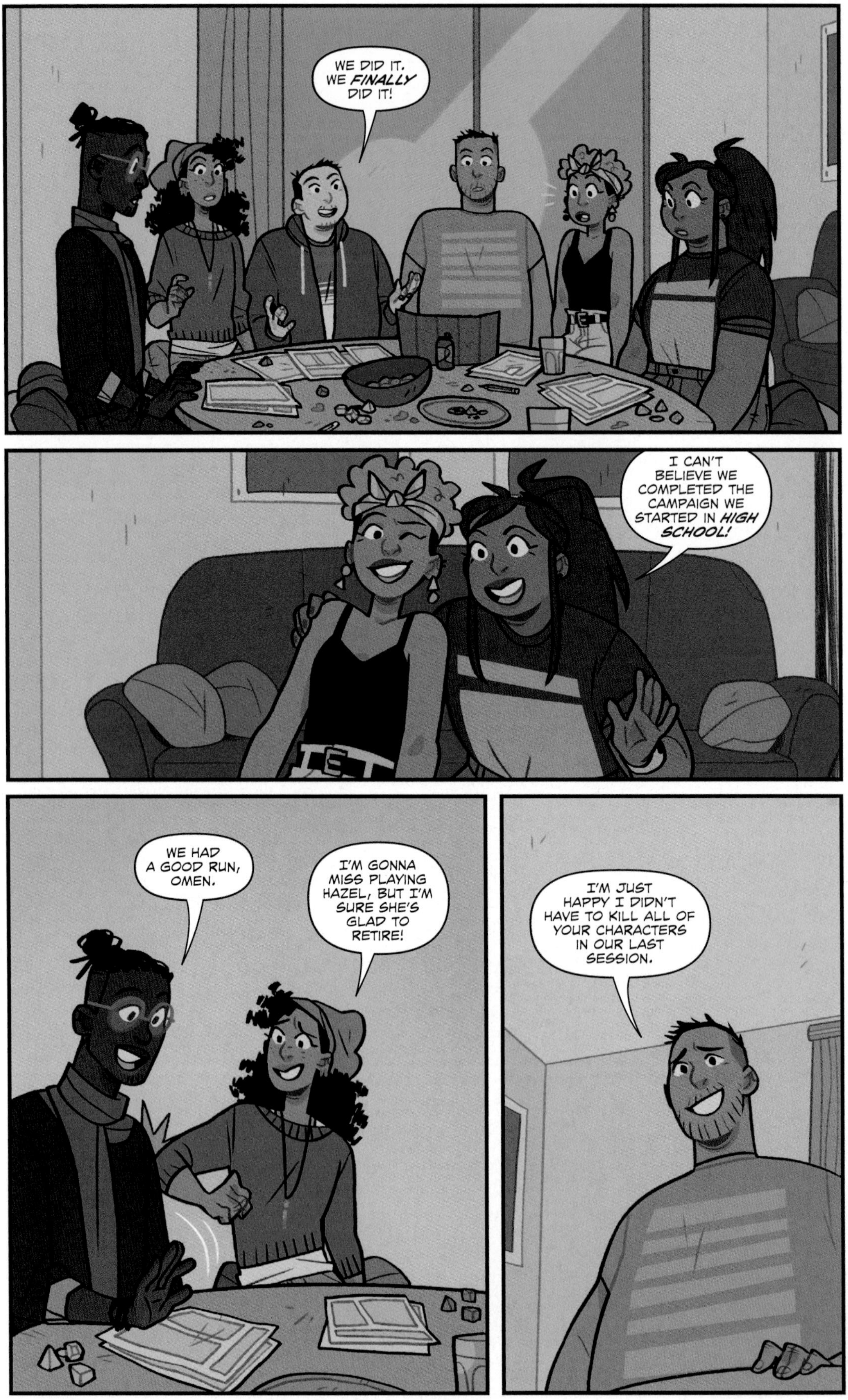
WE DID IT. WE *FINALLY* DID IT!
I CAN'T BELIEVE WE COMPLETED THE CAMPAIGN WE STARTED IN *HIGH SCHOOL!*
WE HAD A GOOD RUN, OMEN.
I'M GONNA MISS PLAYING HAZEL, BUT I'M SURE SHE'S GLAD TO RETIRE!
I'M JUST HAPPY I DIDN'T HAVE TO KILL ALL OF YOUR CHARACTERS IN OUR LAST SESSION.

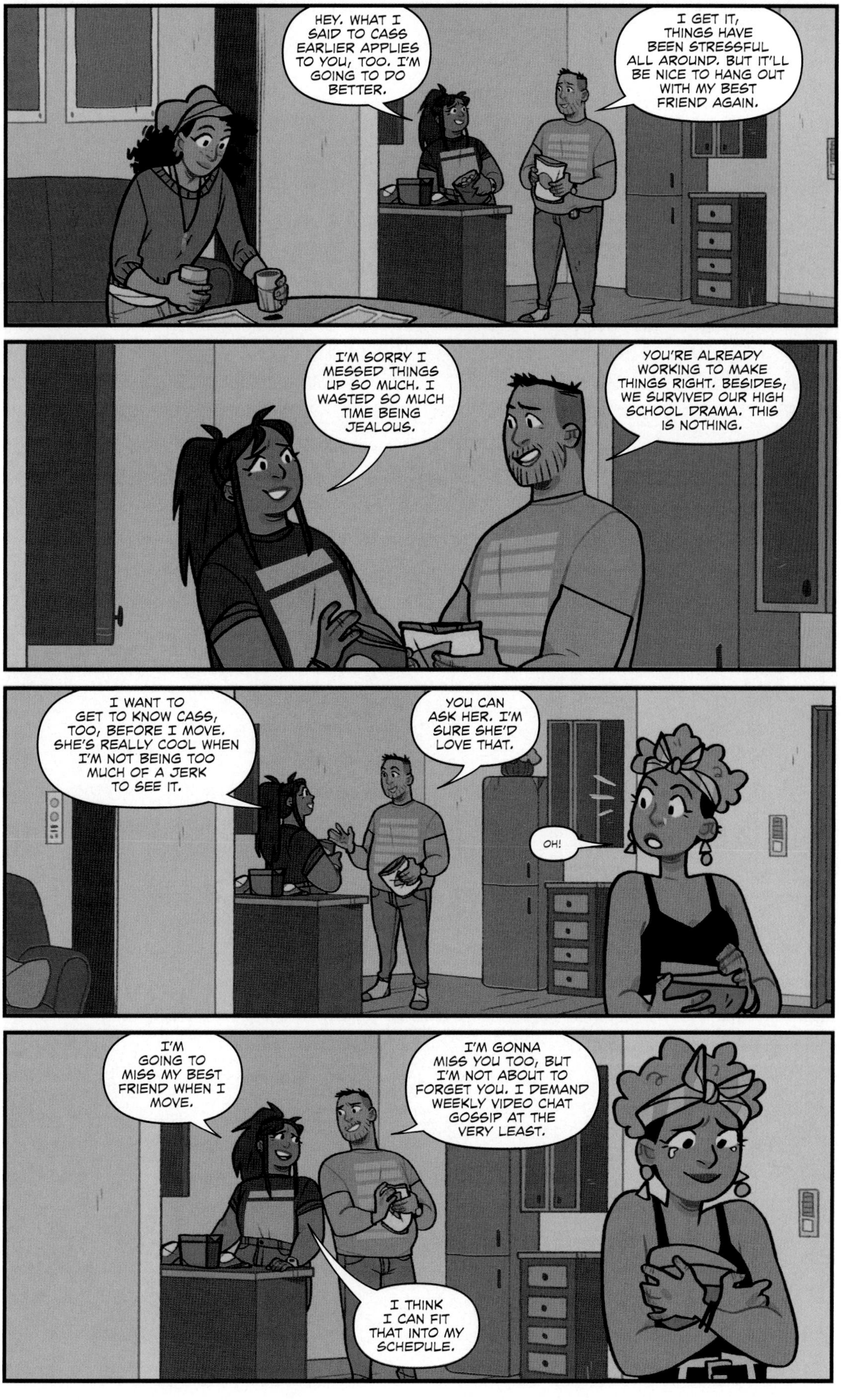
HEY. WHAT I SAID TO CASS EARLIER APPLIES TO YOU, TOO. I'M GOING TO DO BETTER.
I GET IT, THINGS HAVE BEEN STRESSFUL ALL AROUND. BUT IT'LL BE NICE TO HANG OUT WITH MY BEST FRIEND AGAIN.
I'M SORRY I MESSED THINGS UP SO MUCH. I WASTED SO MUCH TIME BEING JEALOUS.
YOU'RE ALREADY WORKING TO MAKE THINGS RIGHT. BESIDES, WE SURVIVED OUR HIGH SCHOOL DRAMA. THIS IS NOTHING.
I WANT TO GET TO KNOW CASS, TOO, BEFORE I MOVE. SHE'S REALLY COOL WHEN I'M NOT BEING TOO MUCH OF A JERK TO SEE IT.
YOU CAN ASK HER. I'M SURE SHE'D LOVE THAT.
OH!
I'M GOING TO MISS MY BEST FRIEND WHEN I MOVE.
I'M GONNA MISS YOU TOO, BUT I'M NOT ABOUT TO FORGET YOU. I DEMAND WEEKLY VIDEO CHAT GOSSIP AT THE VERY LEAST.
I THINK I CAN FIT THAT INTO MY SCHEDULE.

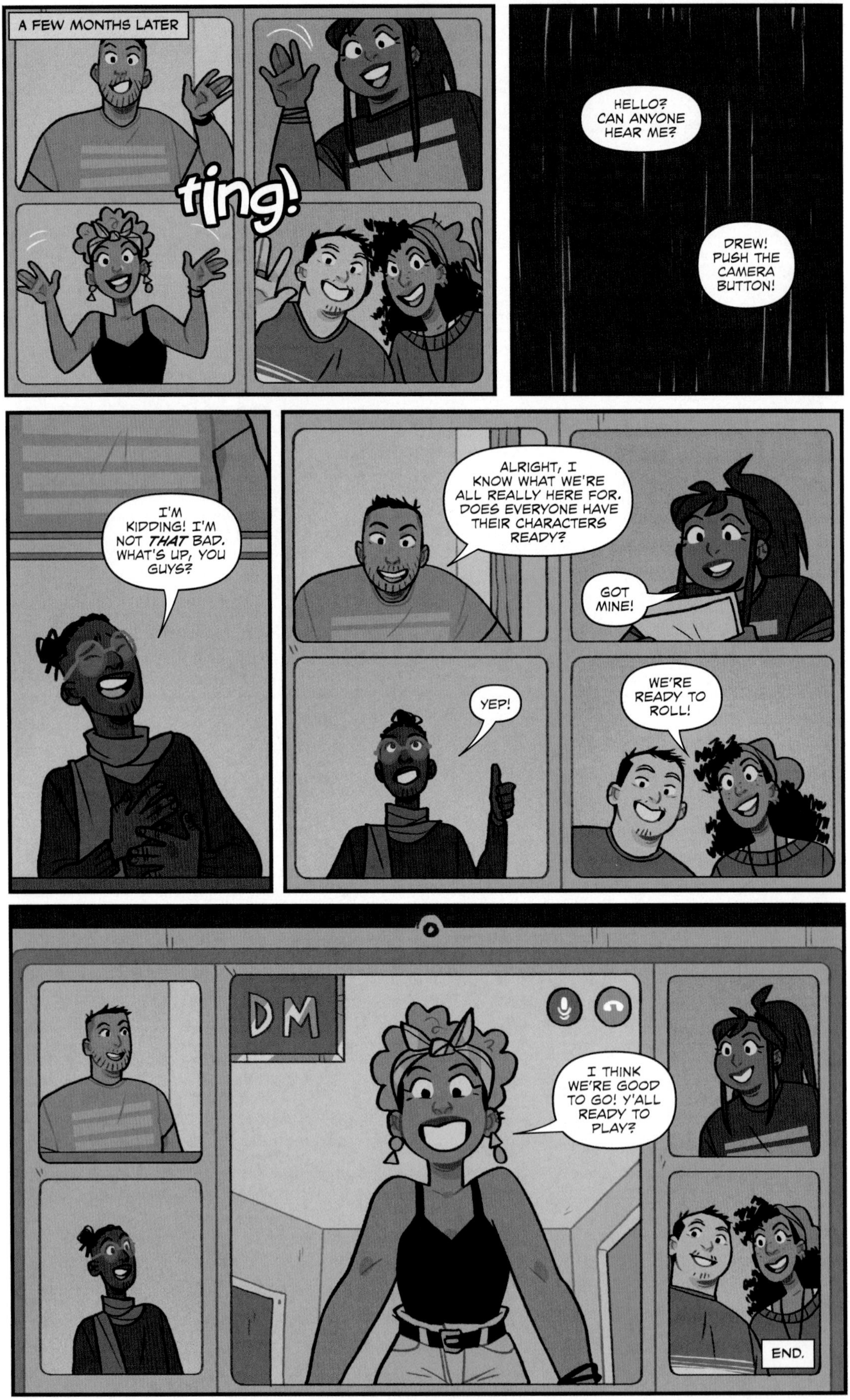
A FEW MONTHS LATER
ting!
HELLO? CAN ANYONE HEAR ME?
DREW! PUSH THE CAMERA BUTTON!
I'M KIDDING! I'M NOT *THAT* BAD. WHAT'S UP, YOU GUYS?
ALRIGHT, I KNOW WHAT WE'RE ALL REALLY HERE FOR. DOES EVERYONE HAVE THEIR CHARACTERS READY?
GOT MINE!
YEP!
WE'RE READY TO ROLL!
DM
I THINK WE'RE GOOD TO GO! Y'ALL READY TO PLAY?
END.

CREATIVE
TEAM

Jasmine Walls
(She/Her)

Jasmine is a California-based writer, artist, and hot chocolate connoisseur with a passion for stories that are fun, engaging, and critical. Her works are unapologetically queer, inclusive, and span across several genres.

Dozer is a nonbinary illustrator, comic artist and bird parent from Germany. They've done work on BOOM! Studios' Lumberjanes, several German TV and movie illustration and animation gigs, and their own wrestling fan-comic. They are always looking for new exciting stories and diverse characters to illustrate!

Dozerdraws
(They/Them)

Micah Myers
(He/Him)

Micah is a comic book letterer who has worked on comics for Image, Dark Horse, IDW, Heavy Metal, Mad Cave, Devil's Due, and many more. He also occasionally writes and has his own series about D-List supervillains, The Disasters.

DISCOVER MAD CAVE

Nottingham
VOL. 1: DEATH AND TAXES

Nottingham Vol. 1: Death and Taxes
ISBN: 978-1-952303-14-2

WOLVENHEART
VOL. 2: A TALE OF TWO WOLVES

Wolvenheart Vol. 2: A Tale of Two Wolves
ISBN: 978-1-952303-30-2

VOL. 2: FATHER'S ARMOR
KNIGHTS OF THE GOLDEN SUN

Knights of the Golden Sun Vol. 2: Father's Armor
ISBN: 978-1-952303-10-4

BATTLECATS
VOL. 3: HERO OF LEGEND

Battlecats Vol. 3: Hero of Legend
ISBN: 978-1-952303-12-8

BOUNTIFUL GARDEN

Bountiful Garden Vol. 1
ISBN: 978-1-952303-17-3

Grimm Tales from the Cave

Grimm Tales from the Cave Vol. 1
ISBN: 978-1-952303-24-1

BECSTAR

Becstar Vol. 1
ISBN: 978-1-952303-16-6

HONOR AND CURSE
VOL. 2: MENDED

Honor and Curse Vol. 2: Mended
ISBN: 978-1-952303-11-1

Battlecats Vol. 1: Hunt for the Dire Beast
ISBN: 978-0-9981215-1-2
Battlecats Vol. 2: Fallen Legacy
ISBN: 978-0-9981215-6-7
Battlecats: Tales of Valderia Vol. 1
ISBN: 978-1-952303-01-2
Midnight Task Force Vol. 1: HiddenVoices
ISBN: 978-0-9981215-2-9
RV9 Vol. 1
ISBN: 978-0-9981215-9-8

Over the Ropes Vol. 1
ISBN: 978-1-952303-00-5
Honor and Curse Vol. 1: Torn
ISBN: 978-0-9981215-5-0
Savage Bastards Vol. 1
ISBN: 978-1-952303-02-9
Hellfighter Quin Vol. 1
ISBN: 978-1-952303-03-6
Dry Foot Vol. 1
ISBN: 978-1-952303-05-0
Terminal Punks Vol. 1
ISBN: 978-1-952303-07-4
Hollywood Trash Vol. 1
ISBN: 978-1-952303-08-1

Knights of the Golden Sun Vol. 1: Providence Lost
ISBN: 978-0-9981215-4-3
Stargazer Vol. 1
ISBN: 978-1-952303-04-3
Wolvenheart Vol. 1: Legendary Slayer
ISBN: 978-0-9981215-8-1
Villainous Vol. 1
ISBN: 978-1-952303-06-7
They Fell from the Sky Vol. 1
ISBN: 978-1-952303-13-5
Pantomime Vol. 1
ISBN: 978-1-952303-09-8

SCAN ME